FIGHTING WINDMILLS

Fighting Windmills
A Quixotic Odyssey

G·A·HARKER

Robert O. Morris

LEGACY PUBLISHERS

FIGHTING WINDMILLS

A Quixotic Odyssey

Legacy Publishers
Post Office Box 62442
Virginia Beach, VA 23466
www.legacypublishers.net
info@legacypublishers.net

Library of Congress Control Number: 2011961038

ISBN 978-0-615-56869-0

Cover illustration by G. A. Harker

Printed and bound in the United States of America.

First printing 2012

Dedication:

This book is for all who have played a major role along my life's journey,

For my many friends, who have so generously given of their friendship,

For my family, whose love has bolstered me throughout the many years,

For my children, who have provided me the motivation for this project,

And for my loving wife, Maka, without whose devotion and support,

Life would not be complete.

CONTENTS

Introduction

I believe that everyone has a story to tell, and that each one of us can benefit from the telling of that story.

According to official figures, there are currently about seven billion human beings wandering this earth. Despite all of the apparent differences that we have, such as different cultures, languages, religions, skin color, and so forth, we all share the same fundamental commonality; everyone of us spends a lifetime trying to find our way. One other common feature we share is that we each, all seven billion of us, have a unique life story to tell, and I am of the belief that any one of those stories would offer some distinct benefit to the rest of us if we were to read it.

Because only a small percentage of our fellow human beings actually record their lives, I submit this reality is our loss. Think about the collective benefit which might be derived if everyone did share the wisdom of what he or she had learned during his or her respective lifetime. Other than being a colossal reading assignment, those collective stories might have an extremely positive synergistic effect on how the rest of us struggle with the challenges that life presents. Perhaps someday we will develop the technological advances through which all of the collective wisdom of mankind can be learned through one comprehensive program to be absorbed during childhood. Until then, however, I guess we will continue to conduct our lives using the current trial and error method.

Whereas this one life story will fall far short of conveying much of the collective wisdom of mankind, my sincere hope is that there will be something of benefit in it for all who do read it. This tale is a story of intrigue and normality, of success and failure, of love and the loss of it, of occasional wisdom and frequent foolishness. On the one hand, it is a unique story, but I would suggest that it is basically similar to the stories of the billions of other individuals who have walked this earth; in essence, it is about living life.

As the title of the book implies, my life has been a continuous odyssey, a seeking of new and different life experiences. I have chosen to call this odyssey "quixotic," which Webster's dictionary defines as "extravagantly chivalrous or romantic, impractical, impulsive, and often rashly unpredictable." For better or for worse, in my case, the definition seems to fit extraordinarily well. The predominant theme and the primary motivation for the title are living with the "affliction" of being a romantic idealist. Just as Cervantes' famous character, Don Quixote, epitomized the quest of chivalry and noble pursuits, and sought the romantic ideal in a thoroughly flawed world, so too has my life been oftentimes characterized by "fighting windmills" of my own creation, as did Don Quixote. It is a proclivity that I do not recommend highly, but it is the story that I have to share.

As I write this book, I have lived some 22,300 or so days already, hopefully with a few thousand more to go. For the majority of those thousands of day, it has been my intention, my dream if you will, to write, and I am finally investing the time to do so. Although, with the blessing of longevity, I hope to create other books in the future, this particular one is intended primarily for my children, family, and friends, although I do hope that many more people will have the desire and the opportunity to read it. Those who do should find some areas of interest in the numerous and different experiences that I have been privileged to have. The content will certainly evoke emotion, frequent laughter, an occasional tear, hopefully not too much anger, and most of all, the sharing of feeling imbedded within the human experience.

With those portions which deal with my career in the Central Intelligence Agency, there is much which I am simply not able to share. In fact, some of the content which I had written has been redacted via the CIA pre-publication review process to which I was required to submit my story. For the most part, the content which has been blacked out deals with the exact locations in which heretofore non- publicized clandestine activities took place. I have also chosen to eliminate names of anyone appearing in this book for whom there might be any unintended embarrassment or simply to protect the innocent. I do hope that these omissions will not detract too much from the story that I am trying to tell. Finally, it is my fervent wish that people who do read this book will, first of all, enjoy it and also find some portions that directly relate to life as they have experienced it. This relevance is the true value of any life story, and I hope that you will find some benefit, however minor it may be, in the telling of this quixotic odyssey.

Best wishes to all of you,

Robert O. Morris

Virginia Beach, Virginia

Footnote: Disclaimer from the CIA.

"All statements of fact, opinion, or analysis expressed are those of the author and do not reflect the official positions or views of the CIA or any other U. S. Government agency. Nothing in the contents should be construed as asserting or implying U. S. Government authentication of information or Agency endorsement of the author's views. This material has been reviewed by the CIA to prevent the disclosure of classified information."

Part I

Inauspicious Beginnings

Prologue to Part I

Moscow, mid-November, 1982

It was a typical November evening in Moscow, already quite cold, but with the full harshness of the Russian winter having not yet set in. The streets were still busy and well populated, with people intently going about their day-to-day business, shopping for hard-to-find foodstuffs, or heading home having completed their tasks. There I was, dressed in my Russian garb and trying to blend into the crowd as best I could, careful not to draw undue attention to myself. If everything fell properly into place according to the well orchestrated plan, in a few minutes, I was to begin my first personal encounter with the CIA's most valuable agent. Any mistake on my part could possibly compromise the operation and subject this brave man to capture, imprisonment, and certain execution. At that point in time, his life and the welfare of his beloved family were entirely in my hands. Although I was careful not to betray my uneasiness, my heart was pounding and my adrenalin flowing at a race car pace. My nerves were tightly wound, and the minutes seemed to pass excruciatingly slow. This meeting was the ultimate test of all of my extensive preparation for this important assignment, and the covert mission was about to commence in earnest.

After two years of intensive training and preparation for my initial CIA field assignment, this outing was my first crucial operational task, a personal meeting on the streets of Moscow with the organization's most productive asset, right under the noses of the all-powerful KGB. This operation was the ultimate reason for my assignment to Moscow, the Agency's most high profile station where an incredible amount of planning and preparation had been invested into my posting there, as a "deep cover" officer. From the historical perspective, the period of my tour, 1982 – 1984, was the very height of the Cold War, with the omnipresent tensions between the USA and USSR at an extremely high peak. The highly compartmented information which this agent had been providing the U. S. Government over the preceding four years had proved to be of immense strategic value to our national defense capabilities. As a result, every time one of our case officers was sent out to meet this valued source, anticipation (and concern) among the senior management of the Soviet-East European Division of the CIA Operations Directorate was palpable.

I had arrived in Moscow for my first overseas posting in July of 1982; my cover job at the ████████████████████ was as an Administrative Officer assigned to the new ████████████████████ project. Cover positions for case officers in denied area tours such as Moscow were all-important because the KGB was normally able to identify who the CIA Officers were by virtue of whether their cover job had been tagged previously as one that case officers normally filled. The concept of establishing a deep cover position was that an Agency officer would be given a clean slot, one that had not previously been used for CIA case officers. The theory was that if a case officer could occupy a clean slot and if he could live his cover properly, then perhaps the KGB would not pay him any special attention. This ploy allowed the deep cover officer the opportunity to stay free of KGB surveillance, and to perform the important operational requirements that he had been sent there to accomplish.

By design, the first two to three months of my tour in Moscow were devoted to the task of living my cover; I was to perform my cover job diligently 100% of the time, and to try not to draw any attention to myself or to give the KGB any reason for suspicion. In other words, my intent was to lull the KGB into a level of comfort that I was simply there to serve my tour as a normal ███████████ and not to cause any covert mischief. Simultaneously, I needed to become as familiar as possible with the lay of the land, so that when the time came to go operational, I would be sufficiently comfortable with the city to move from point-to-point without drawing attention. It was a fine line to be followed, one which required constant diligence to every word and deed, lest the KGB become suspicious of my true affiliation. Living under those fishbowl conditions with the constant threat of exposure should either I or my wife make a wrong move, the pressure was omnipresent, and the cost of the slightest mistake could prove fatal to our agents.

On that November evening, having performed, with my wife alongside, our lengthy and meticulously planned surveillance detection route (SDR), we had determined that we were surveillance free and thus able to go operational. We parked our Russian-made Zhiguli automobile in a place where the ███████████ license plate would not seem out of place and found a secluded outdoor location where we could quickly and easily alter our appearance to blend in better with the local population; we then set out on foot via local mass transportation to perform a final SDR and to move ourselves away from where we had parked the vehicle. At a pre-designated time and place when we had re-confirmed our surveillance-free status, I set off on the final leg of the route to where I would meet the agent, while my wife found a place where she could innocuously kill time while I conducted the brief covert meeting. If all went well, we would meet up about an hour later, move back towards where our car was parked, find a spot where we could return to our normal appearance, get into the car, and return home, hopefully not having drawn the attention of the KGB during any of that time.

Although I had seen a file photograph of this agent, we had never met previously; therefore, he had no idea of how I might look or even whether to expect a male or female case officer. The meeting plan called for us both to meet precisely at a pre-designated time and place, in this instance a certain tram stop, where I recognized him instantly. I approached him with an innocuous verbal parole, which served to identify me as the expected, but unknown, CIA case officer; in turn, he responded with a set parole, thereby closing the identification loop and indicating that it was safe for him to meet. From there he set off from the initial meeting point, and I followed discreetly behind until we came to where his car was parked in a safe and quiet spot; we then got into his car and conducted our brief meeting.

Because he spoke no English, the meeting was conducted entirely in Russian, which required any case officer handling him to be fluent in the language. The case officer also carried a small tape recorder with him to record the meeting in order to ensure that all of the information the agent needed to convey would be properly captured. The agent was already well-seasoned in this process and was used to putting his life in the hands of whomever the CIA decided to send to meet him. From the perspective of the case officer, however, in a tense situation such as that one, with the agent's life on the line and conducting a meeting in a foreign language, the tape recorder was a godsend.

As always was the case in these meetings, I had brought with me a packet of information and operational requirements to be passed, along with whatever supplies and/or funds we had promised to provide him. There was also a level of rapport to be developed and a meeting agenda that needed to be covered within the briefest time span. Omnipresent was the concern that our meeting in the car might come to the attention of some passerby, who, in his Soviet zeal, might decide to report the suspicious circumstance to the closest militiaman. This night, however, having completed the meeting successfully and without interruption, we bid our farewells until the next planned encounter. I then exited the car to proceed to the rendezvous point with my wife, and to begin to make our way back to the relative safety of our apartment.

Back at home finally in the late evening hours, we could afford ourselves the luxury of relaxing, to a point. Because of the constant threat of audio or visual surveillance in our apartment, the operation did not end once we were home. On my person, I carried with me dozens of film cassettes containing highly secret information that was severely damaging to the Soviet State and of significant strategic importance to our USG policy-makers. Because of my cover status, I could not immediately take this intelligence to the ████████ lest I bring attention to myself in the process; in essence, normal ████ ████████████ administrative officers never had good reason to enter the ████████ late at night. Therefore, the information needed to be guarded overnight until the first opportunity to deliver the package safely to the CIA station. Because of the job my wife had obtained ██████████████████████████, she would be able to take the agent's package into the ████████ in the morning, along with my meeting notes written inside the package and safeguard it until the wife of another station officer would be able to meet her and discreetly retrieve the package.

Back in the apartment that night, however, the decompression and euphoria of having successfully completed this initial meeting made for a largely sleepless night. Although we could not discuss the evening's activity inside of the apartment, both my wife and I felt a tremendous relief, plus the intense satisfaction of having performed a mission of significant importance. Moreover, although this was the very first time I had met the agent, from file reviews prior to arriving in Moscow, I had come to understand and to appreciate highly his motivations for working against the Soviet regime on behalf of the U. S. Government.

In essence, he was a romantic idealist, who hated the oppressive actions of the Soviet regime against the Russian Fatherland and the people whom he deeply loved. Fully knowing the risks of spying for the United States and fully aware that he would probably get caught at some point, he was nevertheless willing to risk his own life and the welfare of his family to take action and strike a blow against the oppressor. He was the chivalrous knight, riding his white horse in full charge against a dangerous enemy. He was fighting his own windmills, and from my file reviews and now this initial, brief meeting, I felt like I knew him innately. He and I were indeed kindred spirits with much the same inherent motivations. I had wanted to come to Moscow to fight the Cold War for the very same reasons; the Soviet system deeply offended my values and my love of individual freedom. As I lay sleeplessly in bed that evening, I felt a very close affinity and appreciation for this brave man who shared my sense of romantic idealism. I felt honored to have been given the chance to support this brave patriot and to have the opportunity to help him fight his own windmills.

Chapter 1

Roots of the Romantic Idealist

Before embarking on the quixotic odyssey of this romantic idealist, one begs the question of whether this trait is inherited or is it developed individually. Whether or not it is a generational tendency, it seems worthwhile to explore briefly the histories of those who came before.

Like most Americans, my family roots were planted elsewhere. To my knowledge, we have no Native American heritage nor is there any indication that any branch of the family was brought to America against his or her will on slave ships. Fortunately, we have solid genealogical evidence that all of the various branches of the Morris family came to America from Europe; they came for reasons of either religious prejudice, economic hardship, or simply the desire to seek out adventure and fortune in the New World. Their European origins were in England, Germany, Ireland and Scotland.

The English roots are the best documented ones. James Chilton and family came from the Canterbury, Kent County region in Southeastern England. They were "Separatists" from the established Church of England, who wished to "purify" (hence, the term "Puritans") the doctrines of the Church; however, the Royal Crown forbade the Separatists, who were also referred to as "Pilgrims", to break away from the established Church and threatened them with imprisonment. Thus, the Chilton family fled their home in England to escape the probability of imprisonment and persecution due to their religious views and practices. With a group of like-minded Pilgrims, they fled to Holland and settled in the town of Leyden in 1609. There they developed a life for themselves, and established their Pilgrim Church in keeping with their religious beliefs. In 1620, a group of the English community who had settled in Leyden made the decision to emigrate to America; James Chilton, his wife (believed to be named Susanna) and teenage daughter, Mary, were among this group.

After several aborted attempts to set sail aboard the ill-fated *Speedwell*, which had originally embarked from Holland to England from where it twice suffered failed attempts to sail to America, they eventually joined another group of Pilgrims who were planning to sail there aboard the *Mayflower*. The ship departed from England in September, 1620, and, after a difficult 66-day journey, they finally spotted land in late November in an area of Cape Cod, Massachusetts, now known as Provincetown. They had originally intended to sail further south to the Virginia Colony, but, because winter was nearly upon them, they ultimately sailed further up the Cape and decided to disembark at what is now known as Plymouth Rock. James Chilton had survived the voyage, but died soon after spotting land at Cape Cod. Young Mary Chilton was among the first group of Pilgrims to land at Plymouth Rock. In fact, she is reputed to be the first woman ever to set foot upon Plymouth Rock. Her mother Susanna also survived the voyage but died during that first, very harsh winter, leaving Mary an orphan at the age of 13. Mary apparently made her home with other Pilgrim families until her older sister, Isabella, arrived at Plymouth the following year. In October of 1624, Mary married John Winslow, who had come to Plymouth in 1621, and who would become a well-to-do merchant in the new colony.

John and Mary Winslow remained in Plymouth for the next 33 years before moving their family to Boston in 1657. They both lived well into their 70's and had eight children. Their oldest daughter, Susanna, who was born in 1628, married Robert Latham, who had arrived in the new colony a few years earlier, in 1649. They remained in Plymouth until about 1667, when they moved to what is now known as East Bridgewater, Massachusetts. The Lathams and four generations of their descendents remained in East Bridgewater for nearly 130 years, living there through the Indian wars and the American Revolution, in which several Lathams served and fought against the British. After the Revolutionary War, in the early 1790's, members of the Latham family moved to the small, newly-developing town of Gray, Maine. The Lathams lived in Gray for two generations, spanning 40-50 years. They moved west in the early 1850's to the newly-opening Ohio territory, and eventually settled in Maineville, Ohio, from where future generations of the family would spread across America.

Thus, the English roots of the family came to the New World under the most difficult circumstances in search of religious freedom. They planted their roots deep in New England soil, prospered and begat a solid harvest of new Americans, whose roots intermingled with those of other immigrants to the New World and expanded across the new nation. One of these many descendents from the English ancestral line was Janet Latham Babbitt, my maternal grandmother, who was born on March 15, 1895, in Arlington, Kansas.

From Germany, in the company of his parents and three brothers, came young Andrew Mann, then eleven years of age. The Mann family had lived in the Rheinland-Pfalz region of Germany. Andrew's father, Peter, came from the town of Weinheim, and his mother, Anna Marie, came from Morsfeld. The Mann family belonged to the German Baptist Church. At that time, the only legal religions in Germany were the Lutheran, Calvinist and Roman Catholic Churches; therefore, German Baptists were subjected to persecution. Thus, like many other Europeans, the Mann family decided to leave Germany to seek religious and political freedom in the American colonies. Having made their decision to emigrate to America, the family began their trek from Worms, Germany, in the spring of 1750. They originally set sail from Rotterdam, Holland, in early June and ultimately arrived in Philadelphia on August 15, 1750, aboard the sailing vessel *Royal Union*. The religious climate in Pennsylvania was especially conducive for the Mann family because many German Baptists had already left Germany for Pennsylvania to seek religious freedom during the two to three decades prior to their own departure.

All of the four Mann brothers were children at the time of their voyage. From Rotterdam, the *Royal Union* had sailed across the English Channel to the English port of Cowes, where there would have been a delay of one to two weeks while the vessel cleared English Customs and prepared for the long voyage across the Atlantic Ocean. Whereas the *Mayflower* had carried just over 100 people, the *Royal Union* was much larger and accommodated about 500 passengers; nevertheless, the ship was not really large enough for so many people, and conditions were terrible aboard the ship. The passengers were packed in like sardines, and, without proper food, water and sanitary conditions, diseases like dysentery, scurvy, typhoid and smallpox were rampant. Many, especially the elderly and children, did not survive the 12-week voyage. Combined with the inevitable storms during that time of year and alleged disregard and cruelty of the crew towards the passengers, it is safe to say that this "adventure" of the four young Mann brothers was certainly not a pleasure cruise.

Upon disembarking in Philadelphia in 1750, hardship conditions were not left behind them. Although the Mann family would have almost certainly found a support group in the colony of German Baptists who had arrived before them, they undoubtedly arrived without significant assets to sustain themselves. There are no known records covering the first few years following the Mann family's arrival in Philadelphia, but this period was a time when new land purchases of frontier territory were opening up in western Pennsylvania. Despite the fact that the French and Indian War was being waged in the western region of the Pennsylvania frontier, the promise of land and new opportunity obviously beckoned the Mann family. As a result, during the mid-1750's, they headed west.

According to the few available family records, Andrew's father, Peter, died soon after arrival in Philadelphia, but the remaining members of the Mann family probably joined a wagon train of like-minded German Baptists for the westward trek to the frontier. Family records do reflect that, in 1758, they were located in Marsh Creek, Pennsylvania, about 40 miles west of Philadelphia, and that they reached the Tonoloway Settlement, in what is now Fulton County, Pennsylvania, around 1760. They joined the Tonoloway Primitive Baptist Church, and there Andrew Mann was married to Rachel

Egnor, who had been born in 1745 in Wurtemburg, Germany. The young couple then settled a large parcel of land in what is the Pigeon Cove section of the settlement. Andrew and Rachel had eight children, all of whom were born in Pigeon Cove. During the Revolutionary War, Andrew was commissioned as a Captain in the 8th Pennsylvania Regiment; he survived the War and returned to live out his long life in Pigeon Cove.

Over the next 100 years, four generations of Andrew Mann's descendents were born in Fulton County. In 1835, one of these descendents, Job Mann Winters, was born. In 1856, Job was offered an opportunity to assume a school teacher position in Darke County, Ohio, which was located on the western outskirts of Ohio, about 450 miles due west of Fulton County. Job set out for Darke County soon after accepting the new position, and, upon arrival, he settled in the Richland Township, where his school was located. In 1860, Job married Rhoda Brewer and they had nine children, the first six of whom were born within 10 years.

Added to his enthusiastic support of population growth, Job was equally ambitious in his desire to build a suitable estate for his growing brood. In addition to his teaching duties, Job and Rhoda purchased some property in 1864 on which they eventually built a large and thriving dairy farm of about 340 acres. Rufus Winters was the fourth child and second son born to Job and Rhoda. On April 15, 1890, Rufus married Bertha Burtch of nearby Dawn, Ohio, and they produced three children. The oldest of those children was Owen Burtch Winters, my maternal grandfather, who was born on November 5, 1891.

Owen, known to family and friends as "Obie", was a talented young man and a brilliant student, and because he also came from a prominent family, he was quickly accepted to attend the prestigious University of Michigan, from where he graduated in 1910. Following his graduation, Obie embarked on a highly successful career in advertising, first in Detroit, where he met his future wife, Janet Latham Babbitt, and later in the huge corporate markets of Chicago and New York. Obie's success in the advertising world is well-documented, and he was instrumental in the growth of print advertising during the time of major industrial growth in America between the two World Wars. As a result, Obie was highly rewarded in his efforts and became a very wealthy man.

Obie and Janet were married in Detroit on April 15, 1918; they had two daughters together, the younger of which was my mother, Natalie Ann Winters, who was born in Evanston, Illinois on November 22, 1920.

The union of Obie and Janet, and the birth of their two daughters, officially joined and irrevocably intertwined the English and German branches of the family. Both branches had originally come to America centuries before in search of religious freedom; both branches had also eventually made their way west to the Ohio territory, ironically arriving there within a few years of each other.

In the years following the potato famine in mid-19th century Ireland, during a period of time when starvation, dire economic hardship, and mandated land reform were prevalent, hundreds of thousands of young Irish left their native land for opportunities elsewhere. Migration to Australia, Canada and the United States was rampant, and among the multitudes of young Irishmen who left for America were newlyweds Timothy and Honora Morris. Both Timothy (1837) and Honora (1842) were born in Tipperary County, where their families were employed as tenant farmers on property owned by the landed gentry. Like others before them, they left Ireland primarily for economic reasons. They were already well used to hardship from the famine years in Ireland when they set sail for America, but the perilous and overly crowded voyage across the Atlantic Ocean certainly tested their survival ability.

Timothy apparently arrived first in Boston in the late 1860's, followed by Honora and their two young children, who landed there in August, 1871, aboard the English vessel *Malta*. These were difficult and uneasy times in America, which was still suffering from the aftermath of the Civil War. Jobs in urban America were scarce, but Irish male immigrants were being recruited off of the arrival docks for cheap labor or for service in the Army. There was also significant prejudice against Irish immigrants because of anti-Catholic sentiment; this fact was exacerbated in that the Irish were seen to be taking all of the labor jobs at the expense of more established Americans. Nevertheless, Timothy and Honora managed to find their way. Timothy most certainly worked hard, probably as a laborer, and Honora may have also worked part-time while juggling the demands of motherhood. Between 1872 and 1884, they gave birth to six additional children, bringing their total to eight. The fifth of these children was James Edward Morris, my paternal grandfather, who was born in Boston, on December 10, 1875.

Young James Edward Morris was a strapping and industrious young man, who worked his way into relative prominence. He worked as an editorial writer for the *Boston Post* newspaper and played baseball for the *Boston Post* team. In addition, he was elected as a city alderman at the young age of 22. In 1908, James moved to New York City to accept a position with the *New York Sun* newspaper, where he continued to grow in prominence. He became a leader of the *Sun's* labor union and was attributed with vastly improving the working conditions of the newspaper staff.

Also from Ireland, by way of Scotland, Ellen Cantwell sailed to New York in 1904. She had been born in Glen Boig, Scotland, a mining village east of Glasgow, on April 12, 1885, the oldest of six children. Ellen's grandfather, Edward Cantwell, had been born in Kilbeggan, Westmeath County, Ireland, where, as a young man, he had been working as a laborer. According to family history, he fell in love with Mary Carroll, the beautiful daughter of the village blacksmith, which was considered a position of social prominence, but Mary's father disapproved of the relationship. As a result, in the mid-1850's, with Ireland still in the throes of post-famine hardships, Edward and Mary decided to elope and left Ireland for Scotland. They ended up in the village of Glen Boig, a center of clay and coal mines, where

Edward found work as a brick maker.

Ellen, my paternal grandmother, was only the second generation to be born in Scotland. At the age of 19, she decided to set out for America to seek her fortune; she left with a small group of friends who believed that they would be able to find work as "au pairs" in prosperous New York City. By the time Ellen departed for America, the mode of sea transport had improved greatly over the days of the old wooden sailing vessels, so her voyage was undoubtedly much less treacherous. Nevertheless, it took a great amount of courage for a single, 19-year-old girl to leave her family and everything she knew for the unknown promise of America. A few years after she arrived in New York City and after having established herself in her new country, Ellen met James Edward Morris, a writer for the *New York Sun*. They were an odd couple, in that James was 6'2", and Ellen a mere 5'1", but they fell in love and were married on January 9th, 1910. They lived together happily for 42 years, until James passed away in 1952. They had two children. James Edward Morris, Jr., my father, the older of those two children, was born on October 28, 1911.

Natalie Ann Winters, my mother, was raised in an environment of wealth and luxury, living in a lakeside mansion on Lake Michigan in suburban Chicago. She went to expensive boarding schools, and took private lessons in ballet, which became her passion. Although born of strong-willed parents and with an older sister of the same proclivity, Natalie was inherently shy. With Natalie still at the young age of seven, her parents divorced, and her mother decided to move herself and her two daughters to France, to the Mediterranean city of Nice. There Natalie lived for five years, became fluent in French, and learned the European manner of life. Moving back to the States when she was 12, the family settled in Beverly Hills, California, where Natalie continued to live the life of privilege. The family lived next door to movie stars, and she lived quite a world apart from the norm.

During this time, Natalie also continued to develop her passion for ballet. She was born with an elegant beauty and natural athleticism that helped her to become an accomplished dancer. Nevertheless, despite her blossoming physical beauty and talents, Natalie remained a shy and introspective young lady.

When it came time to move on to higher education, Natalie entered the Washington School of Ballet and continued to follow her passion for the dance. Unfortunately, she was taller and heavier (about 5'7" and 120 pounds) than the prototypical ballerina; she towered over the majority of the male dancers of her day, plus they were normally not strong enough to lift her easily. As a result, despite her prowess as a ballerina, Natalie soon saw the writing on the wall, left the ballet school, and sought other options to pursue her love for dance. With her striking good looks and developed dancing skills, she quickly found that opportunity with the Arthur Murray Dance Studios, which, in those days, was a popular venue for the well-to-do to polish their ballroom dancing skills. She soon found her way to West Palm Beach where she took a position as an instructor in the posh Florida resort city.

My father, James E. Morris, Jr., grew up in a typical middle-class urban environment. His parents had moved from bustling Manhattan to Jersey City, New Jersey, in an effort to provide a better environment for raising children. Jim's upbringing was a traditional one, based on strong Catholic values and emphasizing social interaction and sports. Throughout his school days, Jim was an exceptional athlete, and very popular among his wide-ranging circle of friends. With his uncommon good looks, outgoing personality and exemplary athletic skills, Jim was always the center of attention. He excelled in track and field, in which he was a New Jersey State High School Champion in sprints, and in football, where his elusiveness and speed brought him significant scrutiny from several colleges. He eventually was offered, and accepted, a football scholarship to Catholic University in WDC.

At Catholic University, Jim excelled on the football field and was popular socially, areas that tended to dominate his available time. In truth, away from strict parental influence for the first time and being a "social animal," he gave in to the many temptations surrounding him in the nation's Capital, and devoted very little time to his studies. In those days, prowess on the football field, especially at a traditional Catholic institution, was not accepted as an excuse for academic inadequacy; as a result, his career at Catholic was rather short-lived, although undoubtedly he enjoyed the time of his life.

After departing Catholic, Jim returned home to New Jersey, where, as legend has it, he played football with the New York Giants; this career was also apparently short-lived, when he allegedly suffered a vicious tackle by Chicago Bears star Bronco Nagurski which broke both of his legs. Professional football was not very well-documented in those embryonic days of the sport, so we have been unable to substantiate the facts of the legend, but at least it always made for a pretty good story. In any event, once recovered from his football injuries, Jim began a career as a dance instructor with the aforementioned Arthur Murray Dance Studios. Because of his good looks and athletic grace on the dance floor, Jim moved quickly up the promotion ladder and was eventually offered the opportunity to move to West Palm Beach to manage the Arthur Murray Dance Studio there, where the featured band was often the Jimmy Dorsey Orchestra. It was there, in West Palm Beach, in 1940, that Jim Morris first met Natalie Winters. It was love at first sight for both of them!

Unfortunately, other than a few very nice pictures of Jim and Natalie putting on dance demonstrations together, there is not much detail about their first years together. We do know that they made a striking couple on the dance floor, and we can surmise that the courtship was hot and heavy. They married on February 12, 1941, and their reception was held at the exclusive Breakers Hotel. It must have been a most romantic and colorful event. Soon thereafter, WWII demanded attention. Jim joined the U.S. Coast Guard and was assigned to Connecticut, while Natalie assumed the duties of wife and mother. First son, James Edward III, was born soon thereafter in Greenwich, and daughter, Sheila, came along two years later in New London. Jim spent all of his service time based in Connecticut, so there are no real war stories to relate.

After the war, Jim got into coaching within the Connecticut Prep School circuit, working for several years at The Gunnery School, before moving on to the Kingswood School, in West Hartford. He coached all sports (football, basketball and baseball), and also served as Athletic Director. By all accounts, Jim was a highly successful coach, and his teams all performed very well. He loved his work as a coach, was well respected by his colleagues and players alike, and, at this time, he also began some side work as a broadcaster for local college and professional sports events. With his two children growing and thriving at home, and with Natalie apparently quite content in her domestic duties, things seemed to be going very well. At about this stage, however, Fate introduced some new elements into the mix; Natalie's father, Obie, the successful and wealthy advertising magnate, died at an early age, and bequeathed to the young family a significant sum of money. Despite the sad loss of Natalie's father, this development introduced some interesting new possibilities for the family, which, by this time, had grown yet one more time, with the birth of Robert Owen Morris on August 25, 1950.

With the new addition to the family, and the recent inheritance offering new investment opportunities, Jim and Natalie had some decisions to make; should they stay on their current path, with Jim continuing his coaching career in New England, or should they look into other options? With so many choices available to them, at this point in history (early 1951), they decided to embark upon a new path and narrowed their choices down to two: (1) to purchase a large strip of undeveloped beach property in Florida in what was eventually to become the city of North Fort Lauderdale or (2) to purchase a beef cattle farm in rural Virginia, at the urging of Natalie's mother and sister, who were both living in that area. In retrospect, the beach property acquisition would have been a no-brainer; the Florida coast was rapidly developing, and they could have quickly and easily grown their investment there. On the other hand, the beef cattle industry in those post WWII days was also thriving, and there was the lure of becoming "landed gentry" in the beautiful Shenandoah Valley of Virginia. Notwithstanding the fact that Jim had been raised in Jersey City and had probably never even set foot on a farm and that Natalie grew up in urban elegance in Evanston, Nice, and Beverly Hills, with an equal lack of exposure to the rigors of rural life, they ultimately made the decision to purchase the farm.

Certainly, we have no way of knowing what might have happened should they have chosen to stay put in Connecticut or to invest in the soon-to-be developed Florida beach frontage; however, the choice of these two city-folks to purchase that Virginia farm must rank very close in terms of bad decisions to Napoleon's fateful choice in the winter of 1812 to invade Russia. Both decisions were unwise and equally disastrous.

In a nutshell, everything went very wrong with the farm from the outset. First off, the bottom dropped out of the beef cattle market soon after they closed the purchase of the farm, so they began losing money right away. Secondly, being a social animal, Jim found that life in the country did not meet his inherent need for social stimulation, so he was (too) often in town gallivanting with new-found friends, while Natalie was home taking care of the kids. As might be expected, when money issues mix in with situations where marital jealousy might develop, the results are usually not very positive.

In any event, within four years of becoming country folks, Jim and Natalie sold the farm, at a huge loss, and decided to go their separate ways. Both moved into nearby Staunton, where Jim rented a bachelor apartment while Natalie and the kids moved in with Grandma. For the sake of brevity, this snippet of history is over-simplified, and undoubtedly there was much more involved in the demise of the marriage. However, as with all failed family relationships, many people suffered as a result.

So, here we are, in about 1955, residing in Staunton, Virginia, a charming but sleepy town in the Shenandoah Valley, living with Natalie and Grandma, and with father Jim living just down the street. Our family line had come a long way to end up here. Making the brave decisions to leave the only land they knew and to make the perilous, disease-ridden voyage across the Atlantic, English Pilgrims and German Baptists sought out a land in which the practice of their respective religions would not subject them to imprisonment or persecution. Later, Irish immigrants and transplanted Irishmen from Scotland left severe economic conditions in their beloved land to seek out their fortunes elsewhere. These were all courageous people, making desperate journeys, at tremendous personal sacrifice in search of a dream. It is here, in Staunton, Virginia, where we culminate the respective ancestral paths, and from where the quixotic odyssey will begin.

Chapter 2

"You Were an Accident, Dear!"

When my mother smilingly revealed this interesting tidbit of information, I was already an adult in my mid-30's. Nevertheless, the news of having been born "accidentally" did come as a bit of a shock. Although the thought had never previously crossed my mind, in retrospect, I should not have been too surprised. Brother Jim was eight years my senior, and sister Sheila was six years older, so I clearly did not fit the "every-two-year" planned parenthood formula. This revelation also put things into much better perspective and tended to explain some of the oddities of my childhood.

I had come into the world as an accidental birth, an unplanned yet undoubtedly happy event. In all honesty, I had never felt like an "accident" when I was growing up; on the contrary, although after the economic catastrophe of the farm, we grew up in modest conditions, I do not recall ever wanting for anything. In fact, as my brother and sister used to remind me, almost daily, I was probably a bit pampered and spoiled by my mother as a child. So, accidental or not, life was pretty good.

From the perspective of personality, I did tend to take after Natalie; I was basically shy and introverted, and tended to fend for myself. With my brother and sister being much older and with their own circle of friends and activities, I recall spending much of my childhood entertaining myself, which probably had a great deal to do with the development of a sense of strong independence and may have contributed to the evolution of my romantic idealistic tendencies. Because dad had been raised as a Catholic, (although mom was an Episcopalian), all three of the kids went to the local St. Francis of Assisi parochial grammar school and attended St. Francis Catholic Church. In the little southern town of Staunton, Virginia, there was a very small Catholic community. On the positive side, this reality meant that the teacher to student ratio in the school was advantageous, and the education which we received from the nuns was probably pretty good. On the other hand, the Catholic Diocese tended to send their problem priests and nuns to the smaller parishes, so, charitably speaking, there was a wee bit of dysfunction in the local school and church community.

Almost without exception, every person who attended St. Francis from that era has dozens of stories to tell. We were educated by the Vincentian Sisters of Charity, even though the word "charity" always seemed to be a bit of a misnomer. Although one of the nuns whom I remember was fairly kind and likeable, the rest of them (there were actually only four nuns at the school) were usually ill-tempered and oftentimes abusive. Corporal punishment was universally practiced, and there was one certain nun, Sister Alexis, whose repertoire of punishment practices was, to say the least, highly creative.

I recall one young second-grade girl who made the mistake of telling a lie to Sister Alexis only to have a huge bar of soap jammed into her mouth as punishment. After this startling event, one would assume that she probably never told another lie in her life, so perhaps the punishment was effective after all. Another young boy, who was in truth prone to misbehavior, was turned upside down by this same sister and inserted head-first into a large trash can as punishment. And, like all boys who attended the school for any period of time, I had to drop my trousers on more than one occasion for the administration of the paddle to my backside. Naturally, out of fear of retribution from the dear sisters, no one ever told their parents about all of this physical and verbal abuse; however, when I finally shared this information with my mother years later, she was astounded.

Other than the slightly dysfunctional parochial school which I attended, I can honestly say that Staunton, Virginia, was a good town in which to grow up. I would estimate that the total population in the 50's and 60's was probably no more than 12-14,000 people, and it was a pretty typical small southern town. People were always friendly, drivers routinely waved to other cars on the road, no one ever locked the front door of the house, and car keys were perfectly safe being left in the ignition. The closest thing we had to crime was kids smashing pumpkins on Halloween night.

There was always plenty for children to do. The little league sports programs were well-organized and very positive influences on the kids, and the city park was a center of all sorts of outdoors activity; it contained numerous sports fields, the public golf course, and offered an outdoor summer concert series. The town was simply one of those environments where kids could be kids, could be out and about all day, and parents never had any reason for concern. In summary, it was a great place for raising a family. Like other young people with an inherent wanderlust mind-set, I admit that I was eager to leave the small town atmosphere and to explore the world. Looking back, however, at this late stage in my life, having lived all over the world and experienced much, I find that Staunton stirs in me a strong sense of nostalgia and longing for the quiet life; people there still know all of their neighbors and continue to maintain personal relationships that have lasted a lifetime.

Personally, my grammar school years at St. Francis, which lasted through 7th grade, were primarily sports-oriented. With two very athletic parents, it should not be surprising that I had an affinity and talent for sports. I began playing little league football and baseball at the age of seven and did well at both. I also played basketball every winter at the local YMCA, but I never really caught onto the sport, and was mediocre at best. In general, I was one of the better athletes in my age group and was usually picked for the all star teams. So that was pretty much my life's experience for the first 12 years or so, mostly pre-occupied with successfully surviving the wrath of the Sisters of Charity at St. Francis during the school day, followed by organized sports after school and in the summer, and free-time in the interim.

Looking back on those years, I have a few observations that are clearly different from the experiences my own children have had. First of all, through kindergarten and my first seven years of school, all of my classmates were white of European extraction; there were no black or Hispanic kids in my classes. Although St. Francis was a private school, the same situation was true in the public schools as well because, in the early 1960's, the public schools in Staunton were still segregated. So it was that I never shared a classroom with a non-white student until I moved on to 8th grade at Shelburne Junior High School. This reality was also true of all of the sports teams on which I played; up until that point, the kids who played on the little league teams in those days were all white. Although I recall that the black high school, Booker T. Washington HS, always had exceptional basketball teams, I simply do not believe there were any youth leagues available to them. In fact, it was not until 1963 or so that the public schools in Staunton were officially integrated. That's just the way it was.

Entry into 8th grade and the public school system introduced me to all sorts of new experiences, multi-racial class rooms, teachers who did not wear religious garb and did not beat the crap out of students on a daily basis, and girls. Yes, we did have girls at St. Francis, and there were a few who attracted my fleeting attention, but they did not really have any impact on my life. In those years, girls were simply not a mainstay of my daily concerns or activities. I do, however, recall experiencing my first "puppy-love" in the 7th grade, with a public school girl whom I had met at a high school football game. We attended a party or two together, and had a few innocent dances, but that was pretty much the extent of our relationship. Those were simply more innocent times than today.

Frankly, I do not recall that 8th grade at Shelburne Junior High School changed the girl situation much at all. I was certainly more conscious of them, and I spent more time daily paying attention to my appearance, but I do not recall ever having any serious interest or crushes on anyone in particular. My primary preoccupation was still sports. The only major issue in life during the 8th grade was that all of my friends seemed to be experiencing serious growth spurts, while I simply wasn't. They were apparently making the transition to adulthood, and I was being left behind. As might be imagined, this situation did play an significant role in the way I looked at life during that time.

When I entered 9th grade at Robert E. Lee High School the next year, the situation was still the same. I had made the same transition as everyone else, with the same anticipation as any child finally getting to high school, but my inherent shyness and being behind the growth curve in relation to my peers made the change even more challenging. Perhaps the worst part of it all was in my desire to continue to play football with the same guys with whom I had played throughout the little league years. However, being physically smaller, I still felt and looked pretty much like a little leaguer among growing young men, a situation that seriously affected my psyche. I did give football at Lee High a shot through the pre-school practices, but I simply felt out-of-my-league at the high school level and ultimately decided to quit the team.

As I reflect upon those early years, that event and that period of time in general were really a difficult point in my young life. I remember feeling incredibly embarrassed and humiliated by failing to keep up with my peers on the football field, and I allowed this fact to affect my social outlook. Needless to say, right at the very beginning of my high school experience, this situation set the stage for a somewhat less-than-noteworthy freshman year. I carried with me a feeling of inadequacy that negatively affected my general outlook on life and which dominated my psyche that entire school year. As a result, I largely became a recluse from all school activities, and I felt pretty miserable.

It was clear to at least one of my 9th grade teachers, a kindly lady who was a family friend, that I was unhappy. I remember that she inquired of me one day after class how I was getting along; my response must have caused some concern, and I believe that she contacted my mother about it. It had also become clear to my mother that I was not particularly happy with my experience thus far at the local high school. Some years prior, my brother had the opportunity to go to a prestigious New England prep school on financial scholarship; the Headmaster was an old family friend. Soon my mother approached me with the same opportunity; she had apparently contacted the prep school Headmaster to see if a similar arrangement could be made for me. When she offered me the chance to go there for my sophomore year, I recall that I jumped at the opportunity. I didn't know if things would be better there for me, but I was wise enough to understand that a fresh start would be a good thing. So, the stage was set for me to attend Suffield Academy in the fall of 1965, which would turn out to be a life-altering experience; this move would irrevocably change my perspective of the world from one with a close-up focus to one with a largely panoramic view.

In terms of attempting to put a person's life in perspective, reflection upon the period of childhood is always a useful exercise. Over the years, I have also come to understand that all things in life do in fact happen for a reason. At 15, I would be leaving the one town I had known almost all of my life for an entirely new environment. I would be leaving family and friends for a whole new world as yet totally unknown. In principle, there are some similarities to the fateful decisions which my ancestors had made before me. Like them, I voluntarily left the one home I knew for a brave new world, seeking to improve upon personal circumstances which I found to be unsatisfactory. Granted, leaving home to go to school only 600 miles away is vastly different than permanently leaving one's native land to make a perilous journey of thousands of miles, but the motivation was similar.

What is perfectly clear to me at this point in life is that the decision to leave Staunton for Suffield was indeed a life-changing event. In the course of the next three years, horizons were expanded and expectations of life's possibilities increased. It would be during these coming years that the seeds of a life of wanderlust were planted, from which the quixotic odyssey would eventually evolve. In analyzing the effect of childhood upon decisions to be made in future years, it is probably safe to say that the inadequacies felt in those younger years had a strong impact on the development of a romantic idealist mentality. Like Don Quixote, who was dissatisfied with his common existence, the romantic idealist seeks out opportunities to introduce new elements of adventure and spice to an otherwise lackluster life. In my case, the pattern certainly seems to fit.

As for having been "an accident" at birth, I never really thought twice about this revelation from my mother. I have come to believe that there are no accidents in life. We are all here on this earth for predestined reasons, even if it is not always clear what those "reasons" may be. In any event, in the fall of 1965, I departed my small, Virginia town not knowing what new adventures may lay ahead, but with full anticipation that life's course was about to assume a new heading.

Chapter 3

Broadening Horizons

When I arrived at Suffield Academy just after Labor Day, September, 1965, an entirely new and very compelling adventure was about to begin. At that time, Suffield was a boys-only college preparatory school of some 260 students. The school enjoyed an excellent reputation, and kids were sent there to enhance their chances of getting into a prestigious university. The school grounds were spacious, and beautiful, spreading over hundreds of acres, much like a college campus; the school buildings were numerous and quite impressive. The town of Suffield itself was charming, a traditional New England small town, with picturesque 18th century homes lining the main street around the Academy campus. Needless to say, the first impression I had of my new school was a very positive one.

The vast majority of the students came from very well-to-do families who could afford the price tag of a prestigious boarding school education for their children. Included within the student body were sons and nephews of some famous American families, including Rockefeller, Ford (Motor Company), Tisch (CBS and Loew's Theatres) and many others. The students came from all across the country, plus there was a contingent of foreign students, including some from Europe, Africa, and Asia, making for a highly cosmopolitan group of young men. Finally, there was a handful of local and, like myself, scholarship students, who found themselves in new circumstances living with quite a different circle of folks.

Not only did many of the students come from wealthy backgrounds, but also the school was an intellectual environment of the type that I had not previously experienced. At least half of the faculty had Ivy League educations, and most of the students came to Suffield with a much more well-rounded and finely-tuned educational background than I did. I cannot honestly say that I went to Suffield less prepared academically than the majority of my classmates. However, I arrived there having spent my entire life in a small southern town; hence my view of the world tended to be somewhat limited to that experience.

My intellectual curiosity and capabilities were largely unchallenged up to that point; at Suffield, I was thrust into the midst of students whose perspectives were more widely developed and who were already looking ahead and planning their career paths. By comparison, I had never really questioned my reality and had not given much thought to what the future might hold for me. I had arrived at Suffield in pretty much of a fog, but the wide-ranging exposure which I received in the course of my time there would drastically change this situation.

One of the major changes from life as I had previously known it was the tradition of the school and the comprehensive day-to-day regimen. First of all, the official day began at breakfast and proceeded into a full day of classes, followed by athletics, the evening meal, and after-dinner study hall. Interspersed into the daily schedule was a mandatory work assignment at the school, which could be kitchen, dining room, or grounds-keeping duties. The uniform of the day was a jacket and tie, and the atmosphere was that of a gentleman's institution. Formal team sports or intramural physical activity were mandatory, as was participation at a formal chapel service twice per week. Additional extra-curricular student leadership and/or club participation were also strongly encouraged, so, all-in-all, there was very little down time for anything outside of organized activities. A half-day of classes was held on Wednesdays and Saturdays, the afternoons of which were reserved for sporting events against other prep schools in the region. Officially, Sunday was the only free day, although that day was also largely spent getting ready for the week ahead.

The major benefit derived from an environment such as Suffield Academy, especially for me, was the development of good study habits and time management skills. Students did not have the convenience to enjoy "goof off" time or to plop down in front of a television; this reality was probably a good thing, because students needed to stay on top of academics lest we fall quickly behind the learning curve. The first year for me was admittedly a very challenging one. Not only was there the need to become accustomed to an entirely new lifestyle, but also the course work was demanding. Many of my classmates had either attended Suffield as freshmen and were, therefore, already in sync with the demands of the school, or they had attended other prep schools where the regimen was similar. In my case, I was starting from scratch, and I struggled to keep up the pace during that first year. As a result, out of the 70 or so students which we had in our class, I ended up somewhere in the bottom third in terms of grades.

Sports were also a major endeavor. I was still physically smaller than most, so I was assigned to the lightweight football team, comprised primarily of freshman and sophomores. Still, it was an opportunity to display my football skills that I had developed over the years; hence, I performed well within this structure, which did bode well for later years. I developed Osgood Schlatter's disease in my knee that first season and sported a full leg cast for most of the winter semester, so winter sports were not an option. However, in the spring, I played on the junior varsity baseball team and performed well. These sporting activities helped to rebuild the confidence which had been lost during my freshman year of high school in Staunton, and I finally experienced some of the overdue growth spurt (better late than never) my sophomore year at Suffield, allowing me to regain a sense of prowess in athletics.

With no women on campus, social activities at Suffield were, by necessity, somewhat limited. We had numerous sponsored dances with some of the girls' schools in the region; they either bused the boys to the girls' school or vice versa. Our "dates" were pre-arranged by the social committee, which was clearly an exercise in potluck. Sometimes you met someone with whom you had something in common, but just as often, you did not. Nevertheless, these events constituted a good break from the normal school routine and always made for rollicking conversation for the week following the dance.

By my junior year, I had become quite accustomed to the challenging regimen at Suffield, and, with hard work, my class standing began to improve methodically. This year was the one in which all of the students were actively beginning to consider college choices, so the seriousness of our efforts kicked into a higher gear. We took practice SAT's in the fall and then the real tests in the spring, and those tests, combined with our class results and extra-curricular activities, began to provide the students with the parameters of their future college choices. In addition to improvements in my class work, I also made the varsity football team that fall, and, in an effort to build up my legs and improve my speed, I switched from baseball in the spring to varsity track, where I ran distance races. I was a back-up quarterback on a good football team, where I earned a start or two due to injury to the first team quarterback, but I primarily played "mop-up" in the latter part of games which we had already won by a large margin. In track, I ran well and achieved my objective of improving the strength in my legs, so I was looking forward to a much more impressive senior year in both sports.

In keeping with the development of my wanderlust mentality and my desire to expand my horizons, in the summer between my junior and senior year at Suffield, I got a job on Block Island in Rhode Island, as a cook's helper at a popular tourist restaurant. The owner of the restaurant typically hired high school and college age kids to staff the restaurant. He even had a ramshackle, old barracks-style dormitory where he would house everyone. The pay was pitifully low, but the room and board was provided gratis. This owner was a clever fellow in that he would hire about twice as many kids as he really needed and then quickly weeded them out to a more economical level. For me, at the age of 16, this job was an initial adventure in freedom from the regimen of home and boarding school, so it offered a good lesson in freedom management and maturity. Unfortunately, I was one of the kids who eventually was weeded out, so my adventure on Block Island was more short-lived than I had anticipated. However, it formed the backdrop for the first time in which I really fell head-over-heels in love.

She will remain nameless for the sake of this treatise, but she was purely and simply beautiful. Never mind that she was a junior in college, four years older than me, for I was smitten from the first moment I saw her. She was tall, alluring and very kind; we hit it off well from the outset, and she took me under her wing. Whereas she regarded me as her little brother, being the budding romantic idealist, I was convinced, of course, that she felt the same strong emotions for me as I felt for her. In any event, for the time we spent together on the island, I felt like a puppy following his new master, and I took advantage of every occasion to spend time with her. When the time came for me to depart, I stood on the deck of the ferry, fully-expecting her to come running to the boat after me, but, alas, she never showed. Once I got home, I wrote her several times, and she was kind enough to respond, but she was careful to let me down gently and graciously. Nevertheless, I was truly heartbroken by the experience, which I regard as my first indoctrination into the real world. I never heard from her again after that summer, and I often wondered how her life developed. When the movie "Summer of 42" came out a few years later, it brought back vividly those rueful memories of an impossible love lost.

Back on my feet at Suffield in the fall of 1967, my senior year commenced with great expectations. We had high hopes for another successful year for the football team, for which I planned to play a major role. We had lost a number of good players from the previous year, but we had a new coach and a solid returning nucleus. However, a number of our better players got hurt early in the season, so, even though I had a decent year in the role of running back, we literally limped through the season, losing far more games than we won. In track, based on my productive junior year and tryouts in the spring, I was elected captain of the varsity team, which enjoyed an excellent season. My speed had much improved over the previous year, so I switched to running sprints (440, 220, relays and the long jump), and I performed well. Academically, I continued to improve my grades and class standing throughout the year and increased my SAT scores when I took the test again in the fall. As a result, even though our academy guidance counselor was never very encouraging of my chances to get into a top flight university, I set my sights relatively high.

My first choice for college was the University of North Carolina, for which I applied for early admission; however, even with the prep school background, acceptance at UNC was difficult for out-of-state students, and my application was declined. As back-up schools, I also applied to Whittier College in California (a Quaker school which Richard Nixon had attended), the University of Miami (Florida), and Georgetown University in Washington, DC. I was accepted to both Whittier and Miami while I awaited word from my second choice, Georgetown. Whittier had been suggested by the aforementioned guidance counselor, but I was never very excited about going there; and whereas Miami was attractive to me, even at that young age I knew I would probably have a difficult time keeping my mind on my studies there. So, even though Miami had offered me a financial scholarship package, when Georgetown responded to the positive, I was elated. The prospects of going to a prestigious university in our nation's capital was simply too much to ignore.

So, my mother's wisdom in getting me the opportunity to attend Suffield had seemingly paid off well. Not only had I managed to get accepted into an excellent university, but I had developed some important traits in terms of an improved work ethic and a much more serious outlook on life. More importantly, my view of the world had been drastically altered, from that of a small town boy to one of a member of the global community. My intellectual interests had been greatly expanded, and I had been introduced to a whole new circle of friends. This, in my view, was the most important aspect of my Suffield experience, the close friendships developed during my three years there. Many of those friendships have lasted for a lifetime, and I still consider a few to be the best friends I have ever had the honor to know.

I left Suffield a much-changed person from the boy who had arrived there in September 1965, and I consider the experience to have been one of the most valuable ones I have had during my life. My future was now open to a whole new realm of adventures and experiences, and I entered this new world with enthusiasm and anticipation. What was to lie ahead for me?

Chapter 4

The Big Party

Washington, DC, Late August 1968

After a summer of working in Staunton at hard labor for $1.70 an hour, helping to build Interstate 81, I was off to Georgetown University to commence my college adventure. To set the stage properly, keep in mind that I had grown up in small town Virginia, had spent the vast majority of my high school years in an all-boys boarding school environment, and was now off to college in the vibrant, energetic nation's capital. I was going to "The Big City" with temptations everywhere. Sure, I had developed good work habits and discipline at prep school, but there we did not have a great many choices; there was not much else to do! Now, I found myself in a dynamic new world, and I certainly wanted to experience some of it.

Everyone goes off to college with a great deal of anticipation and excitement, and although I had already had an away-from-home school experience, I was no different. Would I like the college? Would I enjoy my courses? Would I do well in football? Would I have fun? Well, upon arriving at Georgetown that last week of August, 1968, for my freshman orientation, it became clear to me very quickly that the "fun" part would not be a problem. I had arrived as one of thousands of new freshman students that fall at Georgetown plus students at the other near-by universities, who had unanimously come to WDC for the exact same purpose. Fun was a no-brainer.

I had applied for and been accepted into the GU School of Business Administration. Frankly, I do not believe that I had any genuine or special interest in studying business at that point in my life, but I had surmised that it might be easier to get accepted into GU via the Business School, rather than the more renowned Foreign Service or Liberal Arts programs. So, I entered the Business School, and suffered through the customary Introduction to Business and Basic Accounting courses, in addition to the required liberal arts courses such as english, history, and, because GU is a Roman Catholic university, theology and philosophy courses. In a nutshell, although I did learn much during the first semester, and I managed to maintain a C+ average, I was far from captivated by my chosen course of study. Perhaps too many other, more interesting distractions beckoned me. After all, I was an 18-year-old male who had been catapulted into a situation of total freedom in the nation's capital, surrounded by a multitude of attractive females, bars everywhere, and lots of new friends, all eager to take full advantage of every opportunity. There would be plenty of time later in life for discipline and responsibility, but this was the time to let loose and explore.

My one serious diversion from academics and my "social responsibilities" was the football team. I joined the team as soon as school began, and football practice and games became an important part of that first semester. The football program at Georgetown in those days was played at a club level. Whereas Georgetown had been a big-time college football program in the 1930's and 1940's (playing in the 1940 Orange Bowl), like many urban, private Catholic colleges, the maintenance of a large-scale football program became too expensive and demanding. As a result, schools like Georgetown, Fordham, Catholic University, and others, opted to drop their football programs in the early 1950's. However, after an absence of having football on campus for about 13 years, interested students and the school administration combined to create a club football program that began in the mid-1960's. By the time I arrived on campus in 1968, the interest in the club team had grown significantly. The team had hired reputable coaches, had about 50 players, some of whom were as talented as players with major college programs, and had five games scheduled for that year. Opponents that season were Fordham, Seton Hall, Catholic University, Iona, and St. Peters.

We had a pretty good team in 1968. I played halfback in a second-string role behind some talented running backs. We ran a single-wing offense, which concentrated on the running game, and I had numerous opportunities to play during the course of our five games. All-in-all, it was a successful season. We won three of the five games, losing very close contests to Fordham and Catholic, and I was generally pleased with the results of my initial college football experience. Looking ahead into the future, when I returned to the GU gridiron in the fall of 1972, things would be much different; the football program would have become a full-fledged NCAA Program again, playing at the Division III level, with an excellent coaching staff and an improved caliber of players. Personally, I would be four years older, more matured, hardened by my experience in the military, mentally tougher, and 30 pounds heavier and stronger. Back to 1968, however, there was still a multitude of social shenanigans for this young man to experience during that first semester at Georgetown.

In all honesty, the fall of 1968 was largely a blur. With the possible exception of nights before a football game or an important exam, we were partying almost constantly. Although Georgetown had once been an all-male institution, women had been introduced into the student population a few years earlier, and I would estimate that about 30% of the GU student population was female. However, within just a few miles of the GU campus, there were a number of all-girls colleges and junior colleges at our beck and call, and I seem to remember that we found ourselves on those campuses regularly. In addition, the Georgetown section of Washington was a magnet for evening activity, with constant parties all within crawling distance of the GU campus. Sometimes the hardest decision we had to make on any given day was where to go that evening. Usually, the shotgun approach prevailed; we would go everywhere until we found what we were looking for or simply gave out for the evening.

None of the hundreds of young women I met during that freshman year really stick out in my mind; it was like a Swedish smorgasbord in which you know you ate way too much, but no one dish stays in your memory. So it was those first five months at Georgetown. I do recall that I had several dates with the daughter of a very famous professional baseball player, who will remain nameless, but honestly I was more impressed with her last name than with her personally. Repeating, life was pretty much a blur of activity, starting with the groggy effort to get to early-morning classes, recuperating during the course of the day, purging the poisons from my body during football practice that afternoon, and then going out in the evening to poison myself all over again. What a life, right?

Sooner or later, usually during a fleeting moment of relative sobriety, even possessed, irresponsible young men, such as I was, need to sit back and put everything into proper perspective. Where was I going with this style of life? Was this really the way in which I wanted to live? And, how the hell was I going to pay for it? All good questions, and ultimately they needed to be addressed. I think that it became pretty clear to me about halfway through that first semester that my time at GU was going to be a short-lived experience; something would have to change soon. First of all, I did not have the financial resources to support a Georgetown education. Secondly, my C+ average was not going to warrant any scholarship assistance. Thirdly, there were no football scholarships to be had. And, finally, I was not overly invigorated by the academic courses I was taking. In essence, I really had no idea where I was headed, and I needed to grab the wheel to set the ship of life on its proper course.

I had known from the beginning that financial resources were quickly going to become a problem. This period was also the height of the war in Vietnam, and the time of the draft for military service, so the armed forces were always a possible reality of life in those days. As luck would have it, my draft number was very high, which meant that the chances of my being drafted were relatively slim. However, my older brother, Jim, was serving in Vietnam that fall of 1968, living and working in harm's way, while I was celebrating a life of debauchery and irresponsibility. In those rare moments when I allowed myself the opportunity to draw a sober breath and to think clearly, it was obvious to me that something was very wrong with that picture. As a result, I started to consider seriously the option of entering the military.

When, after much internal debate and serious contemplation, I finally called my mother to inform her of the decision I had made, I was completely surprised that she readily agreed with me. I had been prepared for an argument, but there was none. I explained the situation and my thinking to her; I would volunteer for the draft, join the Army, serve my time, get my life into perspective, qualify for the GI Bill, and then return to school afterwards with financial support from Uncle Sam. She listened attentively to my reasoning, never interrupting my pitch; after I had finished, she replied, "It seems like you have thought it all out well. If that's what you really want to do, then it sounds fine to me." Mom always was a wise and reasonable woman. No doubt, with one son already in Vietnam, she was not crazy about the idea of sending another into harm's way, but she always supported her children, and I believe she had faith that I had thought out the situation well. So, the die was cast, and my "career" at Georgetown University (at least as far as I knew then) would be limited to one semester; but what a semester it was!

When I returned to Georgetown in the spring of 1972, things were different. I was a completely changed person, matured by my military experience, and having constructed some firm ideas for life during the course of those years; I also had developed the maturity and self-discipline to excel in the classroom and on the football field, while still managing to have one hell of a good time.

But those changes all came later. Right now, Uncle Sam beckoned, and I dutifully answered the call.

Part II

Wanderlust Unleashed

Prologue to Part II

Moscow, mid-June, 1983

Summer had finally begun in Moscow after a painfully long Russian winter, and I was nearing completion of the first year of my assignment in Moscow Station. There was nothing quite like the feeling a person gets when summer finally arrived there. There really was no notable fall or spring in the northern climate of Moscow; winter lasted from early November until late May, a full 7 months of constant cold and darkness, followed by the quick sprint thru spring into the accession of summer in June. The leaves blossomed quickly and vibrantly, and the world seemed alive once again. The warmer and longer days were certainly a welcome development. From the clandestine operations perspective, however, the change meant that the cover of darkness became shorter and less available, therefore making the conduct of covert activities more challenging. This reality was especially pertinent in the case of "Cable Tap" (not the real code name), the Agency's most sophisticated and important ongoing technical operation, the support of which was one of the primary purposes of my assignment there.

The previous four or five months had been extraordinarily hectic from a clandestine operations perspective, and my evening and weekend hours were comparatively very busy fulfilling important operational requirements; nevertheless, my cover had apparently held up quite well, and I was still generally free from KGB surveillance. With the advent of summer, time was approaching quickly for the next scheduled servicing of the Cable Tap operation, which was a covert wiretap of an underground cable system carrying strategic classified information between the Krasnaya Pakhra Nuclear Weapons Research Institute located in a closed city outside of Moscow and the Ministry of Defense. This operation was an incredibly complex and meticulously-researched and planned inter-Agency project that had been developed and put into action over the previous five or six years.

The most difficult and challenging work of accessing the manhole to implant the wiretap and recording equipment had already been accomplished under extremely-demanding circumstances by preceding Agency technical officers and case officers. By comparison, my upcoming task, to extract the tape recorder and emplace a new one, was relatively simple; however, although there was no human asset involved whose life might be in danger, the stress and "pucker factor" from conducting this highly important operation was just as much a consideration.

By virtue of having been selected prior to my Moscow assignment to assume a deep cover position, I was also chosen to be trained in the conduct of the Cable Tap operation well in advance of my departure to station. The Agency had constructed a mock-up of the operational site at a remote CIA training facility, and I was sent there, along with another designated case officer, to undergo intensive training on accessing and servicing the site. The primary action officers from the Agency's Directorate of Science and Technology, Office of Development and Engineering, were in attendance to ensure that we, largely non-technical, case officers understood the various operative parts of the overall technical operation, as well as the exact sequences which must be meticulously employed to properly service the site. After a very busy and intensive week of training on this operation, I came away with an unprecedented appreciation for the incredible imagination and technical expertise which these engineers and technocrats possessed. This simply brilliant operation was one in which I felt tremendous pride to have been given the rare honor to participate. However, in order to be allowed to carry out my role in support of this mission, I would have to live my cover well enough to still be free of close KGB scrutiny when my time came to go operational.

The key Agency offices involved in the operation and Moscow station management had been planning for months to ensure that all logistical and operational prerequisites were in place in time for the next servicing of the site; however, my final planning rehearsals and review of the operational requirements began just a few weeks in advance. Unfortunately, because of my cover considerations, I did not have the convenience to sit within the secure confines of the station and study the operational requirements at my own pace. The intensive training I had received back in the USA prior to my move to Moscow had taken place almost one year previous, so I needed to refresh my memory to access and replace the recording equipment successfully. In addition, I needed to devise and commit to memory the SDR and subsequent local transportation necessary to get to the site undetected. This requirement in itself mandated extensive planning, for the site was located outside of the Moscow Outer Ring Road in a much less-populated area, about 25 kilometers from city center.

Although I was still very busy with other operational requirements at about the same time, during May and early June, a significant portion of my intentionally limited time within the station was devoted to preparation for Cable Tap. We not only needed to ensure that I properly remembered and could execute the exact operational sequences, but also that I could assure myself and the other station members that I would be able to find the specific site without difficulty. We also needed to plan for getting to and from the site securely, as well as to arrange for the smuggling of rather large, hard to disguise equipment out ▮▮▮▮▮▮▮▮▮▮▮▮▮ and back in again. This task needed to be accomplished without causing any suspicion among the ever-present surveillance teams monitoring all movement in and out ▮▮▮▮▮▮▮▮▮▮▮▮▮▮. The amount of time and team effort which went into the planning of this comparatively simple logistical exercise was impressive and a real tribute to the entire station team.

Because of the restrictions of my cover status, I was forced to study the operational sequences within the safer confines of my apartment; the detailed sequence instructions had been provided to me in a dead drop by the station on water-soluble paper, which dissolved in entirety when placed under water. Accordingly, I identified a secluded spot within the apartment where the possibility of video or audio surveillance would be negated, and I quietly studied the sequences for hours on end until they were indelibly committed to memory. When we finally conducted our final dress rehearsal during one of my visits to the station, I even impressed myself at how completely I had managed to commit everything to memory and could go through the correct sequences without any errors. At this point, we were nearly ready to proceed.

The operation was planned for a weekend in June when the warmer summer weather would provide cover reasons for being outside and when fuller foliage would offer greater concealment of the required activities around the site. ██████████████████████████

██
██
██
██
██
██
██
██
██
██
██
██
██
██
██
██
██
██ This

logistical operation went like clockwork and was highly impressive. Within the realities of planning and executing covert operations in Moscow, all the while under the constant threat of surveillance, nothing came easily or without significant effort.

It was a Saturday afternoon when we finally had everything staged at our apartment and were ready to begin our outing in advance of servicing the operational site. When we left the apartment, we had in our hands, all properly disguised to fit our weekend outing cover story, all of the equipment needed for the operation; this included the properly-concealed Soviet-style backpack which became part of our light disguise, as well as our Russian clothing into which we would change once our surveillance-free status had been determined. Up to the time that day when we left our apartment complex in our Soviet-made Zhiguli, we had enjoyed a lack of surveillance for several weeks; nevertheless, the SDR which we had designed, and the cover for action in conducting that particular surveillance detection route, was conducted carefully and meticulously over considerable time and distance.

The SDR was well-planned and included numerous opportunities to determine correctly either the presence or lack of surveillance on that particular day. By the time we were halfway through our SDR, it was fairly clear to my wife and me that we were surveillance-free. Now, the trick would be to remain that way, not to attract surveillance scrutiny along the route or to arouse any suspicions from police or innocent bystanders. We had pre-selected an explainable location for parking our vehicle, which was close enough to where a ███████████ couple might be enjoying the appropriate attractions of Moscow, but simultaneously far enough off the beaten track (hopefully) not to attract any attention.

After we parked the car and were away from the vehicle, and had safely re-confirmed our surveillance-free status, we found a secluded spot where we could change into our light disguise. We then quickly disappeared into the crowds of Russian citizens enjoying the weekend evening. Once we had donned our local garb, which included the Soviet-made backpack in which all of the necessary equipment (about 30 pounds of it) and our other clothes were packed, we boarded the appropriate sequence of streetcars and buses that would transport us the lengthy distance to the operational site. By this time, after having successfully conducted many clandestine operations already during our first year in Moscow, we were comfortable with our ability to blend into the local populace without drawing any undue attention to ourselves. Nevertheless, the stress and pressure which we felt during this phase of the operation were significant and omnipresent. By the time we finally disembarked from the bus that left us about two kilometers from the site, it was during the hours of darkness, which are few and truly not very dark during June in Moscow, and we felt optimistic. From that point onward, all we had left to do was to locate the well-hidden site in darkness, safely extract and replace the equipment, and then reverse our route in order to get home problem-free within a few hours time.

The actual site was located a few kilometers outside of the outer ring road, just alongside a major highway to the southwest of Moscow. The site was only about 20 meters from the road, but it was concealed from the highway by a narrow line of trees and shrubs. After we disembarked from the bus, we approached the site from the rear, with the final part of the hike being made on the inside of the tree line, along a large open field. Although this route may not have been a normal evening stroll destination for a young Muscovite couple, there was sufficient cover from the darkness and remote nature of the site for us not to stand out.

After the long hike to get to the secluded, well-concealed area, we were pleased to have been able to walk directly to the site without too much difficulty or the need to conduct a wide-ranging search. The concise and extensive prior planning had apparently paid off, for we were able to find the exact spot quickly.

Shortly before reaching our destination, we had taken notice of some male voices engaged in conversation in the general area. Considering that this area was not a very busy one, and that sound can carry for long distances in the quiet nighttime environment, we needed to be extremely quiet in getting to the site and in beginning the operational procedures once we were in place. We were never entirely sure what the hell those men were doing in the area, and we never actually saw them; we just kept hearing snippets of their conversation from an obviously not-too-distant location. Our assumption was that they were just two guys nearby in a parked car, who, having escaped the grasp of their wives and families for one evening, were happily consuming their bottles of vodka while engaging in their erstwhile conversation. On one or two occasions, we ascertained that the fellows had ventured a bit closer to our location to relieve themselves during their drinking escapade, so we needed to "freeze," but otherwise these men never became a threat to our activity. However, they did manage to keep the pucker factor quite high while we executed our tasks.

As it turned out, we needed to be on site for just over an hour in order to complete the requirements of finding and retrieving the old tape recording device and to replace, reconnect, and securely conceal the new one. About halfway through this process, while I was intensely engaged in going through my operational sequences, and my wife was standing guard, keeping her eyes and ears attentive for approaching trouble, something suddenly happened which scared the life out of us! How we managed to remain quiet while our hearts were exploding from fear is still beyond my comprehension.

While my wife was diligently keeping watch for any possible threats, and I was intently involved in my task, out of the quiet and darkness of the bushes beside her, my wife was suddenly and ferociously attacked ...... by two young kittens. How she managed not to scream, I will never understand, but her quiet gasp of fright from just a few feet away did indeed draw my instant attention. The apparently deserted kittens were no more than eight or ten weeks old, and we could only imagine that they had quietly stalked my wife through the bushes when they had spotted her nearby. She may have been mindlessly twitching her fingers or something similar because the two kittens leapt simultaneously from their hiding place to mount their playful attack on her. As difficult as it was not to scream in fright from this unexpected event, as soon as we had regained our composure, it became just as difficult not to give in to the urge to laugh out loud. Naturally, our initial fear was that the KGB had somehow found us and ambushed us. The relief in the realization that these two kittens had not been co-opted by the KGB actually provided some comic relief to the tenseness of our endeavors. My wife successfully managed to keep the two kittens quietly occupied while I completed my operational requirements, and we departed the scene without any further incidents. In the final analysis, the hardest part of the evening was the necessity to leave the two cute kittens behind, but we simply had no other choice.

The return trip via a series of bus and streetcar rides to the area of our parked car, the reverse change of attire, and the safe retrieval of the vehicle for the return to our apartment, all went without difficulty. As far as we could ascertain, we never attracted any undue attention that evening. We did get back to our apartment after midnight, and we were concerned that the lateness of the hour might cause some closer scrutiny and future surveillance coverage from the KGB; but, even though it did not immediately appear, that concern would be secondary to the successful execution of this vital operation. We stayed at our apartment the next day, which was a Sunday, in order to babysit the "take" and ancillary equipment from the operation. Then on Monday morning, we followed the well-planned logistical and circuitous procedures which had been designed to smuggle the old tape recorder and other items back into the safety of the station by additional cut-outs. Once everything was back into safe hands, we finally drew sighs of relief. We had successfully executed our role in completing the requirements of this extraordinarily complex and all-important technical operation, and we felt immense satisfaction and pride for having been able to do so.

The next time we found ourselves back in the headquarters area, which was the following summer, my wife and I were invited to the 7th Floor of the building where we were presented with the "Certificate for Exceptional Accomplishment," which is awarded for "service of exceptional value" to the CIA. The certificates were awarded by the Deputy Director of Operations, and in attendance was a group of senior Agency managers. We were also allowed to invite a very few, witting family members, and my brother, Jim, by now a Lieutenant Colonel in the Army, and my mother were in attendance. Although I had informed my brother of my CIA affiliation in advance of my assignment to Moscow, I had kept it a secret from my mother until just before this award ceremony. Prior to that time, I had seen no need to concern her unnecessarily, and she had been led to believe I was just a normal ████████████████████████. In any event, the world of clandestine operations is one where the convenience of celebration of achievement is rare, and it always takes place behind closed doors; nevertheless, the swelling of pride for both my wife and for me, especially in the presence of family, certainly made all of the effort, stress, and pressure worthwhile. The knowledge that our actions had been of great service and importance to our nation created an indescribable feeling of satisfaction, one that we will certainly never forget.

Chapter 5

Fighting Soldiers from the Sky

I volunteered for the draft in early 1969 and then waited for about five months until my induction date was reached. As far as I can recall, I do not believe that I entered the Army with any preconceived plans or notions of exactly what I wanted to do. I believe that my goals were simply to serve my two years well, try to stay alive, gain benefit of the GI Bill, and then go back to college. As it turned out, I achieved all of my goals, and more.

As indicated earlier, my first semester at Georgetown was not terribly noteworthy. In fact, although I enjoyed my first semester there, and managed to succeed in all of my pursuits, my performance was truthfully a rather mediocre one. In retrospect and in analyzing my formative years, I believe that my romantic idealist tendencies did not really begin to manifest themselves until I entered the Army. Prior to that time, I admit that there was a tendency to be too-easily satisfied with my performance. However, something truly clicked into gear when I entered the service, and I have to credit this time for completely changing the expectations which I began to hold for myself.

I should say just a few words about the time spent between when I took the leave-of-absence from Georgetown (January 1969), until I entered the service in mid-June of that year. In order to pass that time productively, I took a job at the Westinghouse plant just outside of Staunton where workers assembled window A/C units. It was an eye-opening experience, and, although I made some decent money and enjoyed my colleagues, I learned very quickly that such a profession was NOT the manner in which I wanted to live my life. Spending eight hours per day putting components into an air conditioner as it moved its way down the assembly line simply did not excite me.

When the time came in June to report to the regional induction center in Roanoke, Virginia, I did so with some anxiety; frankly, I really wasn't sure what to expect. Once assembled there, we new recruits were loaded onto a bus for the late night trip down to Fort Bragg, North Carolina, where our Basic Training would be conducted. Early the next morning, we were aroused from our fitful bus-ride slumber by a very large and very loud black man screaming at us and urging us to "un-ass the bus." I was soon to learn that this seemingly unhappy and vocal gentleman was Staff Sergeant (SSG) Powell, our Basic Training Platoon Drill Sergeant. He was to be our father, our mother, aunt and uncle for the next eight weeks, and rarely was there a moment when he was not there by our sides, or, more accurately, in our faces. In those rare moments when he wasn't, he was replaced by another Non-Commissioned Officer (NCO), who was twice as large and twice as ominous; he referred to himself simply as "Super Drill Sergeant," and he was one big dude. However, as big as he was, he could never instill the same level of fear in us as SSG Powell did.

Basic Training was an experience of initial culture shock, followed by eventual acclimatization to the environment. Our platoon {3rd Platoon, A Company, 10th BN, 2nd BDE, of the US Army Training Center, at Fort Bragg} was comprised of a real mix of 40 young men of different races, different backgrounds, from very diverse locations, with a wide range of educational levels. Many of the guys in my platoon were from South Philadelphia. Prior to that time, I did not know much about South Philly people, but, believe me, they are a very unique group of folks. There was also a large contingent of country boys from Mississippi, some of whom had never been off of the farm, and this group was even more interesting than the South Philly crowd. Interspersed within this largely-drafted group of young men were a few guys with college educations: one fellow had a PhD from an Ivy League School, another had a Master's degree, and a few (like me) had some varying levels of college experience. All in all, it was a very diverse, and incredibly interesting, assembly of young men.

Some of the guys in our platoon were clearly not a good fit for the Army; others, like myself, took to the regimen, discipline, and hard work like a duck to water. I was quickly chosen to become one of the trainee squad leaders and given the responsibility to keep the squad moving in the right direction. At the end of basic training, based on a compilation of physical training and written tests, my selection as Colonel's Orderly, and exhibited leadership throughout the course, I was selected as Trainee of the Cycle for the Company. It was a prestigious honor, and I was singled out at graduation in front of my mother, sister, and brother, who had just-returned from Vietnam. In addition, based on IQ and personality profile tests that I took during the basic training course, I was also given the opportunity to apply for Officer Candidate School (OCS), for which I was soon selected.

Instead of going to a normal Advanced Individual Training (AIT) after Basic, because I had been selected for OCS, I was sent to OCS Prep for my AIT at the Artillery School at Fort Sill, Oklahoma. I had requested and had been selected for Infantry OCS, so I often wondered about the logic of sending me to Artillery OCS Prep. Nevertheless, the increased discipline and training regimen of OCS Prep prepared me well for the hell I was to experience later at Infantry OCS; moreover, the artillery forward observer training that I received was useful for future infantry officers who may later need to call in artillery support to save someone's butt. In any event, we were there for eight weeks of strenuous and restrictive training, which I remember as a positive experience. I was also training with a platoon of OCS-bound folks, with whom I felt I had much more in common than with some of the guys in Basic. Ironically, however, whereas I had met some characters in Basic Training whom I remember to this day, the guys I met in OCS Prep were not nearly as memorable.

During Basic, I was also given the opportunity to request other preferred training. I was quite interested in Helicopter Flight School, but I was informed that my eyesight did not meet the minimum requirements. I also volunteered for Airborne (Parachutist) School. There was an Airborne training (Jump School) opening that seemed to fit perfectly between the time I was scheduled to graduate from AIT and the time for which I was slotted to begin OCS. Luckily, I was enrolled for Jump School in early November, so I made the trek from Fort Sill, Oklahoma, to Fort Benning, Georgia, where I would also attend OCS. The only unusual aspect of my volunteering for Jump School was the minor fact that I was terribly afraid of heights.

As a part of our basic training, we were often required to run the obstacle course, a timed run over a series of different barriers; one of these was a high, sheer wall that we had to scale by climbing a series of ropes. The height of the wall scared the hell out of me, and, frankly, I shook the entire time I scaled the wall and while descending the other side. I was ashamed of this fear and decided to take steps to overcome it. My mother had been petrified of heights, and I assume that I learned this behavior from her. Mind you, I was never as badly affected by heights as she was, but I inherited enough of this phobia to have it negatively affect my self-perception and pride. Jump School seemed like it would provide an easy cure for this unwanted affliction, and it did.

Airborne School was indeed a challenging course. It consisted of three weeks of intensive physical training, a thorough introduction to parachutist techniques with emphasis on proper exit of the aircraft, parachute landing falls, guiding the chute, and then the final "jump week" during which each trainee made five static-line jumps. The course was hard work, but I completed it successfully and without incident. Naturally, there was the added consideration of my fear of heights which was a constant companion. Whereas the lead-up to jump week had its fearful moments, such as repeated jumps from the 34-foot mock-up tower, and the trial jumps from the 250-foot towers, my epiphany came on the first actual jump.

Our first jump was from a C-119 "Flying Boxcar" propeller aircraft. I thought the Army quite wise in having chosen this particular aircraft for the initial jump, for the shaky, bumpy and fear-inducing flight aboard this ancient craft made jumping from it the lesser of two evils. On the approach flight to the jump site, I had also successfully convinced myself that, if it was indeed in God's plan for me to die while jumping out of an airplane, so it would be and there wasn't much at that point I could do about it. The jump-master also kept everyone so successfully distracted with pre-jump banter and involved with preparing for the jump that, before anyone had much time to focus on it, we were out the door and floating the 1,500 feet towards mother earth. The relief I felt upon reaching the ground was significant, but it was overshadowed by the pure thrill I felt from the experience of the jump. Still to come were one more jump from a C-119, two from a C-130 cargo aircraft, and then one from a C-141 jet aircraft, all of which ended successfully, without incident. Amazingly enough, by confronting my phobia head-on, I had largely conquered my fear of heights from that point forward. This experience was indeed a good life lesson in how to deal with fear, and one from which I have benefitted throughout my lifetime.

I had only to move across base at Fort Benning to relocate for my OCS course. I arrived there with an additional source of pride and confidence in that I sported my new Airborne Wings. Among the 240 aspiring officer candidates who arrived at 94th Company, Ninth Student Battalion, The Candidate Brigade, U. S. Army Infantry School, I was one of a very small handful who wore the wings. As I recall, it probably took the OCS Tac Officers all of 30 minutes to negate any special pride and confidence I may have felt from Jump School, for they methodically cajoled, harassed, and reduced us from individual soldiers into officer candidates. As they reminded us frequently, the only thing lower in life than an officer candidate was fish-shit on the bottom of the ocean. The 23 weeks to follow were, as devised, pure hell. For six months, we were harassed for 20 hours per day, sleep and food-deprived, and re-programmed from enlisted men/NCOs into infantry lieutenants. Looking back on all of the various experiences which I have had over 60 years, I can honestly say that the only one which I would really not want to do over again is OCS.

We began OCS in early December 1969, and graduated in late May 1970, with a two-week break for Christmas at about the three-week mark. As I recall, of the original 240 or so officer candidates who began in December 1969, there were only about 64 of us left standing when it came time to become infantry officers. The attrition rate was high and rapid. The vast majority of those who left were judged not to have what it took to become an infantry officer, were washed out of the program and returned to their previous enlisted ranks. Many others simply decided that becoming an officer was not worth the "BS" and left of their own accord. At one point or another, almost everyone toyed with the idea of quitting; honestly, I thought very seriously about it more than once. One time at a point of perceived desperation, I was truly ready to throw in the towel, but a phone conversation with my (then Army Captain) brother convinced me to stay the course, and I made it through successfully.

Noteworthy recollections of the OCS experience were the constant challenge of actually staying awake during our infantry classroom training; we were all so sleep-deprived that it took incredible effort, plus hundreds of elbows in the ribs from classmates, to stay awake so that we could learn how to command an infantry unit and keep our soldiers alive. I also recall the pugil stick competition as being especially memorable. This event was simulated bayonet fighting using long poles with padding on each end, while we wore protective helmets. I managed to win our company competition by being the last one standing. The finals were between me and another younger candidate, with whom I shared a mutual dislike. He made the mistake of giving me a strong thrust to the head at the beginning of our duel, after which I went into a frenzy of pure hatred and pummeled him to the ground, from where the other candidates had to pull me off of him. Frankly, the level of intense hatred which I generated against this person disturbed me, but that instance was not to be the last time that I experienced such a level of strong negative emotion.

Once it was clear (between the 12th and 18th weeks) that the vast majority of those still in the program would actually become commissioned officers, we started to look at our post-OCS career opportunities. Many of our group went on to become normal infantry officers, serving in traditional infantry units; others were allowed to transfer to branches other than infantry. For me, the budding romantic idealist, nothing but what I perceived to be the very best was going to be satisfactory. Service in the Army Special Forces, the Green Berets, captured my fancy from the very beginning of my service experience, so I volunteered for a Special Forces (SF) assignment. Because I already had the requisite Airborne training and a solid service record, I was pretty much a shoo-in; thus, after graduation from OCS, I was assigned to the 6th Special Forces Group (Airborne) at Fort Bragg, North Carolina. My first job there was as Executive Officer (XO) of a SF Operational Detachment A, typically called an "A-Team" in those days; the A-Team was comprised of two officers (a Commanding Officer, usually a Captain, and his XO, usually a 1st Lieutenant) and 10 Non-Commissioned Officers (NCOs), who ranged in rank from E-5 to E-8, but who were all proven soldiers of the highest caliber. So, there I was, dressed in my officer garb, with my shiny "butter bar" designating my 2nd Lieutenant rank and second in command of one of the world's most elite military detachments, all three months shy of my 20th birthday.

I must admit that I was a very gung-ho soldier, well-suited for the U.S. Army, and I could not have been prouder than to be associated with the Army Special Forces. Very soon after arriving at my unit, I was slated to begin the Special Forces Officer's Course (SFOC), which at the time was a 12-week course intended to prepare Army officers to command an A-Team or whatever other assignment they might obtain within SF. Honestly, whereas the SF NCO qualification courses were highly challenging, sometimes requiring over one year of intensive training in their selected fields, the SFOC was pretty much a gentleman's course and not nearly as much a challenge as what the NCOs faced. Of course, in those days, SF was not a career branch for officers; it was considered a one-time lateral tour for career officers, or intended for those officers who placed a higher emphasis on a quality experience over the potential for promotion. In my case, I simply did not want to be anywhere else.

Soon after completion of the SFOC, I returned to my unit, and, like most soldiers in those days, began preparing for my upcoming assignment to Vietnam. Although my dream was to be assigned to the 5th Special Forces Group in Vietnam, I soon received orders for the Military Assistance Command Vietnam (MACV) as an advisor to one or another South Vietnamese infantry company. The deployment date was set for April, 1971, so I began to prepare myself accordingly. In the meantime, during the early days of my assignment to Fort Bragg, I had heard that a team was being assembled for an unnamed special mission. The team was to be formed under the command of Colonel "Bull" Simons, a legend in the SF community, and the commanders were looking for SF soldiers with significant combat experience. Despite being a rookie, with no combat experience, I volunteered my name for the mission; I had no realistic hope of being selected, but, being a gung-ho, romantic idealist, I threw my name into the hat anyway. As it turned out, this was for a mission to liberate American POWs allegedly being detained at the Son Tay prison camp in North Vietnam, for which the raid took place in November, 1970. Although there were no POWs at the camp at the time of the raid, it was a bold and courageous attempt, and I was proud to know several of the superb troops who were selected to participate in the mission.

Between the completion of the SFOC course and my intended deployment, it seems that I was almost constantly in training. I took the Jungle Warfare Training Course, which was conducted at Fort Sherman in Panama and which was an excellent preparation for combat in jungle conditions. This training was also my first international experience, and, although we were not allowed off-base more than two or three times during the course, the exposure did create in me the desire to experience more outside of the United States. The other formal course that I took during this period was a Physical Security Course at Ft. Gordon, Georgia, which was concerned with establishing and maintaining base camp security in a combat situation. These courses, in addition to the many other internal training exercises in which we participated over that period, did produce a highly-trained Special Forces soldier, ready for any number of assignments that would come his way in the future.

As Fate would have it, in early 1971, my orders for the MACV assignment in Vietnam were rescinded. Those were the initial days of de-escalation of the Vietnam War, and the demand for infantry officers in theatre began to decrease. In my case, the Department of the Army decided to enact these cut-backs by selecting certain Infantry OCS graduating classes for cancellation of their orders to Vietnam. One class would continue with their orders, while another would be rescinded; my class was one of the latter. For me, gung-ho as I was, this development was a major disappointment, and I immediately contacted the officer personnel department at Fort McNair to see what else might be available for me. Soon thereafter, I drove up to Fort McNair and met with a group of the personnel officers to plead my case. I still had about 16 months left on my active duty tour, so I thought there must be something exciting available where I could put my training to good use. I was pushing for a tour with 46th Special Forces Company in Thailand, thinking that this would put me a lot closer to the action, but allegedly no slot was available with them. However, the personnel officers did offer that, if I committed to an additional four years of active duty, that they "could have me in Vietnam by next Christmas." I pondered the offer, but fairly quickly decided that it did not meet my long term objectives. Thus, I returned to Fort Bragg with the realization that unless some other unplanned opportunities arose in the near future, I was destined to simply serve out my time stateside, and return to civilian life in 1972.

During that final year, again as part of the scale-back of forces in Vietnam, the 5th Special Forces Group was transferred from Vietnam to Fort Bragg; the 6th Special Forces Group with which I had been assigned was officially disbanded, and we were integrated into the 5th. Also during my final year, as always, there was a preponderance of training. The best example occurred in the fall of 1971 when my A-Team was chosen to take the 6-week SCUBA training course, which was conducted in Key West, Florida. This training was an excellent, demanding course, which, despite the rigorous physical regimen, was also a highly enjoyable endeavor. The purpose of the course was to train us for any assigned mission that would require underwater infiltration. Whereas no such assignment ever evolved for me, the training was superb, and at least provided excellent qualification in a sport that I would enjoy in my post-Army years.

Another significant event which happened during this period of time is that I became highly interested in all things Russian. My team Intel Sergeant, who had been a member of the aforementioned Son Tay mission and who was the consummate Special Forces soldier, was a naturalized citizen with his roots in the Ukraine. During downtime on our numerous US-based training exercises, we discussed his heritage and the realities of life in the Soviet Union; I became fascinated. As the USSR was (on paper, at least) part of the possible Area of Operations for our Special Forces Company, I was also able to participate in some Russian language courses that were available through my unit. As a result of this newly-found fascination, when I elected to take an early-out from my tour of duty to return to college, I had decided to pursue further studies in Russian and Russian Area Studies. This decision was not entirely logical in that there was no real envisioned career path in mind; I was simply responding to an impulse that seemed to meet my current desires. As a result, when I was re-admitted to Georgetown University for the spring semester in January, 1972, I entered the School of Languages and Linguistics and designated my major course of study as Russian; this decision had a major impact upon my personal and professional life, one that I ultimately owe to those many after-hour discussions with this model SF soldier.

Upon my return to Georgetown, I also decided to join a Special Forces Reserve unit (the now-disbanded 12th Special Forces Group) that had a sub-unit at Andrews Air Force Base, just outside of Washington, DC. This decision was a positive development, for it not only enabled me to stay involved in an undertaking of which I was very proud, but also it provided me the means to earn some extra money to support the high cost of a Georgetown education. Again, it was more of the same, lots of training, good camaraderie with other Special Forces reservists, and a positive experience. Between that spring semester at GU, and the upcoming fall semester, I was also able to take a 6-week Military Intelligence Staff Training Course at Fort Meade, Maryland, which provided good training for the future, as well as much-needed funding for Georgetown. However, I also very much wanted to return to the gridiron when football season began, and the monthly week-end drill requirements at the unit conflicted with this desire. As a result, I reluctantly opted to leave the reserve unit in favor of the full University experience, and my Army career was officially closed

In retrospect, the decision I made in 1968 to take leave from Georgetown and to volunteer for the draft was the wisest decision

I have ever made. I entered the Army in June of 1969 as a boy, uncertain of what the future might hold for me, and I left as a man, with a highly positive experience and a purpose and goals to pursue. Needless to say, being a young officer in one of the most elite military forces in the world created an incredible learning experience for me. The professional NCOs and officers with whom I had the honor to serve took me dutifully under their collective wing and helped me avoid the mistakes of inexperience and to perform my job well. I was indeed fortunate and gratified from this experience. The self-confidence, work ethic, and leadership skills that I developed during this period have served me very well ever since.

I admit that I do regret that I never experienced combat. I left the Army as a highly trained, capable soldier, who never had the opportunity to exercise in real conditions the ultimate skills that I was able to develop. However, I am enough of a realist to understand that romantic idealists, like me, often do not emerge unscathed from combat conditions. Almost certainly, the inherent urge to mount the heroic charge, to lead brave soldiers into fierce combat, and to vanquish the ideological enemy may have led to my demise. Perhaps Destiny had other plans for me, I surmise, and I am reconciled to this fact. However, I often wonder how many of my Army colleagues from Basic, AIT, OCS and the SF units, may have ultimately lost their lives in the course of their service to the nation; many certainly did, and I am grateful and proud to have had the opportunity to serve with them.

Chapter 6

Hoya Saxa!

Washington, DC, January, 1972

Prior to returning to Georgetown University in January, I had determined that I wanted to transfer from the Business School to the School of Languages and Linguistics (SLL) to study Russian. In that regard, I had arranged an appointment at GU in November with the Head of the Russian Language Department, Dr. Robert Lager, to pave the way for the school transfer. Although I had withdrawn from GU in good standing in January, 1969, I wanted to ensure that I would have a proponent at the SLL who could assist in that endeavor, if needed. Accordingly, I dressed in my Army dress green uniform and green beret for the meeting, in the hope that it would make the right impression. I suppose that the ploy did work to my advantage, for Dr. Lager and I hit it off from the onset, and he assured me that the transfer to the SLL would not be a problem. I think that he also liked the prospect of having someone with my background and with my clearly-defined goals in his classes. I had learned previously that Dr. Lager was a demanding professor with somewhat of a dictatorial reputation in the conduct of his classes, and I think we both left that first meeting with the idea that we were kindred spirits.

After I was re-admitted to GU for classes in January, 1972, I needed to resume taking required freshman courses, plus a few electives; I would not be able to begin my intensive Russian language courses until the upcoming fall semester. When they began, it soon became clear that Dr. Lager's reputation was well-earned, but I very much appreciated and enjoyed his highly-demanding approach to his classes. Whereas most of his students were young, right out of high school, and intimidated by his approach, with my military experience, I felt right at home. Like my military instructors and

Special Forces comrades, Dr. Lager expected excellence from his students and accepted nothing less. He challenged us, and we either responded, or took a hike. To this day, I consider him to be one of my most esteemed mentors.

Back to spring semester, as stated previously, I had returned to GU with a renewed purpose and direction in my life and with a strong motivation to excel. I had rented an apartment just across the Potomac River from campus and set up my life as a serious and determined student, but one who was still intent on having a good time. Contrary to my previous tenure at Georgetown, I now had the maturity, dedication, and time management skills to be able to do both. As for financial support to afford expensive GU, I had the GI Bill to assist, but I knew that I was still going to have to work part-time to be able to support myself. I had joined a Special Forces Reserve unit at nearby Andrews Air Force Base, which, between once-per-month reserve week-ends and summer training, helped to finance my education for that first semester and the following year. I also applied myself diligently to my studies, and, although some of the required courses were not terribly stimulating, I managed a 3.5 GPA that spring semester and made the Dean's List. I also created a rather active social life for myself; I had taken in a roommate from my reserve unit, who also worked hard and liked to party when time availed. In addition, I met a beautiful young lady from a neighboring college, who really caught my fancy. So, all in all, those first four months back in a university setting were really positive. Life was good.

The summer of 1972 was spent with two weeks at Army Reserve Summer Camp at Camp Pickett, Virginia, followed by an 6-week training course in Military Intelligence at Fort Meade, Maryland. As noted previously, however, due to my compelling desire to play football again at GU, which conflicted with my reserve weekend drills, I eventually opted to resign from the reserve unit. When I joined pre-season practices with the GU football team, a great deal had changed with the program over the preceding three years. First of all, the team had graduated from "club" status to a fully-recognized NCAA Division III program. Although there were no athletic scholarships available at that level, the size and quality of the team had increased significantly, and the schedule had been expanded from five to eight games per season. Despite the fact that the coaching staff was part-time and with only token compensation from the university (all of the coaches had full-time jobs in addition to their coaching duties), they were first class. The head coach, Scotty Glacken, had been an All-American quarterback at Duke University and had played several seasons of pro football. The assistant coaches also had excellent college careers at Duke, UNC, North Carolina State, University of Maryland, and East Carolina, and several of them had played professionally as well.

When I returned to the gridiron that late August of 1972, I was a different person in many ways from when I had first played at GU in 1968. For the sake of comparison, during my last year of football at Suffield, I was a 155-pound running back and still growing. By the time I arrived at GU that fall of 1968, after a hard summer of construction work on Interstate-81, I had increased my weight to 170 pounds, but was still rather slight. By 1972, when I began summer football practice at GU, I had beefed up to 200 pounds, by no means a behemoth by college standards, but much stronger, tougher, and perhaps a wee bit meaner, by virtue of three years in the military. Because I had been a running back or quarterback in all of my previous football experience, I chose to compete as a running back. We ran a wishbone offense and already had a strong contingent of halfbacks, so I was asked to play fullback. This position constituted the first option in the triple option offense we were running, but I was more often than not a blocking back. In any event, I split the role with another fullback who had played the position the previous year, and we enjoyed a decent season.

The team finished with a 4-3-1 record that year, and I performed well enough. However, my major disappointment, and most significant memory from that year, is from the game against Fordham at their field in New York. Trailing by one touchdown late in the game, I got the ball on the 1-yard-line twice on dive plays against the middle of the Fordham defense, and failed both times to get into the end zone. We lost that game to Fordham 14-7; that defeat left a sour taste in my mouth and was a huge motivator for me in future games against them.

The most important life impact made upon me during this football season was the many new, life-long friends that I made. There is a strong inherent bond made among men both in the military and on the football field, and this was especially true of my time at Georgetown. As I write this particular segment, I have recently returned from a football reunion at Georgetown during which I saw several friends with whom I have kept in frequent touch over the years. I also re-connected with many others whom I hadn't seen since we last played together. Nevertheless, even with those guys with whom I had fallen out of contact, the bond of comradeship was fully intact, and we were able to pick up the conversation just where we had left it some 40 years previously. Back to the fall of 1972, those close friendships, which began to develop that year and which persevered over the years to come, made a special impact on my life.

Off the football field, life during that fall semester at Georgetown went well; I took 18 credit hours that semester, including the 6-credit Intensive Russian I course, which was incredibly demanding, but I loved it. I was gratified that I had been so wise in my choice of curriculum. The other aspect of my Intensive Russian courses that I found much to my liking was that, among the 25 or so students in the class, I was one of only three males; and, of the 20-plus females, most of them were both bright and attractive. Suffice to say, there were some definite fringe benefits contained therein. I had to be very careful to keep my flings discreet, however, lest the girls begin to trade Morris stories among themselves, which they eventually did. Alas, there are drawbacks to all honorable pursuits in life! In addition to the intensive Russian course, I took 12 other credit hours, including Russian history (which I loved), economics (which I didn't), and two other required courses. Despite playing football, and, therefore, having much less free time for study, I was still able to ace the semester with a 3.5 GPA and once again made Dean's List.

Ironically, during spring semesters, I never did quite as well as in the fall when I had more demands on my time. I did find an excellent part-time job during spring and summer sessions, working at an upscale WDC apartment house as a front desk receptionist between 4:00 pm to midnight five nights per week. This job allowed me ample time for study, but I simply found that I tended to manage my time much more efficiently when I had less of it free. This fact is ironic to be sure, but it is a reality that I continued to find to be true over my lifetime. My grades did drop a bit, and I did not make the Dean's List that spring semester, but I maintained a 3.0 GPA. With my full-time evening job, combined with the GI Bill and some student loans, finances were also not a problem. Although the combination of classes, study, and my job certainly limited the quantity of time for social activities, the quality remained high; I dated around quite a bit and found a few ladies whom I liked enough to date several times, but nothing of a serious nature. Life, therefore, continued fancy free, as they say.

Because I did not begin my Intensive Russian courses until my sophomore year and was, thus, a year behind my contemporaries, I took Advanced Intensive Russian I & II, both of which were 6 credit courses, during the summer of 1973. In essence, that course was as close to living in Russia as a person could get without actually being there. These intensive classes were equivalent to the normal 4-month courses condensed into 6 weeks each; as a result, I had about four hours of class time each morning, followed by hours daily in the language lab, and then topped off by my evening job 5 nights per week. In between, there was time for workouts at the gym, trying to get prepared for the upcoming football season, so it was indeed a busy time. Somehow, I managed to do especially well in the Russian classes, achieving a 3.75 GPA over the course of the summer. I simply really enjoyed the courses, thrived under the dictatorial approach of Dr. Lager, and, not to forget, had a classroom full of attractive females to assist me in those all-too-rare hours of down time.

From the perspective of academics and social life, the next two years, from the fall of 1973 until graduation in May of 1975, went well and in keeping with previous notations. Academically, I remained serious about my studies and maintained over a 3.0 GPA, graduating with a 3.155 overall average and an induction into the National Slavic

Honor Society. My social life continued to be active, gratifying, and free-flowing; good friendships prevailed, and lots of good times were had, but nothing too serious on the romantic front. There were a few flings that had the potential to become something more, but Destiny simply did not have that in mind, at least not yet. As for football, however, life did indeed introduce some change, which, as it turns out, did have a major effect.

Frankly, I do not recall if it was during the spring practice of 1973 or during late summer practice sessions when our head coach, Scotty Glacken, decided that the team needed some additional help on the defensive side; therefore, he asked me to make the switch from fullback to defensive end. Mind you, although I had increased my weight to about 210 pounds by this point, I was far from meeting the image of a hulking defensive lineman; however, our defensive alignment (a 5-2-4 defense) allowed for smaller and quicker defensive ends, who filled the requirements for the pass rush and containment of efforts to run to the outside. Because I had been a running back previously, I was certainly quick enough, and the coach felt that I was strong and athletic enough to fill the position well. So, I began the season as the starting left side defensive end, a position that I had never played previously, but one in which I had grown sufficiently comfortable in the practice sessions and scrimmages leading up to our first game. The season would prove the wisdom of this move.

The first game of the 1973 season was played in Boston against Boston State College, not to be confused with Boston University or Boston College because it had no affiliation with either. Although we had also played against them the previous year at GU and although I was fairly familiar with schools in Boston, prior to playing them in football, I had never heard of this institution. Be that as it may, Boston State fielded a pretty good football team, much on the same qualitative level as ours. Although we had beaten them handily, 32 – 6, in 1972 at the GU campus, the game in Boston in September of 1973 was a hard-fought contest that we ended up winning, 7 – 6.

During the heat of a football game, especially one playing on defense as opposed to running back, a player never fully appreciates how effectively he may have played until film sessions on the following day. After the game, I had thought that I had played pretty well, but the film session that Sunday morning back at the GU campus showed that I had actually played this new position much better than I had realized. No one had run around my left end that game, and I recalled that I had two sacks of the Boston State quarterback, but the films showed that I had made some excellent plays in the process.

One play in particular had the coaches raving about my performance. Boston State ran one option play in my direction in which the quarterback faked a dive play to his fullback into the line and where a blocker came to kick me outside. I fended off the block with my hands, putting the blocker at my feet, when the quarterback pitched the option lateral out to the halfback for the end run. Having successfully fended off the block, I wheeled around clockwise and ran straight down the line of scrimmage to tackle the runner near the sideline for no gain. I had never practiced that move before, but somehow, I just executed it instinctively. The coach played back the film several times, exclaiming more than once, "Morris, that was an All-American play!" I must admit that I impressed myself with the athleticism and speed that I had demonstrated to make that difficult play. After that film session, with many of my teammates congratulating me on the excellent game I had played, I began to think that the coach must have known what he was doing when he switched me to defensive end. Perhaps there was some method to his madness after all?

After that first game, we lost four of the next five games we played, the last of those games being on November 3rd against arch-rival Fordham at GU. This match was my 3rd game against Fordham; we had lost to them in 1968, 31 – 6, during my freshman year, and, as noted previously, in 1972, at Fordham, when I had failed to score the tying touchdown on two one-yard-dive attempts. Not only was I out to score some revenge this time for my own failings the previous year, but also I had become incensed by some of the predictions I had seen in the newspaper by two of Fordham's star running backs, Owen Ward and Pierre Davis. They were quoted as saying that they were going to "run all over" us. I took those predictions personally and made the pledge to myself that I was going to punish those two individuals at every opportunity. Given the chance, I promised myself to attempt to decapitate either one of them if they tried to come around my end. Obviously, it was a foolish idea, but I was going to do my damndest to fulfill the pledge. In the spirit of the title of this book, I had transformed these running backs into "windmills" of my own creation; I had nurtured an intense hatred for these adversaries, and I would mount my imaginary white horse to fight them to the death. Funny to be sure, but, for better or for worse, that is the mind-set I had as we began that contest.

We indeed entered the game as the underdog. Not only was Fordham heavily-favored to win, but we had also lost our star running back, Johnny Burke, the previous week, and he was out for the season. Listening to my customary pre-game mental-preparation music, "Bolero" and "The 1812 Overture," I was psyched and mentally ready to play the game of my life when the opening whistle blew. The adrenaline flowed furiously throughout the game, and, true to my pledge, I was indeed trying physically to punish the enemy at every opportunity.

Using my right arm regularly as a club against the opponent's head whenever the possibility availed itself, early in the game, I felt that I had injured my arm rather seriously. However, the combination of hate and adrenaline, combined with a high threshold for pain, compelled me to continue to play. Again, later in the first half, after administering another arm-club to the head of a Fordham player, I realized that I must have broken my arm; the pain had become more severe, and my use of the arm became more limited. Nevertheless, I continued to play into the first part of the second half.

Finally, when a Fordham player came out to put a block on me, and I tried to fend him off with my right arm, I experienced the *coup de grace*; I not only felt a significantly-increased level of pain, but also I heard the remaining remnants of a partially-shattered arm give way completely. When I came off the field, I went to our team doctor on the sideline, Dr. Fred Burke, and matter-of-factly informed him that "I think I may have broken my arm". He did a quick examination, started to chuckle due to my calm demeanor and confirmed that the radius bone seemed to be shattered; that was the end of the day, and the season, for me. By the way, we lost that game to Fordham, 13 – 0. Hence, I was now a three-time loser to the hated adversary.

I had the arm placed in a temporary cast over the weekend, with the plan to perform surgery on the arm the following Monday. The timing was really poor in that I had a date after the game that Saturday with a beautiful young woman. After the temporary cast was applied, and I was given a full supply of powerful pain pills, I still managed to make the date, which was a dance, with R&B star Percy Sledge performing, at the GU gymnasium. The pain was severe by that time, and no amount of pain pills seemed to help, but we (somehow) managed to enjoy a nice evening. We also got together for another date the next day, but because of the persistent pain and a complete lack of sleep the previous evening, I was not much fun to be around. Oh well, such is life! Monday morning I was admitted to GU Hospital, and operated upon to repair my shattered radius bone. The surgeons needed to implant a steel plate to put the bone back together, and I still have the nearly foot-long scar on my right arm to show for it.

GU won one of the two remaining games we had that season, and the team finished the year with a disappointing 3 wins and 5 losses. We had expected to have a much better season, but injuries, a lack of depth at key positions and a tough schedule worked against us. However, the story of my having played most of the Fordham game with a broken arm became a bit of a human interest story, and apparently caught the imagination of the coaching staff and the sports information director. In any event, the account was publicized quite a bit, and there were several articles in the press. Much to my surprise, at the end of the season, I was notified that I had been selected for the Kodak All-American Team (Division II).

Prior to the 1974 season, I was selected by my teammates as one of the captains for the upcoming season, so we all prepared ourselves for the challenges ahead. By that time, my arm was basically healed, and the steel plate had been removed, but I still wore thick padded protection for the arm the entire season. We entered the season with high expectations, for we had most of the offensive and defensive teams intact from the previous year, plus we had added a solid freshman class to the roster. The entire roster was still comprised of only about 45 players, so we were very thin by today's standards, without the convenience of much depth at each position; therefore, we knew that any serious injuries would drastically hurt our chances for a winning season. Nevertheless, the skill level (at least for the starting teams) was quite high, and I was of the staunch opinion that, with a little luck, we might very well go undefeated. This opinion was widely shared, and, with that level of optimism in mind, we entered the season confident and enthusiastic about our chances for success.

Although we knew that we had a strong defensive team, our offense was potentially dominating. We still ran the wishbone offense, which primarily focused on the running game, and we had two superb running backs, Johnny Burke and Danny Lopez, leading the charge. We also had a solid fullback in Brian Melody and a skilled quarterback in Tom Gargan, who was a highly accurate passer when needed. The offensive line was a veteran one, and our receivers were quite competent, so, as long as everyone could remain healthy, we were poised for a solid season. On defense, we had a quick and highly-aggressive team. The defensive line was solid, the linebackers were quick and tough, and the defensive backfield was highly skilled. The greatest advantage which we had, however, was our knowledgeable and experienced coaching staff, whose extensive background in the college and professional ranks had prepared us well for the upcoming campaign.

We won our first three games that season, against Duquesne, Manhattan, and St. Peters by a combined runaway score of 131 to 26; the offense averaged nearly 44 points per game, and they were largely unstoppable. Johnny Burke and Danny Lopez combined for hundreds of yards rushing per game, and Burke personally scored four touchdowns in the St. Peters game. Honestly, we had fully expected to win those games at the outset of the season, but even we were a bit surprised by the potency of the offense. The defense played strongly in each game, as expected, and shut out Manhattan entirely. The fourth game was against Salisbury State (MD) whom we knew to be a staunch opponent; they had beaten us soundly (53 – 13) the previous year, despite an 89-yard touchdown run by Johnny Burke to begin the game. Contrary to the Ivy League ambiance of Georgetown, Salisbury was a tough Maryland state school, made up of big farm boys, so we travelled there with the knowledge that this would be a tough game. We were right.

We played the game against Salisbury on their home field on October 19th. They knew that we had a potent offense from the results of our previous 3 games; however, Salisbury had a much larger roster than we did (65 players as opposed to 45), and the average size of their offensive and defensive lines outweighed our players by 20-30 pounds each. Nevertheless, we were quick, skilled, and determined to win this game when the opening kick-off came.

The game was a hard-fought contest. Despite being significantly outsized, our defense played extremely well throughout the game, and held them to only one touchdown through the first three quarters. Our offense sputtered against their strong, aggressive defense, however, and could only manage one touchdown themselves through the first three quarters. In the fourth quarter, their size and depth on offense eventually wore our defense down, and they scored again to make the score 14 - 7. Unable to mount any noteworthy drives, our offense did not score again, and the game ended with Salisbury victorious by that score. We had been defeated by a larger, and, on that day at least, better team, but we had played valiantly. We were beaten up fairly badly during the course of the game and suffered several injuries, but, luckily, the next week was an off-week, so we would have two weeks to lick our wounds and to prepare ourselves for our archenemy, Fordham, on November 2nd.

The next two weeks of practice and preparation for the Fordham game were intense. While the players who were injured during the Salisbury game had some extra time to heal, the rest of us were getting mentally prepared for this important game. Having lost to Fordham the previous three times I had played against them, I was especially primed and ready for this upcoming game; I promised myself that

I was NOT going to lose to them again, and I reminded the team daily. In fact, on the Thursday afternoon practice just prior to the game, I sensed that the team was not demonstrating the seriousness of purpose necessary to defeat Fordham, so I stopped practice, called them all together, and lit into them. I reminded them that I was not going to lose again to these guys and implored them to stop the grab-ass and get serious. I believe that my admonition hit home, for the quality of the practice picked up demonstrably. The game was to be held at Fordham field; it was their Homecoming weekend, and they were expecting a crowd of 15,000 fans, which would be the largest crowd we had ever played before. We boarded the bus to travel to New York on Friday morning and arrived that afternoon.

We had a light practice at Fordham on Friday afternoon, mostly to stretch, walk through plays, and get familiar with the field. Afterwards, there were more chalk talks to review the game plan and make final preparations. When we arrived at our locker room at the Fordham field the next morning, I sensed that we were mentally-ready for the game. After pre-game warm-ups, we returned to the locker room for our final prep; personally, my adrenalin was flowing at a frantic pace, and I was psyched and ready to kick some ass. I called the team together and made an emotional, impassioned speech, which (I was told later) helped to elevate the level of readiness for many of the other guys. When we finally did run onto the field for kick-off, there was no question about our preparedness; I was so pumped that I felt like I was flying. My father was in attendance, and he remarked after the game that he could tell by the way we ran onto the field that we were ready to play. He was right.

Fordham was the favorite to win. It was their Homecoming game, and they had the large crowd of fans supporting them. They were also enjoying a good season, despite two losses already. They had a very potent offense, and their star running backs, the previously mentioned Owen Ward and Pierre Davis, were enjoying stalwart seasons. In addition, their record in recent years against Georgetown was a solid one. Like most of our other opponents, they had a larger squad, more depth, and much bigger players; however, we came to their turf completely ready to play football.

From the opening kick-off, we dominated. Our offense hit the ground with all cylinders burning. Johnny Burke and Danny Lopez rattled off one long run after another, and our defense, inspired as we were, shut them down entirely for the most of the first half. Halfway through the 2nd quarter, we had amounted a 21 – 0 lead. On their final possession of the 2nd quarter, however, the Fordham offense began to show signs of life; they drove methodically down the field and finally scored just before the end of the half. Personally, although I had been playing on adrenaline throughout the game, I recall beginning to tire during that final drive of the first half. When we entered the locker room at halftime, I felt terribly fatigued and wondered if we would be able to sustain the positive pace during the second half. However, we took the second half kickoff, and the offense again marched down the field for another touchdown. Propelled forward by an offensive line which dominated the bigger Fordham defenders, the running tandem of Burke and Lopez made several long runs en route to the end zone. As I believe the entire defense was, I was incredibly inspired by this tremendous offensive display, which helped dramatically to get my adrenaline flowing anew. When the defense returned to the field, we shut them down again, as we did for the remainder of the game. And, when the final whistle blew, we had defeated our arch-rival convincingly, 35 – 7.

As I write this chapter 37 years later, and as I have felt so many times previously when recollecting this event, I become inspired all over again. This victory was a tribute to the human spirit, the innate ability of a collective of like-minded individuals to overcome the odds and to work as a team to accomplish great things. This victory remains today one of the proudest moments of my life, a feeling which I know was shared by all of us on the field that day. There was not much written about the game in the sports pages the next day, and no one other than the players involved and the fans who witnessed the game really took much notice of what had transpired; however, we knew what had happened on that November day, and the feeling of collective pride was immense.

The following Saturday, we had a home game against Hofstra University. Typically, Hofstra had a larger squad and bigger players;

they had also played Fordham earlier in the season, and that game had ended in a tie, 21 – 21. Because we had dismantled Fordham so convincingly, we were considered the favorite to win the game, but we knew that Hofstra was a team to be reckoned with. We needed to play once again to our maximum potential, but we were healthy and equally determined to be victorious. I was personally motivated by the fact that my entire family was to be in attendance, including my older brother, Jim, who had not seen me play previously. Because Jim had always been a role model for me, it was important that we performed well, and I wanted to play the game of my life.

As usual, our offense started the game fast and effective. Almost every time we had the ball, the offense scored. In particular, Johnny Burke had the game of his life, scoring four touchdowns and averaging 13 yards every time he ran the ball. The offense played lights out the entire game and scored 40 points. The defense also played well against a much larger offense; we limited Hofstra to 20 points and won the game handily. Personally, I was playing against a much larger offensive tackle, who admittedly outplayed me for the majority of the game; he was athletic and strong, and I had a difficult time getting around him. I did finally get a couple of sacks on the quarterback by breaking the rules and taking the inside route on a few occasions, but, otherwise, I was frustrated by the lack of more impressive results in front of my family and especially my brother. It was a humbling experience, to say the least.

The next game was against Gettysburg, on their home field. We were 5 and 1 at that point, but we entered the game knowing that this would be our greatest test. Although Gettysburg was suffering through a sub-par season (they were 3 and 5), this game was their final one of the season, and their last chance to finish their season on a positive note. Gettysburg, as usual, was bigger than we were, had a more-established program, and was ready to show our upstart team how football was played. Unfortunately, they came out of the starting gate quickly and never slowed. Gettysburg dominated the game at every turn, completely shut down our highly potent offense, and scored four times against our defense. The final score was 27 – 0, and we returned to Washington, truly humbled by the experience, but with the determination to regroup and to end our season on a positive note.

Our final game on the following Saturday was at home against Catholic University. The football program at Catholic, like ours at Georgetown, had been rebuilt along the same timeline. Like many urban universities, they had dropped their football program in the early 1950's, had re-started it on a club level in the mid-1960's, and had worked their way up to the NCAA Division III level. Georgetown had played them almost every year since 1966, and with one exception (my freshman year when we lost to them 7–6), Georgetown had beaten them soundly. This year was to be no exception. Once again, our offense rambled virtually unobstructed, with Burke and Lopez running wild, and our defense rebounded from a lackluster performance at Gettysburg to shut out Catholic completely. Our defensive team played with tremendous energy and aggressiveness and never allowed Catholic's offense to gain any momentum. At game's end, when we had won 32 – 0, the opposing quarterback, whom I knew personally, came up to me and said, "You guys were everywhere!" It was a gratifying end to what had turned out to be a successful season.

Our team ended the season 6 and 2. We had not gone undefeated as was our goal prior to the season, but, by all measures, we had been highly successful. At season's end, we were ranked 10th in the east among Division III schools for the Lambert Cup, which had been established by the ECAC (East Coast Athletic Conference) to recognize colleges competing outside of Division I. Accordingly, the 1974 season constituted a major accomplishment for Georgetown football. Also three Georgetown players received All-American recognition of one sort or another that year, including Johnny Burke, defensive back and fellow Captain Jim Chesley, who won an Academic All American award, and myself. We were all proud and gratified by the recognition the team had received, but I was most proud of the way that this team had worked so diligently together and achieved the success which we enjoyed. To this day, the accomplishments of our 1974 football team are a source of tremendous pride for me. I am honored to have had the privilege to compete with these players, under the tutelage of our outstanding, and highly dedicated coaching staff. *Hoya Saxa!* ("What Rocks!")

In the real life outside of the world of football, I graduated from Georgetown in May of 1975 with a Bachelor of Science degree in the Russian Language and a minor in Russian Area Studies. Although I was at this point unsure of where this degree would lead me on my career path, I was confident that Destiny would eventually show me the way. Rather than go right away into the work force, I had been accepted to participate in what was for me a post-graduate program at Leningrad State University in the USSR intended to take my Russian language skills to a higher level. I was also eager to experience firsthand the harsh realities of the Soviet Union and, therefore, I was looking forward to the forthcoming adventure. Little did I know at that point what kind of a life-altering adventure it would really be.

Chapter 7

The First Man I Met in Europe was Myself

Europe, June 17 – August 28, 1975

This was to be the trip of a lifetime! Although it did not turn out exactly as planned, it certainly did not disappoint in terms of the final results. It had started as a summer-long study abroad program in Leningrad, USSR, intended to improve my Russian; it evolved into a ten-country, unplanned backpacking escapade, which became an exercise in intensive introspection and the ultimate development of a life-plan for the future. This last statement will probably require some explanation, which will follow in due course.

To begin, what happens when a bunch of young, rambunctious college kids are put together on a trip of dreams? Do I mean other than the non-stop sexual maneuvering, heavy drinking, and all-night partying? What else is there, you might ask? Well, I should mention at the get-go that the group of 60 or so college students from five university hubs who left New York's JFK International Airport on June 17, 1975, for the Summer Russian Language Program in Leningrad, were mostly serious and dedicated students of the Russian Language. They were investing the entire summer and not a small amount of money to vastly improve their skill levels in a subject of importance to their career development. However, let there be no doubt, even serious, dedicated students can largely be counted upon to engage in their share of the aforementioned activities, and some, such as yours truly, more than others.

The first stop after JFK was Paris, where we spent two days prepping for the continuation of the trip to Leningrad. In Paris, we got to know each other and received the required "what to do / what not to do in the USSR" meetings, and took language tests to determine level of proficiency; however, what we mostly did during those two days was to visit the normal tourist spots of Paris, and to consume copious amounts of beer and wine. We were there for two nights, and those two nights were devoted to debauchery at the highest allowable level. And, why not, you ask? In just two days, we would be flying into the womb of the Soviet Union, the main enemy of the United States and a police state, where debauchery of this sort would be highly frowned-upon! So, we might as well have lived it up while we could, right? Well, as my diary from that day so vividly reflects, the sins from our last night in Paris had placed me in a painfully hung over condition as we sat in Warsaw Airport, our last stopover before continuing to Leningrad. Some might think that this condition was a most appropriate one from which to suffer while waiting to enter the USSR. In any event, this time certainly proved not to be the last occasion during the summer when I suffered from similar afflictions.

By the way, the very best thing which I did during that eventful summer of 1975 was to keep a personal journal; otherwise, most of the shenanigans and noteworthy memories from that time period would have long since vanished from memory. Over the 36 years which have separated that eventful summer and today, I have re-read that journal about a dozen times, and the memories and insights that it conjures up are a priceless gift. In retrospect, I am very grateful that I invested the time and effort to record my thoughts; they are very telling and explain a great deal about what was to come in my life.

Back to the story at hand, we arrived in Leningrad on the evening of June 20th. In addition to the aforementioned hangover which accompanied me on the last leg of the trip, there were also the trepidations and inherent anxiety upon entering the enemy's lair. I am not sure how the other, more normal, college students felt about the situation, but, after all, I was a former Green Beret who had studied the USSR as a potential military target, so I admit that I entered the closed country with a certain level of suspicion and paranoia as an ever-present partner. We had been briefed in Paris that we could expect the Soviet students and teachers with whom we would come into contact would all be reporting on our every action to the KGB; and we were all duly warned about the possibility of provocation to entrap us into some sort of coerced cooperation. Personally, as my journal reflects, I entered the USSR expecting that there may be some sort of trouble to be found, which only proves the premise that our thoughts do often become a self-fulfilling prophecy. In fact, trouble was actually just around the corner.

We arrived in Leningrad just before the summer Equinox, during which the Russians celebrate the "White Nights" festival. Because of Leningrad's northern location, during the period of the White Nights, there are only about four hours of darkness per day; the result is that people tend to find themselves out on the streets, celebrating with their comrades, and doing the normal sort of universally comradely things, such as sexual maneuvering, partying, and drinking. Naturally, we American college students fit right into that environment. Although we started our daily language classes during that first week in Leningrad, all of which came with required homework assignments, we always seemed to find the time for evening activities.

One night, we pulled an all-nighter on the streets when we had befriended a group of young Soviets who had a guitar and a few bottles of vodka, which are both prerequisite to the singing of time-honored folk songs. One small detail that had helped our decision to stay out all night is that, during the White Nights festival, the authorities lifted all of the 900+ bridges in the city at midnight; therefore, unless people found themselves on their designated solid ground or felt like swimming across frigid rivers, they were pretty much stuck where they were until 0600 the next morning when the bridges were lowered again. Considering all the fun we had, there were worse outcomes to be sure.

At the end of that first week, we had a weekend excursion planned to the northern island of Kizhi, which is a UNESCO World Heritage site; there the Russians have assembled a marvelous collection of ancient buildings such as Orthodox churches, museums, towers, and so forth, which reflect the unique architecture of 17th-20th century Russia. It is really a wonderful open air museum, and one very much worth seeing. The trip to get there from Leningrad, however, is a lengthy and, as we later discovered, potentially a very adventurous one.

We left Leningrad on a midnight train for the eight-hour trip to the city of Petrozavodsk, located on the shore of Lake Ladoga, northeast of Leningrad. Naturally, preparation for an eight-hour overnight train ride with a group of college students required us to stock up on all of the necessary supplies, such as snacks and several bottles of wine and the ever-present vodka. Typically under such circumstances, as might be expected, the night ride to Petrozavodsk turned out to be quite an adventure. Without going into much detail, let it suffice to say that, after arriving in Petrozavodsk at 0800 that morning, followed by a two-hour tour of the city and a one-hour boat ride on the hydrofoil from the city to the island of Kizhi, I was still pretty much inebriated upon disembarking onto the island. In a nutshell, we consumed way too much vodka, so much that I honestly could not remember very much of the train ride that had taken us there. It was probably just as well.

Here are the positive things which developed from that trip. Firstly, I finally sobered up in sufficient time to enjoy the beauty of Kizhi. Secondly, I somehow succeeded in meeting the young blonde American girl from our group whom I had previously targeted, prior to leaving Leningrad, as someone I surely wanted to meet during the trip. In fact, we were finally uniquely introduced as I was lying face down on a small pier on Kizhi, throwing lake water onto my face in an effort to sober up and clean up from the previous nights activities. She unceremoniously stepped on me as she was backing up to get a better view of the wooden cathedral she was trying to photograph. Hung over and smelling of stale vodka as I was at the time, I shouldn't have expected to make a positive impression under such circumstances, but I must have managed to do so after all. After a day of touring on the island, where I managed to have a few more brief encounters with said blonde, I did maneuver myself to sit next to her on the return hydrofoil ride to Petrozavodsk and to continue to develop our embryonic relationship. As for the return train ride to Leningrad, it was also a night ride, during which, this time, I slept the entire way.

There were also some not-so-very-positive things that evolved from that historic excursion to Kizhi. During the train ride up to Kizhi (remember the part of the trip which I did not), I apparently got involved in some vodka-motivated mischief, a bit of a "dust-up," which need not be detailed to any great degree. Suffice to say, any type of mischief by Americans visiting the USSR in those days was not highly encouraged. To make a long story short, the American program management and I decided that my misadventure on the train ride might possibly create later repercussions, so it was decided, for the best of all concerned, that it would be wise for me to leave the program. Needless to say, having invested a considerable amount of money to participate in the program, with the goal of perfecting my Russian language skills, this development was not a desirable outcome. It was also quite a humiliating turn-of-events, of which a person can never claim to be proud. Nevertheless, such is life, and we take the bad with the good and try to make the best of the situation. Finally, the last not-so-positive development that evolved was the fact that, having just made some progress towards my desired relationship with the aforementioned young blonde girl, I was suddenly about to lose contact with her. In any event, I made rapid arrangements to depart the USSR that same day and landed in Helsinki, Finland, later that evening. Thus, my initial adventure in the Soviet Union lasted a full 10 days! Furthermore, I had been correct about the foreboding feeling that I had concerning impending trouble. Talk about a self-fulfilling prophecy!

Before proceeding to the next destination, I would like to jot down the words I wrote in my journal on June 26, 1975, at approximately midnight, after a full day of classes and witnessing an evening performance of the Siberian Dance Ensemble: "I have more or less concluded that my destiny lies with the Soviet Union in some still unknown way. Something is going to happen in the near future to show me the way, I am sure." As future chapters will illustrate, these words too were quite prophetic, to say the least.

The next insert in my journal originates from Helsinki, which was the most expedient destination from Leningrad. Because my departure was an unexpected development and my entire USSR summer program was already paid for, one of my first considerations in planning for the rest of my adventure was monetary. I had only a few hundred bucks in my pocket and nearly two more months before my ticketed return flight to the States could be used, thus there was much to consider in my planning.

This was my first visit to Helsinki, and, as my journal indicates, the strongest impression made upon me there was the strong allure of the young female population; it seemed like everywhere I turned, I saw another magnificent, blue-eyed blonde with a wide smile of white teeth contrasting against well-tanned skin. Had I died and gone to Heaven? Would I ever really want to leave this paradise? Well, for one reason or another (which is not entirely clear to me as I write this), I made the decision to leave for Stockholm, Sweden, just one day after arriving in Helsinki. The decision must have been based largely on my financial situation; otherwise, for me to leave so abruptly simply wouldn't have made any sense. In any event, on the evening of July 1st, I found myself on an overnight ferry from Helsinki to Stockholm.

Having just emerged from an adventure created largely out of a vodka bottle, I was not really looking for any such stimulation; however, to be sure, I was probably the only human being on the boat that evening (with the possible exception of the crew), who was not knee-walking drunk. I thought that the Russians were heavy drinkers, but the boatload of Scandinavians that evening put the Russians to shame. Whereas I had hoped to find a quiet seat on the ferry and to get a good night's sleep during the crossing, I was awakened not once, but several times, by drunks falling across my lap while trying to get to their seats. Once daylight arrived, and we were travelling through the Swedish Archipelago of thousands of islands just east of Stockholm, the dysfunctional nature of the preceding evening was well gone from my memory. The natural beauty before me was breathtaking, and I was mentally ready for new sights, new sounds, and new adventures.

I arrived in Stockholm on the morning of July 2nd and had decided that I would stay in the city for a few days and make an effort to find a job. I knew that I did not have sufficient funds to make it through the entire summer without finding work, so I thought Stockholm would be a good place to look. The downside of Stockholm was that it was quite expensive, so I needed to get lucky quickly or to pack up and head to the next destination. I did manage to find a few job leads, one that sounded promising, but unfortunately nothing developed. Although I located a nice youth hostel that was reasonably priced for bed and breakfast, and I found the Swedish Cooking School to be a good source of excellent, low cost evening meals, it became quickly apparent that I needed to get to a cheaper city. My plan was to head for Innsbruck, Austria, a place I had always wanted to visit, so I left Stockholm on the morning of July 4th. The first phase of the plan was to hitchhike as far as Copenhagen, Denmark.

I learned a good lesson in human kindness on that 4th of July, a fitting day on which to do so. After less than an hour of trying to hitch a ride south to Copenhagen, I was offered a lift by a young Englishman in his VW bus. He did ask for 50 Swedish Kroner as a gas-sharing donation, but I pled poverty and offered him 10 instead, which he accepted. We hit it off very well and the ride was full of good conversation. We stopped for food at a charming roadside restaurant, and he bought me lunch, which undoubtedly cost him more than the 10 Kroner I had given him. Once we arrived in Copenhagen and were about to bid farewell, out of the goodness of his heart, he gave me another 50 Kroner to help me out with my travels. Frankly, I felt like a cheap bastard at that moment because, in truth, I could have afforded his full price at the beginning, but it was a good lesson in human kindness; from that time forward, I have often reciprocated to other young people in need with this gentleman's kindness fully in mind.

I decided to hang out in Copenhagen for a few days and purchased a train ticket to Innsbruck for July 7th. I enjoyed Copenhagen as well; it is a beautiful city, full of public parks, with many entertainment opportunities. Tivoli Gardens was a highlight of my visit, and I went there each day. I wished I could have spent more time in Denmark, but my heart was set on going to Innsbruck, so the next afternoon I was off, headed for the Austrian Alps.

The combination train/ferry/train ride to Innsbruck was much more eventful than I had anticipated. After the train departed Danish soil and pulled onto the ferry for the crossing of the Baltic Sea to Germany, I met onboard the ferry a very attractive Finnish girl, who was en route to Munich. She didn't speak very much English, but we somehow managed to communicate effectively, and I bought her dinner on the boat. Once we reached the German port of Warnemunde, she joined me in my berth for the still-lengthy overnight trip to Munich and then to Innsbruck. We enjoyed a very pleasant, yet broken, conversation on the train ride before nature began to take its course. She had become quite affectionate and, before I knew it, I was being "aggressively (yet pleasantly) attacked". There was an elderly German lady who had been riding with us in the berth, but she apparently took exception to the romantic interlude nearby and left; all I could do was shrug my resignation to being "victimized" in this manner and smiled sheepishly as she left. In a nutshell, it was one hell of a train ride.

The young Finnish lady and I parted ways at Munich station, professing undying affection and promising to meet again as soon as possible. Unfortunately, although we spoke by phone a few times over the coming weeks, we never saw each other again.

Upon arrival in Innsbruck the morning of July 8th, the first order of business was to find a place to stay. I came upon a private home where I could rent a room for about $3/night, so I rented it for one week and decided that I would make this my operational base, and find a job to tide me over financially. The next day, I began my job search and actually found a few good possibilities; however, they were all looking for someone who could stay thru October, so none of the jobs worked out. Towards the end of the day, I began to feel really fatigued and weak, so I went back to the house to rest. Awaking the next morning, it was immediately clear that I had become quite ill; I had severe stomach pains, accompanied by a nasty diarrhea. My landlords gave me some home remedies, but when it became worse they called a doctor to come visit. The medication which the doctor gave me did not help much either, so the next morning I made my way to the Innsbruck University Clinic, where I was diagnosed with

Giardiasis (Giardia), which I undoubtedly had contracted from the water in Leningrad. The illness can take from seven to fourteen days to take effect, but, when it does, it feels like being hit by a freight train. I spent the next week in the clinic where I received exceptional attention and was thoroughly cured. The medical staff was also kind enough to bill me for the services, with the understanding that I would pay them as soon as possible upon my return to the States. Once again, I was vividly reminded of the potential of human kindness.

So, it was July 17th when I emerged from the clinic, healthy and energetic once again. My landlords had kindly held my room for me, so I still had a place to stay. I also landed a lead on a job with Avis and was offered an opportunity to take a train down to Milano, Italy, on the 19th, from where I was asked to drive one of their cars back to Innsbruck. This gig turned out to be as enjoyable a job as I could have imagined; unfortunately, they had no follow-on opportunities in the coming days, so I decided to leave Innsbruck after those two weeks, and to continue my odyssey.

When I awoke the next morning, my intention was to take the train to Munich, but somewhere along the line I changed my mind and decided to board a train for Vienna. So much for the benefit of planning! In any event, I arrived in Vienna on the evening of July 21st and settled in for a few days. By this time, I had decided that I would need to borrow some funds in order to stretch my money through August, so I wired home to my brother for a loan while I was in Vienna and received it on July 25th. It was during those four or five days in Vienna when I irrevocably caught the international bug and decided that my career would definitely be spent in the global theater. I really enjoyed the atmosphere of Vienna and spent a very pleasant time there. This point was also about the half-way mark in my summer travel, and, bolstered by the additional funds I had received from home, I was now more able to keep afloat my last month and looked forward to the adventures ahead.

On the evening of July 26th, I boarded a train for Zurich, Switzerland, where I arrived the next morning. After walking around Zurich for a very short time, I decided that it held nothing for me, so I jumped a train in the direction of Geneva, which took me through the Swiss Alps. This portion of the trip offered without a doubt the most breath-taking scenery I had ever seen, and I decided to stay awhile. I disembarked in Lausanne, Switzerland, on the north bank of Lake Geneva and spent a few days there, enjoying the small mountain village ambiance. I thoroughly loved Lausanne, although I pretty much spent my time alone; so, by the time I was preparing to board the train from Lausanne to Spain on the evening of July 31st, I was really in the mood for some human companionship.

En route to Valencia, I spent one night in the beach resort of Calella del Mar and the next night in the beach town of Castellon de la Plana. I then set off for the small city of Vall de Uxo, where I met a traveling group of German girls. They had decided, as I had, that the youth hostel in Vall de Uxo was a dump, so we all left together the next day for Valencia, where we spent the day at the beach. It was nice finally to have some companionship on my travels, but I quickly found that it seriously encumbered my independence. Although I had hoped that I would enjoy Spain, as well as have the opportunity to practice my Spanish, I honestly was not overly impressed by what I found there, so I decided to leave for other locations the following day. The first stop would be in Paris, where I could drop off some of my belongings until the time of my scheduled departure for the States, and then I planned to head to Ireland. But first, there was the 24-hour bus trip from Valencia to Paris.

With the exception of the fact that I fell deeply in ineffectual love during that 24-hour bus trip to Paris, it was largely uneventful! "Why," I asked myself the entire trip, "have I not studied French instead of Russian and Spanish! What a dumb ass!!!" Sitting in front of me the entire bus ride was perhaps the most sensual, young beauty on whom I had ever set my eyes. It was clearly God's punishment for me that she spoke nothing other than French, and I knew no more than a small handful of words in the language. What was obvious, however, was that we both wanted very much to communicate, but we were ineffective in doing so. Thus, the end result was 24 hours of pure frustration, and, upon arrival at the bus station in Paris on the morning of August 8, we unhappily parted ways. Life can be so cruel!

I stayed in Paris just long enough to store some of my things there until I could return in a few weeks for my flight to the States. With the intention of continuing to Ireland, I made travel arrangements to London; however, my travels from Vienna to Switzerland and then to Spain over the past two weeks had put a huge dent in my finances, so I once again made travel plans according to what I could afford. Upon arriving in London, a sober look at my wallet convinced me that further travel to Ireland would not work, so I decided to rent a bicycle in London, and just start peddling south.

I spent the next two weeks in Jolly Ol' England. My bike ride took me as far south as the village of Abinger Hammer, a charming town between Guilford and Dorking, about 40 miles south of London. After camping out the first night, perhaps the coldest night I have ever spent in my life, I quickly decided that, if I wanted to live long enough to get home, I needed to find more habitable shelter than a hilltop in the national forest. That Sunday afternoon, watching a cricket match on the village green, I decided that Abinger Hammer might be a good place to settle down for awhile, to find a place to stay and a suitable job, and to enjoy the last two weeks of my summer adventure. Going into the pub next to the village green, all of my requirements were quickly answered: I got a good lead on a place to stay (a local farmer who took in boarders) and on a couple of jobs. Who says good things never happen in a pub?

These two weeks were a happy ending to my travels. I had looked into two jobs, one as a domestic helper and the other as a gardener, and chose the latter one. It was good, invigorating work (at 60 pence/hour plus lunch), and I was able to build up my quickly dwindling purse; the lodging at the farmer's house was excellent, and I paid 2.25 British Pounds per night for a nice bedroom with a bountiful English breakfast every morning. I really felt like I had fallen into a great circumstance; moreover, I was there long enough to really get to know my landlord's family, my gardening employer (a wonderful lady with a nice family), as well as the villagers who hung out at the local pub. My stay there was a pleasant segment of my travels, and I genuinely enjoyed it.

After bidding good-bye to the folks in Abinger Hammer, I peddled my way back to London; and, with a few superfluous quid in my pocket, I decided to "live it up" a bit in London before heading to Paris, from where my flight to the USA would depart. The last few days were enjoyable, but it was more importantly an opportunity for introspection and to analyze the activities and impact of the past 10 weeks. In retrospect, what had transpired over that one summer and the decisions that resulted from it were truly life-altering for me.

First of all, just prior to my premature departure from Leningrad, I had decided that the Soviet Union would play a major role in this lifetime, which, as later chapters will show, it truly did. Secondly, while pondering life in Copenhagen, I had decided that the young blonde whom I had met in Leningrad would somehow become a part of my life; later, she did in fact become my first wife, and the mother of my two oldest children. Thirdly, while touring the town of Leopoldsberg within the Vienna Woods, I had come to the personal conclusion that my career would be an international one, and indeed it has turned out to be so. Finally, while on that last leg in London, I had noted in my journal that I also had an inherent desire to write, and to author a novel someday. Well, as it turns out, finally at the age of 61, I am embarking along that career path as well. So, I can surmise that this period was indeed an important, prophetic portion of my life's existence, a time of reflection and introspection, an opportunity to take a blank canvas, and to paint upon it my future life's path.

The first man I met in Europe was truly myself. For better or for worse, the quixotic odyssey to follow jumped into full swing as a result of that fateful summer of 1975.

Chapter 8

International Meanderings

Arlington, Virginia, Early September, 1975

As indicated previously, when I returned from my summer odyssey, I had come to some firm conclusions about the life that I was planning to pursue. I had decided that my future would somehow revolve in part around the Soviet Union, would certainly involve international pursuits in general, would include the young lady whom I had met (only briefly) in Leningrad just prior to my departure from the study program, and would involve the calling to write. And, as I sit here today writing this chapter, I continue to be amazed by how accurate my predictions and inclinations have become. Maybe I have a bit of Nostradamus interwoven into my DNA? Probably not, but, nevertheless, my life's path does go to prove that if we listen attentively to our inner yearnings, we do certainly have a say over how our lives will manifest themselves.

Having made all of those major life decisions, however, upon returning to my Arlington apartment at the conclusion of my summer wanderlust, I honestly had no earthly idea how all of this would come to pass. I was a Georgetown graduate with a degree in Russian but with no job prospects in view, and I had declared my romantic intentions for a woman with whom I had only fleeting contact more than two months prior; I also had no firm clue on how or where to contact her. Obviously, I had my work cut out for me if I were to bring all of these high-minded intentions to fruition. Nevertheless, being a true romantic idealist, I purposefully set out on an uncharted course, armed with only a sense of destiny that all of my plans would eventually come to pass.

The first course of action was to track down and somehow charm the aforementioned female to whom I had pledged my undying devotion.

I don't exactly recall just how I managed to get her coordinates, but I was able to accomplish that very soon after my return. When I first contacted her family at their home in Michigan, I found out that she had decided to take a cruise ship back from Europe to the United States and that she was not expected for another few weeks. On top of that, as I was informed later, when I left the message with her parents for her to contact me when she got back home, the message was intentionally destroyed. Coincidentally enough, as it turned out, I had the exact same name as her previous boyfriend, whom the parents despised; they had mistakenly assumed that this Bob Morris on the phone was that same reprobate whom they had tried diligently for several years to eliminate from their daughter's existence. No way in hell were they going to pass her my message! So, after several weeks of not hearing from her, and knowing that she should have returned by that time, I called their home again and, luckily, she answered the phone herself.

The initial task I had in the opening of our conversation was to remind her who exactly I was. After some prompting, she said that she did remember me, and much of what turned out to be a lengthy conversation revolved around what in the hell had happened to me and how we had spent our respective summers. It was largely a get-reacquainted conversation, but I left the discussion with the realization that whatever spark I had detected back in those fleeting encounters in late June was in fact still present. At the conclusion of the call, I asked her if she had received the message that I had called previously; she said, "no." Only weeks later did I learn of the coincidence about the name of her former beau, and the resulting resistance from her parents. In any event, the dialogue had been successfully initiated, and our relationship was to be a work in progress.

On the job front, I easily got my job back at the upscale apartment house where I had previously worked as an evening front desk receptionist, so I almost immediately had resolved the issue of having an income to support myself while I looked for bigger and better endeavors. As it was when I was a full-time student, this job also enabled me more than ample time to besiege the corporate world with job applications, as well as the opportunity to maintain an ongoing written and telephonic dialogue with the young lady in Michigan. Granted, this position was neither a career-enhancing nor overly inspiring one for a college grad to have, but it definitely served multiple purposes.

On a lark, about that same time, I had also written to my congressman, Virginia 6th District Representative Caldwell Butler, inquiring if he might be able to use his influence to find me a suitable position within the federal government. Naturally, I played up my prior service as an Army Special Forces Officer and my exploits on the football field while an honor student at prestigious Georgetown University. Soon thereafter, to my delight and amazement, I actually received a positive response. When I went to the Congressman's office to discuss the job with one of his staffers, I was told that it was certainly not a job worthy of such a "distinguished graduate," but that it would offer the chance to get my foot in the door to a life of government service. The proposed job was at the Veteran's Administration as a file clerk; the position itself was certainly not awe-inspiring, but the salary was not so bad, and it would at least liberate my evenings for pursuits more enjoyable than playing houseboy for the folks at the apartment building. In any event, I was pleased and gratified by the responsiveness of the Congressman's Office to my request; it demonstrated to me that, in fact, the system did work.

The job was at the Department of Veteran's Affairs (VA) headquarters on Vermont Avenue in downtown WDC, just two blocks north of the White House. I admit that there was an element of excitement when I first reported to the VA for my new job. After all, I was a veteran myself, so working at the Federal Department responsible for veterans' affairs seemed potentially interesting and appropriate; perhaps I could make a difference there. Unfortunately, it did not take very long to discover that the job itself was not going to be either challenging or rewarding.

My job was located somewhere in the basement level of the building, in an office populated by seemingly endless file cabinets and uninspired workers, who had long since lost interest in performing their duties. They had become nameless bureaucrats, just filling in their time with as little activity as possible until the day would arrive when they could retire with their government pension. Naturally, being young and full of piss and vinegar, I approached the mundane position with energy and a determination to do the job to the best of my ability. Quite soon after I began my work there, I was approached by my supervisor and advised not to act so busy in the workplace, lest I make the rest of the office workers look bad. Her suggestion was both perplexing and confusing to me, but I decided to try to be less obvious in my dedication to the task and not to rock the boat too demonstrably. I did notice, however, that one elderly gentleman in the office clearly seemed to be a lot busier at his desk than the others. When I chose a quiet moment in which to inquire discreetly why it was that he was so busy while no one else seemed to be doing anything, he showed me how he spent his day, busily figuring mathematical odds on paper. He offered to show me how, but I politely declined. What an introduction to the U. S. Government bureaucracy at work! Whenever new government programs are proposed by our politicians as a means to manage anything having to do with the common good, I think immediately of that kindly, but ineffectual, government worker.

Because I had determined that the Soviet Union was going to be the primary thrust of my professional efforts, I sent my resume to all US companies and agencies conducting any sort of business or government activity with the USSR; ironically enough, for whatever reason, the CIA was not one of them. In any event, this period was the era of "détente" (initiated during the Nixon Administration) between the two nations, and trade and other types of exchanges were growing. Finally, towards the end of 1975, I received a positive response from the Pullman Corporation, which was a Fortune 100 Corporation headquartered in Chicago, with the invitation to arrange an appointment for an interview at their Swindell-Dressler Division in Pittsburgh. As I came to learn, Pullman was the first

US Corporation to have been accredited by the Soviets to open a commercial office in Moscow just a few years prior. By this time, the company had several large engineering and construction projects ongoing in the USSR as well as in Poland. The Swindell-Dressler Division had won a contract to design and engineer a steel foundry at the Kamaz truck-building facility in southern Russia, and it had won a similar contract for a foundry in Huta Katowicza in Poland. Another Pullman Division, M. W. Kellogg in Houston, had also won several contracts to design and build ammonia fertilizer plants in the USSR, so the Pullman Corporation had already created quite a significant footprint in this previously forbidden land for American business.

By virtue of its unique position in having commercial offices in both Moscow and Warsaw, Pullman had initiated a strategy to offer sales representation in the USSR and Poland to other American Corporations wishing to explore business opportunities in those countries. Pullman was seeking qualified employees for this embryonic business activity for which I would be interviewed. At the time I received this invitation, the Christmas season was just around the corner, so we agreed that I would come to Pittsburgh after the New Year for two days of interviews and to meet the entire staff. In the meantime, the progress of my romantic pursuit had been developing positively and moving rapidly forward.

Having re-established contact with the aforementioned young lady, and having developed a steady discourse through written and telephonic correspondence, the next step in the attack plan was naturally to arrange some face time. After all, we had not seen each other since late June, so by mid-October meeting face-to-face seemed to be a logical next step. Accordingly, after significant long distance development of the relationship, I invited her (several times) to come to Washington for a visit, to which she finally acquiesced. Her initial visit to WDC, a long weekend, went exceedingly well; although it was strictly platonic in nature (as it turned out, she was "old school"), the weekend ended with the realization, for both of us, that the relationship was worth pursuing. That weekend was followed by daily and quite expensive telephone chats and the agreement that I should go to Michigan to visit at her family home for Thanksgiving. That four-day visit further cemented the relationship, and managed to move it past the platonic stage. In fact, it moved forward so quickly that we agreed she should pack her bags and move to Arlington after Christmas to take up residence with me. Hence, the attack plan was successfully completed, and the die was cast for the immediate future.

Back on the job-search front, my interview at Swindell-Dressler in early January went very well and Pullman offered me a position soon thereafter. The job description seemed to be just what I was looking for, a responsible entry-level management position, dealing within the international markets in which I was most interested. The prospect of travel to both the Soviet Union and Poland on behalf of their growing East European business segment was there too. Although the salary was attractive enough, it really was a secondary consideration because I was more than ready to abandon the stifling environment of the VA for a prime job in the real world. So, my new live-in girlfriend and I packed our collective stuff into a U-Haul truck in mid-January and headed from WDC to Pittsburgh, Pennsylvania, our new home to be. Mind you, we had no idea where we would live as yet, but we planned to start that search once we got there. In the meantime, life was looking pretty good. My pledges to (1) secure the female of my choice, (2) to get a job in the international theatre, and (3) to deal with the Soviet Union, had all come to pass within a six-month time frame. During that drive from WDC to Pittsburgh, I had to smile and congratulate myself that I had managed to bring my primary life goals to fruition in rapid succession. Not so shabby, I felt!

After arrival in Pittsburgh, we purchased a local paper and started searching the "for rent" advertisements, looking for a furnished, reasonably-priced apartment. Luckily, we found one that met our needs very early in our search. It was an upstairs apartment in a private home, and the landlady with whom we spoke on the telephone sounded like a very nice, elderly Irish woman. Considering the situation before we actually went to meet her and to tour the apartment (it was 1976 and she sounded like a good conservative, Catholic lady), it occurred to me that we might be wise to lie just a wee bit and tell her that we were married. After we checked out the new digs, the landlady did indeed pop the question, and the fib flowed quite easily out of our mouths; but, of course, we are Mr. and Mrs. Morris, and quite happily so, thank you very much. To this day, I believe that the lady was more worldly than we gave her credit for, and she probably understood immediately that we were stretching the truth; however, we were a charming and friendly young couple, and I am sure that she wanted to rent the apartment to us, even if we were ("God forgive them!") living in sin.

We unpacked the truck, organized our new home, and started life in lovely Pittsburgh. Despite all that I had been led to believe, Pittsburgh was indeed a charming city; its reputation of being a smog-filled steel town must have persevered past the time when it was actually true, for I do not recall ever seeing any hint of smog. The only aspect of our new home that eventually became somewhat irritating was the fact that our apartment was within a few blocks of the Pittsburgh Zoo. The lions had the unwelcome habit of roaring much too damn early in the morning for my fancy. Whereas it was cute in the beginning, and we loved being close to this charming zoo, being awakened at 0500 every morning by the lions started to get on our nerves. I confess that I gave serious thought to buying a hunting rifle to take care of them once and for all, but ultimately we decided just to go to bed a bit earlier and to live peaceably with our version of urban roosters. Otherwise, we were perfectly happy with our new situation, living in sin as we were. I found my new job to be thoroughly interesting and challenging, and my "wife" soon found a job downtown as a travel agent; all seemed to be working out pretty well.

During the first few months of my assignment to Pittsburgh, I made several familiarization trips to Pullman's Chicago headquarters, where I met all of the big bosses. Although I was living in Pittsburgh under the tutelage of the President of Swindell-Dressler, my official boss was actually the Executive VP of Pullman, Donald Morfee, who had been one of the primary proponents of establishing business links with the Soviet Union a few years prior. I also made initial introductory trips to both Moscow and Warsaw in June of 1976 to meet all of the team members manning our offices in both cities.

The Moscow office was managed by an American expatriate, who was supported by a Dutch petroleum engineer and a Russian staff of about 10 people. The Russians were mostly nice-looking ladies, surely under direction of the KGB to keep a close eye on the comings and goings of all the dangerous Pullman-associated foreigners traveling to Moscow. The office was well-appointed, nicely equipped, quite modern, and set in an excellent location within the Garden Ring Road, not far from the USA Embassy. Naturally, although this marked my first visit ever to Moscow, my previous visit to the USSR for my study in Leningrad had not exactly been a sterling one, so I was very cautious not to make any waves during this visit. In any event, all went well during this initial trip to Moscow, and I was off to Warsaw right afterwards for my familiarization visit there.

As in Moscow, there was an American expat, of Polish extraction and perfectly bilingual, heading up the Warsaw office, which was equally well-appointed and in a very good location. Once again, as in Moscow, the office staff was comprised of a number of quite attractive ladies, with most likely the same behind the scenes duties as their Russian comrades, who manned the office and managed the administrative requirements. Other than a quick stop at Warsaw airport en route to Leningrad the previous summer, this trip was my first one to Poland, and I was quite impressed with Warsaw itself and the people. In those days, Warsaw was a typical Communist city, with architectural style having been imported from the USSR with all of its Socialist Realism charm. In fact, Warsaw had been largely destroyed by the Germans during WWII. The Soviets had taken control at the tail end of the war, so they generously imported all of their socialist preferences and imposed them upon the Polish people. However, the one glowing exception to this stark communist façade was the way the Poles had rebuilt the *Staroye Miasto* ("Old Town") section of the city. They had meticulously studied all of the available photos and architectural drawings from the original 13th (and later) century buildings, and rebuilt this section of town as close to an exact replica of the original as possible. This renovation was truly an impressive feat, one which was duplicated in all major Polish cities, and a tribute to their national pride.

Back in Pittsburgh towards the end of that summer of 1976, it soon became evident that I might be better off moving to Chicago to work out of the Pullman headquarters office. Because my boss was located there, it seemed to make a great deal of sense. More than the need to pack up our stuff for another move, this anticipated change also had a greater impact on our personal lives. Although we had been planning to get married at some point in the near future and had been discussing how and when to do it, the impending move to Chicago compelled us to take action quickly. We did not feel comfortable making another move under the pretense of being married when we actually weren't, so we decided to bite the bullet. Thus, on September 21, 1976, in front of a Justice of the Peace in Pittsburgh City Hall, with two complete strangers as witnesses, we were married. Soon thereafter, we packed up and moved to The Windy City.

Pullman's office in Chicago was located downtown on The Loop, just off Lake Michigan. Whereas our offices at Swindell-Dressler in Pittsburgh were comfortable, yet modest, Corporate headquarters in Chicago was quite a bit more upscale. Because my new wife and I could not afford to live in the downtown area close to the office, we rented an apartment in the suburb of Arlington Heights, about 25 miles northwest of downtown. Each day, my wife dropped me off, and picked me up, at the Arlington Heights train station from where I would take the Northwest Commuter Train back and forth to the office. Then, she went on to her new job at a suburban travel agency where she had quickly found employment. My position with Pullman was entitled International Marketing Coordinator, which sounded much more important than it was, but that was the way my boss had wanted to present me to potential clients. My primary responsibility was to identify, seek out, and recruit new retainer-paying corporate clients for representation in the USSR and Poland through our offices there. It was truly a great job that entailed significant responsibility and corporate exposure for me. Accordingly, for any corporate aspirant, it was by any definition a great position for a young 25-year-old. However, for a romantic idealist with quixotic tendencies, working in the Ivory Tower, although interesting, left a great deal to be desired. My spirit eventually yearned for adventure and wanderlust, and I soon began to seek them elsewhere.

Although my position allowed me to travel extensively, domestically as well as periodically overseas, my strong desire was to gain one of the expatriate positions in either Pullman's Moscow or Warsaw office. Unfortunately, the expat positions that the company had budgeted were fully spoken for, and the chance of one of those positions opening up for me was, at best, years away. Mind you, I was not terribly unhappy with either Pullman or my position; I simply had a deeply embedded yearning for something more. It had become clear to me that my spirit was not made for corporate life; it cried for more adventure, something more out-of-the-ordinary and less predictable. In any event, on a client recruiting trip to New York City during the summer of 1977, I met with the President and Founder of Ferrex International, an export management company located in lower Manhattan, close to the World Trade Center. This gentleman, Andrew Ferretti, impressed me greatly. He was a true, highly energetic entrepreneur, who had built his company from scratch into one with a global presence. I developed an instant admiration for this gentleman and thought that it would be excellent to work in such an entrepreneurial and energetic environment. As a result, when I returned to Chicago and discussed this idea with my wife, as always, she was more than willing to consider the possibility. You see, for better or for worse, she also shared my quest for adventure.

Whereas my original pitch to Mr. Ferretti had been to use Pullman's offices to support sales of his product line to the USSR and Poland, this approach simply did not match his business model. His business was based upon finding indigenous distributors who would buy and resell his products within a specific market; and, in those days, privately-owned distributorships did not exist within the socialist economic model. When I later wrote to Mr. Ferretti suggesting that I was interested to join his company, he responded noting that they were looking for someone to handle sales representation in Africa. This position would require moving to Africa, establishing a central base of operations, traveling the continent to support current distributors and to recruit new ones to sell the Ferrex equipment line {Note: Ferrex International represented a stable of small and medium-sized US manufacturers for international sales}. I had become fascinated by Africa over the previous few years, thanks in large part to having become enamored with Wilbur Smith's novels, which I first discovered as a patient in 1975 in the Innsbruck University Clinic. I informed Mr. Ferretti that I would indeed be interested; however, he stated that he would not be able to hire me without first obtaining approval from my current boss, Don Morfee.

When Mr. Morfee received the letter from Mr. Ferretti, he called me into his office. He asked in his unwavering kindly manner what was the background behind the letter, and I explained as best I could where I was coming from. I should note that Don Morfee was one of my true role models in those days, and he remains one of the few persons whom I hold in the highest personal regard today. Even though he must have thought that I was a bit crazy, I believe that he did understand my reasoning and my yearning for adventure. He emphasized that there were no anticipated openings in either of the offices in Moscow or Warsaw, although he assured me that I would be a leading candidate to fill one when/if it opened up. He also stated that he would not stand in my way if this was what I truly wanted to do. In turn, I assured him that I was eternally grateful for the opportunity that he and Pullman had given me and that I would not leave the position until I had helped to find a suitable replacement. He agreed to this suggestion, and I set out to begin the process of finding someone to take my place.

I recall vividly how I felt when I wrote out my job description to use when advertising for my replacement. As I read it, I thought to myself that it sounded like THE perfect job for anyone who wanted to work in the field in which I had been dealing the previous one and a half years. I asked myself, "What kind of a dumb ass would willingly give up such a job?" Nevertheless, the spirit was moving me in a different direction, and I felt the overwhelming urge to answer the call.

I had always been personally interested in the Thunderbird School of Global Management in Arizona, so one of the first places I went to interview potential replacements was there. The school generously accepted my request to come there to conduct interviews and helped to arrange a list of suitable candidates. I recall interviewing about a half-dozen candidates who were all highly qualified to fill the position, and I carried my recommendations back with me to Chicago. The young man in whom I had been most impressed was eventually chosen to assume my position, so I felt that I had met my responsibility to fill the void which I was creating. As a result, once everything was deemed in order, we again packed up our things and headed east to assume my new responsibilities with Ferrex International. I remember wondering to myself if this life-style was really what my wife had in mind when we got together. After all, this was her fourth move within the two years since she had originally come to Washington to live with me, and the fifth one was already scheduled for the New Year when we would be relocating to Africa. I also recall wondering what her parents must be thinking about this apparent wanderlust? Thankfully, for better or for worse, my wife seemed to share this (dysfunctional?) tendency too.

My plan with Ferrex was to spend the first couple of months getting acquainted with the company and going to visit the stable of manufacturers whom they represented in order to acquire product knowledge. Because I would be traveling most of the time, rather than find a place to live in New York City, we decided to rent a place on the Jersey shore, and we found a charming furnished house in Monmouth Beach. On those days on which I commuted to and from the Ferrex office in lower Manhattan, this trip necessitated a two-hour train and subway ride each way, but we enjoyed our down-time on the Jersey shore. Otherwise, I was on the road for the majority of the time, traveling to about a dozen manufacturers all over the country. The pace over those few months was fast and furious, but we were both very excited about the adventures that were ahead of us.

Ferrex had already developed several solid distributorships in French West Africa for the log skidder tractors that they represented worldwide, and the African headquarters of this distribution company was in Abidjan, Ivory Coast. Abidjan was also the most developed and strategically-located city from where I would be able to manage distributor sales, so, once the Christmas holidays were completed, we set off in early January, 1978, for Abidjan. Back in September, I had signed a one year agreement with Ferrex as an independent contractor, from which I would be paid a base salary plus commissions on sales; my territory was all of Africa, except for the North African Islamic countries, and all of my travel expenses would be paid by the company. Assuming that my sales activities would be successful, the contract offered a potentially-lucrative commission arrangement, but the base salary was not large enough to afford the expensive expatriate housing in Abidjan. As a result, we worked a deal with the Forum International Hotel on the outskirts of Abidjan for long-term rates on a small room. It was crowded, to say the least, but it did offer comfortable and safe lodging, with all of the conveniences of a luxury hotel. Needless to say, we made very good use of the swimming pool in the tropical conditions, and, although space was limited in our room, we found it to be quite a satisfactory arrangement.

My always industrious wife also quickly found a job with the Ivory Coast Tourism Board, teaching English to aspiring Ivoirian Tour Guides. Her new job not only supplemented our income but also provided her with enjoyable employment. This development was especially useful because I was traveling a majority of the time, and she could immerse herself in work she enjoyed while I was gallivanting across the continent. During the following eight months, I traveled often to countries such as Ghana, Nigeria, Cameroon, Gabon, Zaire, Sudan, Kenya, and others; South Africa was also a territory of mine. Because the apartheid government was still in power, I had obtained a separate passport to travel there in order to keep my travel segregated; unfortunately, however, I did not manage to make a trip to South Africa during that time.

Travel in Africa during those days was indeed a challenge. Flights between countries were infrequent, and they could also be quite adventuresome. I recall well one flight for which I had a ticket from Libreville, Gabon, back to Abidjan, and for which I literally had to fight my way on board; I developed a whole new appreciation for the concept of overbooking on that particular trip.

Travel to Nigeria was always an adventure, not so much getting in and out, but rather navigating within the country. On my initial visit there, the taxi ride from the airport to my hotel, a trip of only about 10 kilometers, took more than four hours, in a cab that had no air conditioning despite the tropical conditions. During that cab ride, I noticed what seemed to be a dead body along the side of the road, with people passing by normally. I asked the driver if he thought that was a dead body, and he said, "Sure." When I asked why no one had removed the body, he replied that anyone stopping to do so could very well be accused of having committed the homicide, so discretion was the better part of valor. Amazing! During that same visit, I rode up-country to visit a customer along with the distributorship's driver. When we passed through a small village, a group of villagers started to chase our vehicle and soon forced us off the road. I didn't know what the hell was going on, until my driver informed me that they were actually after him for some alleged past infraction of local protocol. After the large group of unhappy Nigerians surrounded us, I got out of the car to speak with the leader of the angry mob. Somehow, by the grace of God, I was able to convince them to find forgiveness for the young man and to let us go. As we drove away from the crowd, I was still shaking inside, wondering what in the world I was doing there! Welcome to Nigeria, I thought.

I also made several trips to Ghana during that time period; once, planning to attend a trade show in Kumasi in northern Ghana, I decided to drive across the border rather than fly. During the border crossing from Ivory Coast into Ghana, I came to the Ghanaian border post, where an armed soldier awaited me; border guards in Africa had a notorious reputation in those days of always expecting bribes on the spot for the privilege of entering their country. When this particular border guard asked me what I had brought him that day, I replied, "My everlasting friendship and best wishes!" He laughed so hard that I was afraid he might mistakenly pull the trigger on his rifle, but, good-naturedly, he just waved me on. As I glanced back in my rear-view mirror, he appeared still to be laughing out loud.

During this same trip, the government refinery just happened to encounter equipment problems, and gasoline became unavailable for a few days. At the conclusion of the trade show, my Ghanaian colleague was informed the problem had been corrected and that gasoline trucks would be coming to Kumasi that day to refill the gas tanks. After several days without gas, however, the demand was quite high, and drivers were stationed for miles along the Accra-Kumasi highway to follow the tanker trucks to their destinations in order to get a good spot in line. Because I did not have enough gas in my vehicle to get back to Ivory Coast, we did the same; however, by the time we got word of a tanker truck coming to a nearby station, the line for gas was already several miles long. While I hopefully held my spot in the queue, my Ghanaian colleague walked to the front of the line to try to find a sympathetic person, who might sacrifice his place in line for an unfortunate foreigner who needed to return to Abidjan to his wife. He soon returned with a young taxi driver, who, although his livelihood depended on being able to drive his cab, was willing to give up his spot for me. When I asked him why, he responded that his allocation of gas would be used up that same day anyway, so he considered it more important for me to be able to drive home. I was indeed touched by his generosity and gave him a good tip in exchange, but I know that his gesture was genuine and not motivated by the prospect of money.

I could probably go on for many pages writing about the unusual occurrences that happened to us in Africa; the continent offers ample opportunity for unique experiences, far more than any other place I have ever been. Without babbling on too much further, however, I will share one additional anecdotal story that is worth telling.

It happened during a visit to Libreville, Gabon, where I was meeting our local distributor, a French-owned company that was selling our log-skidders into the local timber industry. The French manager of this distributorship was a congenial gentleman, who, after a morning of business discussions, took me to lunch at the local expatriate beach club. There we sat in a small, thatched-roofed pagoda on the beach, where our table was set. While engaging in conversation, I noticed that there was a stunning young lady sunbathing topless not too far from our pagoda. Naturally, I tried not to look at her too directly, lest I offend my host, but it was certainly difficult not to allow my eyes to stray in that direction on occasion. About 10 minutes later, the aforementioned alluring, and scantily clad, beauty got up and began to walk directly to our table. When she arrived, my host introduced me to his 17-year-old daughter, who had been sunbathing while waiting to join us for lunch. She sat down with us at the table, in all of her naked glory, and joined in the conversation, apparently without a thought of covering those perfectly perky boobs. The French consider lunch to be the main meal of the day, so lunches tend to be quite lengthy affairs, especially in tropical Africa. I can honestly say that experience, spent eating a wonderful two-hour lunch with this nubile beauty sitting next to me, was by far the most uncomfortable time I have ever spent in my life. I am guessing that my host understood perfectly my discomfort in the situation, and, no doubt, it certainly provided him many hours of pleasure in relaying the story to his French compatriots. *"Oh, Les Americaines!"*

As we approached September, 1977, my one-year contract was nearly at an end, so we returned home for some well-deserved R&R and to conclude my contractual obligations with Ferrex. Although my time in Africa had been highly interesting and reasonably successful, we frankly did not know if we wanted to sign on for another year. Therefore, we sold the car that we had purchased in Abidjan and packed up all our belongings, yet again, to return home, not knowing what the future would hold. Back in NYC at Ferrex headquarters, they paid me the commission that was due me under the contract for the past year and offered me the opportunity to renew my contract, albeit on terms which were less-advantageous for me. Once our business with Ferrex was concluded, we left NYC to spend time with our families and to ponder whether we wanted to return to Africa or to find some totally new adventure to pursue. Little did we know what Destiny had in mind for us next, but, based on recent history, it was probably a pretty good bet that it would be unconventional.

Chapter 9

The Country Innkeeper

Bath County, Virginia, late-September, 1978

My wife and I had just returned from our time in the Ivory Coast, and, after paying proper respects to family members, we decided to take some time off alone in order to ponder whether we would return to Africa for another year or change to some other endeavor. I had purchased some mountain property after I left the Army in 1972, and, although it was not developed, it was ideal for some Spartan mountain camping. So we packed up a tent, sleeping bags, and other basic camping essentials and headed for the mountains of western Virginia.

Although the weather had been warm up until that point, soon after arriving at the property, we realized that a cold front had come in, and we suddenly decided that we would be much more comfortable somewhere inside. My wife remembered finding a nice country inn in nearby Hot Springs just a few years before, so we promptly chickened out under the threat of cold weather and headed straight for Hot Springs and the Vine Cottage Inn.

I didn't recall ever having noticed Vine Cottage Inn during my previous trips to Hot Springs, but I became enamored at first sight. The building was a beautiful, turn-of-the-twentieth-century Victorian building and looked very elegant from the exterior. When we entered, we were greeted by the owners, an elderly couple who had purchased the Inn a few years previously. The husband, Henri Ribet, a retired French pastry chef from the famous Homestead Hotel nearby, had envisioned the inn as a suitable hobby. As it turned out, we were the only guests that night, so we received a first-class tour of the entire inn, all three floors and 20 rooms of it. On our tour with Monsieur Ribet, during which I continued to be impressed, he mentioned that they had decided to sell the inn. Out of curiosity, I inquired what price he had in mind. His response immediately caught my attention and started my mind to work. The price he had disclosed seemed extraordinarily low, if from no other perspective than basic real estate value. Accordingly, once we retired to our room for the evening, our discussion was uniquely focused on the prospect of becoming innkeepers.

It has been said by friends that I can tend to be a wee bit impulsive; there may indeed be some credence to that opinion because, in the spirit of full disclosure, we presented our offer to purchase Vine Cottage Inn within 24 hours of having entered the premises. Firstly, we were both convinced that the real estate alone was hugely under-priced at the quoted level, which it was. Secondly, with our youth and energy, plus some imagination and hard work, we believed that we could quickly refurbish the physical plant, which was not actually in bad shape, as well as vastly improve the occupancy rate. We had some savings from our past year in Africa, and we were able to solicit some small loans from our families in order to finance the down payment. The owners agreed to hold a First Deed of Trust for the remainder of the debt, so we all reached agreement quickly. Talk about Destiny taking hold of one's life! In the short span of a few days, we negated our plans to return to Africa for another year, agreed to purchase a hotel, and embarked head first into a business in which we had no previous experience. Impulsive? Nah! The spirit simply moved us.

I must admit that we were both really excited about this new endeavor. We were proprietors of our own business, a really charming property in a famous resort area, and a business that we believed we could make successful, all the while greatly enhancing the value of the enterprise and property. We also had quickly ascertained that we had an available work force to come to help us with this new undertaking. My mother was not overly content with her life in Washington, DC, at that time, so she was more than happy to move to Hot Springs to help us with the inn. Later, my half-sister, Cathy, also agreed to move south from New Jersey to help out, so we quickly became a family affair. In addition, we had ample part-time help available from the local community, so we were in pretty good shape in terms of necessary hotel staff.

During the late 1970's, country inn-hopping was very much in vogue. People looked for quaint, personable lodging alternatives to motels, and there were several guidebooks in circulation those days pointing out such establishments; "Country Inns and Back Roads" was the most popular of such books, but there were several others. The profession of innkeeper was also considered to be the ideal job, one where the master of the house could don his tweed jacket and, with pipe in hand, play charming host to hundreds of interesting guests from across the world. Although there was certainly some truth to this concept, the stark reality of being an innkeeper was sometimes altogether different.

I would like to add a few words about our new chosen home, Hot Springs, Virginia. The village of Hot Springs and the entire area of Bath County in general are absolutely a beautiful, peaceful environment. The world famous Homestead Hotel is the centerpiece of the region, around which a thriving tourist industry has developed. The vast bulk of the county is either National Forest land or large private tracts and farms, so real estate development has been minimal. Historically, the area of Hot Springs and nearby Warm Springs, both known for their natural hot sulfur baths, were a haven for wealthy families, who built their lavish summer mansions in the cool Virginia mountains, and simply took turns entertaining their friends. The region is blessed with clean, trout-filled streams and rivers, beautiful hiking trails running through the mountains, superb golf courses, excellent hunting, and ski slopes for winter travelers. It is truly an outdoor paradise and everyone enjoys the frequent opportunity to bask in nature, unless, of course, he or she chooses the occupation of innkeeper.

Perhaps I should qualify that last statement from the outset. If an innkeeper is independently wealthy, is not overly concerned about the profitability of the enterprise, and has plenty of help to support and maintain the establishment, then the profession is not so challenging. In such a situation, in which the innkeeper can consciously assume the role of congenial and charming host, the profession actually may be one of the ideal career pursuits anyone could choose. On the other hand, for someone who is not independently wealthy and who needs to make the business profitable in order to survive, the lifestyle, albeit still enjoyable, can be much more challenging. This is especially true in the case of "Ma and Pa" businesses, such as ours. Commenting on the myth that the job of country innkeeper was the ideal professional pursuit, I recall an article which was published during that time in a travel magazine, which stated that the divorce rate among couples who run an inn together was about 75%. I can understand why.

When my wife and I purchased Vine Cottage Inn, I had just turned 27, and my wife was about to turn 25. Although it did not occur to us at the time, in retrospect, the job of innkeeper is probably an ideal retirement job; however, for those who are still infected by the wanderlust, it may be a bit premature. In total honesty, both of us being control-freak workaholics, we were most probably our own worst enemies. We worked 18 hours a day, 7 days per week, and lived right in the inn itself. After a short while, we began to feel more like prisoners in our own castle than masters of it. We were wise to divide our duties, thereby limiting potential areas of conflict; after we became settled, my wife handled the day-to-day operations of the inn, while I threw myself into managing the refurbishment of the building and the sales and marketing requirements. This division of labor seemed to work out fairly well, although there were still plenty of opportunities for conflict within this closed environment.

What we lacked in hotel management experience, we made up for in energy expended and pure hard work. We put a great deal of effort into cosmetic changes for many of the rooms, repainting where appropriate, or simply adding flair where we could. Major structural improvements, other than new shingles for the roof, were thankfully few, because we did not have the capital to support too many costly projects.

Fortunately, having been raised in nearby Staunton, I had contacts who were happy to help us with publicity. We were featured in the Staunton newspaper as the young couple who had met in Russia, lived in Africa, and had chosen to purchase the historic Vine Cottage Inn.

With that, and other publicity channels, we were able to make a splash from the very beginning, and, as a result, our occupancy rate started to grow methodically. We especially took maximum advantage of group bookings, which featured golf groups throughout the year, hunters in the fall, and ski groups during the winter. This trend was also the most profitable method we had because such groups usually filled up the inn, the capacity of which was about 50 people. In addition, group packages always included breakfast and dinner, for which we had pre-set menus and full attendance, which cut down on waste and increased our profit margin. In the very beginning, we hired a chef to assist us with the meals; however, I quickly realized that his skills were really not much better than I could do myself, so I soon decided to let him go and assume the title of "iron chef" myself. In fact, we did manage reasonably well in that respect, and we saved a great deal of money in so doing; however, on the negative side, running the kitchen ourselves introduced additional, largely unanticipated stress, as well as some truly comedic situations.

The most hilarious predicament in which we found ourselves was our decision to make Eggs Benedict for a Sunday morning seating of about 50 folks. Anyone who has made Eggs Benedict knows that timing is the key to success. The eggs need to be poached precisely when the English Muffins and Canadian Bacon are stacked and ready and as the Hollandaise Sauce is just close to perfection, and ready to pour on top. So, picture the chaos and delay that can be created if the Hollandaise Sauce suddenly separates and needs to be started again from scratch, which necessitates re-poaching 100 eggs, ensuring that the muffins and bacon are still warm and presentable, etc, etc. Although I do not believe that the 50 breakfast customers really noticed that anything was wrong, the chaos in the kitchen while trying to rectify this situation could have been a great episode of the *The Three Stooges*. After we resolved the dilemma and finally got everything cleaned up and put away from that breakfast, we immediately broke out the Bloody Mary's and decompressed for the next couple of hours, laughing all the while once the stress of the moment had dissipated.

Over the course of the two years or so in which we owned and operated the Vine Cottage Inn, the greatest pleasure we received was the quality of the guests whom we were able to host and to know. Inn-hoppers are usually very interesting and well traveled folks, who are looking for more in a lodging experience than simply a room and a bath. We had so many wonderful visitors that it is an impossible task to go into much detail. One visitor, however, clearly sticks out in my mind, one who was not only highly enjoyable, but whose visit also turned out to be quite prophetic in nature.

There was a stage in our development when we decided to offer lunch for the local business community, in addition to any guests for whom it might be convenient. Our method was to have a pre-set and unique (usually ethnic) menu each day, and, more often than not, we attracted a pretty good crowd. Once per week we would offer a Russian-style lunch with traditional Borscht (thick beet soup) and Piroshki (small meat-filled pies), which turned out to be especially popular with our guests.

One afternoon, as we were preparing the Borscht for the next day's meal in the kitchen, we heard a booming male voice from the lobby, loudly exclaiming, "I SMELL BORSCHT!" When I exited the kitchen for the lobby to identify the source, I came face-to-face with Vasya (last name unnecessary), a distinguished looking gentleman in his mid-50's, and his attractive family. Vasya couldn't believe that they had just walked into a small inn in Hot Springs, Virginia, to find his favorite native delight being prepared on the stove. As it turned out, Vasya, who was born in Russia, had just retired from a successful career in the CIA, and he and his family were merely taking a summer jaunt in the Virginia countryside. Not only was he amazed to find Russian cuisine in this remote location, but to find two young Russian speakers running the establishment blew his mind. From my perspective, especially in retrospect, I found it equally amazing that we had accidently attracted a CIA case officer into our castle. Little did I know at the time that within one year of Vasya's visit, I would be discussing employment with the CIA myself. Years hence, life has taught me that there is no such thing as coincidence and that everything happens for a reason. This episode was one of the best examples I have experienced of this philosophy.

I also remember fondly the many ski groups that came to the inn. One in particular included a small band of traveling troubadours from the WDC area, who unexpectedly broke out their musical instruments one evening in the inn's living room. They put on such an impressive performance and enjoyable sing-along that we decided they needed to come back on a regular basis to entertain our groups. Accordingly, we offered them free room and board in exchange for entertainment on whichever winter weekends they could fit into their schedule. They were simply great entertainers; they made everyone smile and have a wonderful time, and we became close friends. Those were certainly some of the most memorable times at Vine Cottage Inn. Some 32 years later, recalling these evenings of camaraderie and music brings a wide smile to my face. They were good times indeed!

On the other hand, some of the times we spent at the inn were more challenging. As indicated previously, although we were certainly living in God's Country, and running what some people believed was the ideal business, we soon started to become disenchanted with the endeavor. Largely because of our own somewhat dysfunctional modus operandi, and truthfully also motivated by our inflexible financial situation, we had imprisoned ourselves in the business and did not allow sufficient time for enjoying the area. I did make one wise move in that I also obtained my real estate sales license very soon after purchasing the inn. Whereas I never made a great deal of money in this side venture, it did give me the opportunity to escape from the building from time-to-time to review or show beautiful mountain property, which I really did enjoy. All the while, however, we became more and more cognizant of the fact that we were too young, and the world too wide and inviting, to want to spend the remainder of our lives running an inn, albeit in a wonderful location. Thus, as we passed our first anniversary as owners of the inn and into our second year, we began to think seriously about selling the business.

Old and close friends can often provide motivation for introspective examination. About this time, within weeks of each other, I was visited at the inn by two good buddies, Randy Osgood, my classmate from Suffield Academy, and Johnny Burke, my close friend and football teammate from Georgetown. Ironically, both of them had been struggling with battles with cancer. Randy's disease seemed to have gone into remission at that point in time, but it was clear that Johnny was in the midst of a desperate battle. In fact, Johnny probably should not have been traveling at that point, but he really wanted to take a break from WDC and to visit with me. In both cases, I regard their visits as divine intervention, and we spoke at length about life and the pursuit of happiness, as only close friends can do. I came away from those visits not only grateful for their friendship, but convinced from our conversations that life is short and that we should follow our destiny elsewhere if current circumstances were not meeting our needs. Their visits were truly timely and pertinent, and, to this day, I am convinced that they were sent by the Universe to help guide me on my destined path.

We will read more about this unhappy development in the next chapter, but Johnny Burke soon lost his battle with cancer. He passed away within months of his visit with me in Hot Springs. However, at his funeral in WDC in the spring of 1980, during a conversation with Johnny's brother-in-law, I revealed to him that we were thinking about selling our inn. He became immediately interested because his younger brother was a professional in the hospitality industry, and he, a successful stock trader from Chicago, was looking for such an investment opportunity as ours. To make a long story short, over the next few weeks, we did come to an agreement to sell Vine Cottage Inn to Johnny's in-laws. This development was welcome and appeared to be a win-win situation for all concerned. For me personally, however, it was only one of the first times in which John's spiritual presence had seemingly come to offer me guidance; it was clear to me then and much more so today.

Back to the situation at hand, having reached the decision to sell the inn and having identified a buyer, our major consideration became, "okay, what comes next?" Up to that point, we really hadn't given our future plans much consideration. I had applied to the MBA Program at the University of Virginia on a lark, having decided that I could possibly juggle both endeavors, running the inn and studying for my MBA simultaneously. As it turned out, I was accepted into the program, so this option was a possible one. Prior to receiving that acceptance letter from UVA, however, I had researched and applied for a number of international business opportunities that had come to my attention; one of these was a position opening for international sales representatives interested in living and working overseas, much like I had already done in Africa when I worked for Ferrex International. The only odd thing about this job advertisement, which appeared in the Wall Street Journal, was that it specified a set salary scale for the position. Because like most international sales reps, I had worked for a base salary plus an established commission schedule, this advertisement struck me as a bit strange, but, what the hell, I decided to apply anyway.

Within a few weeks, I received a call from a gentleman in response to my application for the international sales representative position. We conducted a rather lengthy telephone conversation during which we both asked the typical job interview questions when he suddenly asked me, "So, Bob, what would you say if I told you that I am really calling you on behalf of the Central Intelligence Agency?"

My response was fairly immediate, "I am not really surprised, since your advertisement specified a set salary base, which seemed strange to me in terms of a sales rep position."

He chuckled, and responded, "Yes, I hear that frequently."

Nevertheless, we continued the conversation awhile longer, at which point we mutually agreed to begin the formal application process. My interlocutor informed me that the process would be a lengthy one, with extensive background information to be provided and numerous security-related interviews which would need to take place; nevertheless, the concept sounded interesting to me, so we proceeded accordingly. At that point, (it was about mid-April of 1980), we now had a number of potential options to consider during the months ahead. First, I had been accepted into the UVA MBA program; secondly, the CIA was now interested in considering me for a position; and, thirdly, my wife had inquired into a possible teaching position at the local high school, for which she had received strong encouragement. So, there was much to consider, while we moved towards the closing of the sale of Vine Cottage Inn, which was to occur in early June.

By the time of the closing, my wife had accepted the teaching position at the high school for the coming school year, so, at least, that piece of the puzzle was set. Because she was going to be teaching French, she decided to spend much of the summer brushing up on her language skills, so she enrolled in a foreign study program in Aix-en-Provence in the south of France. Even though we had already begun the due diligence process with the CIA (submitted all of the required background information, and traveled to WDC to take the psychological tests, and lifestyle polygraph examinations), we were informed not to expect any firm decision for several months. As a result, I decided to spend the summer in Charlottesville at UVA; I had been advised by my MBA program counselor to take an advance course in Quantitative Analysis at UVA to prepare better for the beginning of the program. Frankly, I did not know how I would ultimately decide if or when the CIA actually came back to me with an offer of employment.

The Colgate-Darden MBA Program at UVA was a prestigious one, and successful graduates of that program could usually expect excellent job offers with huge starting salaries, so that option was certainly attractive. On the other hand, with my Special Forces background and strong interest in foreign languages, cultures. and expatriate living, a career in the CIA certainly also appealed to my sense of adventure and inherent quixotic nature. In any event, time would tell, and we took one day at a time until Destiny revealed itself.

After my wife departed for her summer study in France, I moved to Charlottesville, along with our Golden Retriever, Christy, and set myself up in a basement apartment in a private home. I soon began my class in Quantitative Analysis at the university, which not only involved my first exposure to calculus and statistical analysis, but also my initial exposure to the computer world. I can honestly say, without any embarrassment whatsoever, that I have never felt as absolutely clueless and lost as during that class. The professor of the course was great, and, because he was the uncle of a boyhood friend of mine, he took a personal interest in helping me along. Nevertheless, I never caught up to the flow of the course, and quickly came to the conclusion that this was simply not my cup of tea. About that same time, the CIA personnel department contacted me and advised that my application had been accepted, although there was still no indication of when I would be able to start the Career Trainee (CT) program. My interlocutor said that they still needed to determine when they would be able to fit me into the CT entry program, but, in the meantime, they wanted an expression of interest from me. Because I was completely lost in my first exposure to the MBA world, I concluded that, although there was nothing definitive as yet from the CIA, God was clearly speaking to me; therefore, I gave the Agency my agreement to join forces with them and decided to withdraw from the UVA MBA program.

When my wife returned from her studies in France, we found a place to live in Hot Springs, and she proceeded to begin her teaching position at the high school. I was still waiting for the Agency to give me a start date, so I decided to fill my time with some interesting projects. With the profits from the sale of Vine Cottage Inn, we had purchased a beautiful mountainside lot right within the village of Hot Springs, and we had been investigating the type of home we wanted to build on it. I heard of a Post & Beam building course that was being offered in Bath, Maine, so I handed Christy off to the wife and headed north to invest my free time in interesting and worthwhile pursuits.

At the conclusion of the Post & Beam building seminar, which was fascinating, I decided to enroll in a two-week French Language program in the village of Jonquiere, in northern Quebec, close to Lac Saint-Jean; it seemed like a logical decision, for the French language skills would certainly come in handy in my work with the Agency, and I wanted to improve upon the basic French that I had learned while living in the Ivory Coast. In addition, the prospect of a sojourn into beautiful Northern Quebec was also quite appealing, so off I went in late September for two weeks of intensive French language instruction. It was a good program, and I enjoyed the experience, but, by this time, I was growing quite impatient and anxious that I had not received a start date from the CIA; I decided that I needed to help the clearly bureaucratic process along a bit.

At the first opportunity after my return from Canada to the States, I phoned my contact at the CIA and asked again for a prognosis on when I would be able to begin. When I got another "I don't know" response, my impatience and frustration with the lengthy process got the best of me, and I gave the personnel officer some insights into my frustration level plus a slight ultimatum. In a nutshell, I informed the officer that if I did not hear something definitive from them within the next few days, that I was simply going to do something else with my life. I guess the ultimatum finally caught their attention, because they contacted me quickly afterwards to inform me that they had identified an opening in the CT class to begin on October 20th and asked me to confirm that I could and would be able to take the slot. Without any hesitation whatsoever, I agreed to do so. Thus, the die was finally cast, and the next phase of my wanderlust life was about to begin. In anticipation of this unique opportunity to work on behalf of my nation as a professional intelligence officer, my quixotic spirit was primed and ready for the unknown adventures to come.

Chapter 10

A Jolt Along Life's Path

Chevy Chase, Maryland, March 21, 1980

There are indeed certain dates that stand out in our memories because they made a strong impact upon our lives. Like September 11th, 2001, and November 22nd, 1963, for me and many others, March 21st, 1980, was one of those days. Unlike the other two, however, which were entirely unexpected and tragic events, we knew that the event of March 21st was inevitable, but that did not make it any easier to bear when it happened. Thirty-plus years later, the memory of it is still indelibly engraved in my memory. That was the day on which my close friend, John David Burke, finally succumbed to his lengthy bout with cancer.

Johnny Burke was 27 when he died. It's tragic enough when any human being dies prematurely, but Johnny was not your normal human being. John David Burke was very special.

For his family, his many friends, and the multitude of others who knew him, the mention of John's name brings a knowing smile; it is simply recognition that we were uniquely blessed in having had the privilege to know him. John is not so easy to describe for those who did not have the chance to meet him; I know, for I have tried. Although a person can never make a statement such as this one without igniting some indignation and controversy, and although I admit that I have my own definitions in this regard, of all of the tens of thousands of human beings whom I have met over my 60 years, John David Burke most closely met my image of a Christ-like figure.

Let there be no doubt, Johnny was human like all of us; as his close friends knew, he could misbehave and/or be as mischievous as any of us. During the years that I knew him, I admit that I was personally responsible for much of that mischief. But as human as he was, there was a quiet, spiritual presence about him that exuded pure peace and brotherhood.

Saying that everyone liked Johnny somehow seems insufficient; it is more accurate to say that everyone was drawn to him. He had a personal magnetism that was undeniable and which most vividly manifested itself when he was with children. John had a unique ability to communicate with children at their level; kids were like putty in John's hands, as he was in theirs. To witness Johnny's uninhibited affection for his large family was also touching. The expression of love and brotherhood in all of his inter-personal relationships was something which, contrary to many of us, simply came easily and naturally for John.

I met John for the first time in August of 1972 during preseason practice of the Georgetown University football team. This was my sophomore year and first football season at GU since my return from the Army. Although he was also a sophomore, it was John's first year on the team because he had decided not to play football his freshman year to devote himself more thoroughly to his studies. We were both competing for a position at running back, but it became quickly clear to me that John's skills were at a much higher level than mine. Johnny was barely 6' tall and played at just 175 pounds, but his speed and instinctive elusiveness were superior. It was evident from the beginning that John would be a special running back at Georgetown, just as he had been during his high school years.

Over the three years which he played there, even though his junior year was cut short by injury, he went on to set every rushing record at GU for total yards, average yards per carry and rushing touchdowns. Watching him run was like seeing a thoroughbred horse in full stride; he was poetry in motion. He made Honorable Mention All-American after his senior year and was later inducted into the GU Athletic Hall of Fame. However, as good as he was on the football field, and although football was the venue through which we became close friends, this is not a treatise on athletic prowess. This chapter is about making a powerful impact on humanity.

John died over 30 years ago, and I am still not able to think about him without tears welling up in my eyes. Mind you, I have lost other good friends to premature passing, as well as a brother and both of my parents, but nothing affects me quite as emotionally as thinking about John. And, to be clear, it is not so much the sadness of his passing away prematurely which brings the tears to my eyes. The best illustration I can conjure up in explanation is the scene at the end of the movie *Saving Private Ryan,* where the then-elderly Ryan is standing before the grave at Normandy Cemetery of Captain Miller (the character played by Tom Hanks), the man most responsible for saving his life; Ryan is in tears in this scene, asking the spirit of Captain Miller if he has been worthy of the sacrifice which Miller and the other soldiers made in saving him. Had he, Ryan, lived a good enough life to somehow justify the premature death of Miller and the other soldiers? Paraphrasing Ryan's thoughts, it is the essence of this question which I find myself asking so often of Johnny, and it usually produces the same tearful effect, for very much the same reason.

Within the scope of his 27 years, Johnny lived a full and inspiring life. A testimony to his impact upon people was the crowd of thousands who attended his funeral in the spring of 1980. John had married just a few years prior to his passing, and he had hoped to have a large, nurturing family of his own, just like the one in which he had been raised. At the time of his passing, Johnny was studying to become a lawyer, although I was never convinced that his heart was fully in the pursuit. John's passion was more in his creative side; he wrote poetry, some of which was published, and took up carpentry and painting in his last years. The results of his woodworking were masterful, as were his paintings, which glorified his love of life and nature. Despite the intense pain that he was experiencing during those last few years, John was determined to make the most of every minute, which he certainly did.

*"When I find myself in times of trouble, mother Mary comes to me,
speaking words of wisdom, let it be.*

*And in my hour of darkness she is standing right in front of me,
speaking words of wisdom, let it be."*

- The Beatles -

Over the years, I have firmly come to believe that everything in life happens for a reason. Reflecting upon the pain which I and so many others felt with the passing of John Burke, I have often pondered what could possibly be the "reason" for his death at the all-too-early age of 27.

Although he did not live to create the large family that he and his wife had wanted, Johnny unquestionably lived a full and happy life. He personified all that is important in our life's existence. He loved people, and people loved him. Everyone who came to know him was better for the experience and was seriously impacted by his death. For me, Johnny's passing was truly a life-changing event. Although I'd only known him for some seven years, his friendship had become an important part of the foundation on which my life had been structured. Similar to the feelings which I had felt when President Kennedy was assassinated and then again almost 40 years later when the events of 9/11 transpired, Johnny's passing created a time of serious introspection and questioning of the "meaning of life."

I do know this; my life has been blessed because I had the honor of knowing Johnny. He was a role model in many respects, but mostly from the perspective of brotherly love and compassion. His friendship gave me strength and helped me to see the best in my fellow man, as he had always done. With his passing, although a cause of great pain for me, he has also become a source of spiritual strength. When I find myself in "times of trouble" or in a personal "hour of darkness," Johnny is the spiritual being from whom I seek strength and wisdom. I often pray for his guidance and his support as I continue to run the gauntlet of life's challenges. For those who might question this practice, allow me to share the following experience.

It was in January of 1992. I had been living and working in Warsaw, Poland, at the time and was scheduled to return there that evening from Washington Dulles Airport. Before leaving for the airport, I had stopped into Georgetown University Hospital to visit with my prep school friend, Randy Osgood, who had been hospitalized in his losing battle with cancer. When I reached Randy's hospital room, he had apparently just fallen into a coma, from which he never emerged. I had really hoped to speak with him and to communicate to him how much his friendship had meant to me. My inability to do so hit me very hard. I was in a daze at the time, and I don't remember how exactly it happened, but I soon found myself in the GU Hospital office of Dr. Fred Burke, Johnny's father. Mind you, I had no clue where Dr. Burke's office was located, nor was it on my mind previously to go looking for him. But, there I found myself, crying on his shoulder, seeking his comfort. Dr. Burke consoled me and volunteered to call Randy's father to offer emotional support, and eventually I was comforted. There is absolutely no question in my mind how it was that I found myself there; a guardian angel, my departed friend, John, had taken me by the hand "in my hour of darkness" and led me there.

Just moments before Johnny passed away on that day of March 21st, I am told by family members who were gathered around his bed at their Chevy Chase home that his last words to his beloved family were, "I won! I won!" By all possible measurements, John David Burke's life on earth was an unquestioned victory. He led a brief yet thoroughly exemplary life, and the positive impact which he had on thousands of his fellow human beings, and continues to have, is one of the miracles of our collective experience. I would submit that therein, making a positive impact within one's immediate community, exists the true meaning of life.

Part III

Romantic Idealist in Action

Prologue to Part III

A Modern-Day Don Quixote

Warsaw, Poland, June, 1976

{Author's Note: As in the tradition of Don Quixote, there are moments when the true romantic idealist, in his unending pursuit of chivalry, becomes unintentionally humorous; I debated at length whether to include this particular excerpt, but I finally decided what the hell! It is true, after all, regardless of how comical it may make me look.}

I made my initial visit to Pullman's Warsaw office in the summer of 1976, following an introductory visit to our office in Moscow. Although Warsaw was under the firm grip of the Soviet Union in those days, it was still a much more cheerful place than Moscow, and there was much more to do. At the time of this visit, we had a new Director of the Warsaw office, and the Director from the Paris Office, who was generally in charge of all of Pullman's East European business, was also in Warsaw at the time. One evening, after we had all gone out to dinner, we decided that we would drop by the Bristol Hotel where there was a popular (with foreigners) discotheque and where we could have a few drinks and enjoy the ambiance. The disco was also one example of the means through which the totalitarian authorities could keep tabs on the expatriate population by allowing selected hotels and restaurants to cater to foreigners.

Although I do not recall exactly, I believe that it must have been a weekend evening, because the disco was particularly busy that night; there were expats aplenty, some well-connected Poles, and numerous females. My colleagues and I were standing aside together, chatting about nothing in particular, when, all of a sudden, I spotted what seemed to be one of the most beautiful young women I had ever seen in my life. Amazed by the pure and innocent pulchritude that had appeared before my eyes, I nudged my colleagues and pointed her out to them. I commented several times to my colleagues about how beautiful I thought she was and how I was surprised to see such an innocent young lady in this vile bar. Finally, one of my colleagues had heard enough and stated flatly, "Morris, she's a hooker!"

I was aghast by the accusation, and promptly informed him that he was full of crap! She was simply too pure and innocent to be a hooker! I tried to convince my colleagues of my version of reality but was unable to sway them from their opinion. Finally, one of them said, "If you don't believe me, just go ask her." At that point, I had no other alternative, so I left my group of friends, approached the young woman, and asked her to dance. She smilingly accepted. And, what a stunning smile it was!

It was a slow dance, and the band was playing a soft ballad, so I engaged her in conversation. I addressed her in Russian, but she asked me to speak English, which she spoke haltingly but said she preferred. We bantered about in the usual small talk, while I considered how I was going to prove I was correct in my assessment that she was certainly not a professional on the make. I saw that my colleagues were watching us from across the room and noticed several times how they were chuckling at my apparent dilemma. Although she was a charming girl, and I was certainly enjoying her company, I was not making much headway in my intelligence mission. However, when the music stopped, and the band played another slow dance, we continued our conversation.

By that time, I felt that we had established sufficient rapport so that, with my finely-tuned diplomatic skills, I should be able to broach the point in a manner that might not offend her. As we were dancing, I nodded in the direction of my colleagues, and asked, "Do you notice my friends over there?" She nodded to the affirmative.

"Well", I continued, "when I saw you enter the room earlier, and I commented how beautiful you were, they told me that you were here working, …. as a prostitute. Is that true?"

She looked up at me with her stunningly deep blue eyes, with a look which I interpreted as being extreme regret, and she nodded, "yes". I was stunned, and found myself speechless. As the dance continued and I tried to figure out what to say next, if anything, I finally asked her, "So how much do you charge?"

She replied, "$50.00." Again, I was unable to find a proper response, so I continued to dance without speaking.

When this dance finally stopped, I asked her to wait a minute, and I reached for my wallet; and, as discreetly as possible, I pulled out a $50 bill. I surreptitiously gave it to her and said, "Look, I would like it very much if you would take this $50 and just go home." She glanced at the money and then looked at me with incredulity, saying nothing.

I reiterated, "I mean it. Please just take the money and go home. It would make me happy." In response, she reached up and lightly and ever so sweetly kissed me on the check, and then left the discotheque. At that point, feeling noble and chivalrous like I had rarely felt in my life, I returned to the company of my colleagues.

One of the guys, who had been watching us covertly, asked me what had happened, and the others in the group turned their attention to me as well. I said, "Well, you guys were right. I can't believe it, but she's a hooker! I wanted her to get the hell out of here, so I gave her 50 bucks and just asked her to go home."

They all replied together in amazement. "You did WHAT?!?" one of them asked.

I repeated, "I gave her 50 bucks and asked her to go home."

At that point, they all erupted together in harmonious laughter, so hard that it looked like they were having difficulty breathing. At last, one of them gathered enough oxygen to be able to say, "Morris, you idiot! She'll be back here within 15 minutes!"

I vehemently disagreed, fully confident that she would be satisfied with the money I had given her and with the realization that she would not have to earn it the normal way. All the while laughing, my colleagues apparently decided not to belabor the point any further, other than to assure me with a "you'll see!" Nevertheless, I continued to bask in my self-assured feelings of nobility and chivalry, knowing in my heart-of-hearts that I was right; I had indeed performed a noble deed, saving this beautiful young lady from having to indulge in her sinful trade, at least for this one night.

As predicted, almost to the prognosticated minute, the young beauty returned to the dance floor to hunt for new customers. I looked her way a few times, but she never seemed to look back towards me. I was humiliated and a bit angry with myself for being so foolish; however, that was a day in which I learned the lesson that I truly did look at the world through different eyes.

Years later, living in Madrid, Spain, when I was telling this same story to my close friend, Eduardo, and his brother, they erupted in uncontrolled laughter in much the same way. Eduardo put the picture into proper perspective when he said to his brother, "Oh, my God! He's Don Quixote, born again!"

Chapter 11

The Spy Who Jumped into the Cold

Langley, Virginia, October 20, 1980

When the day finally came to report to work at my next career endeavor, I admit that I was truly excited. I had been to CIA headquarters previously during the job application process, but here I was being officially admitted into the fraternity of spies, and it was indeed an exhilarating feeling. I could not imagine any career choice that would more perfectly meet the high-minded expectations of a romantic idealist than this one. What could possibly be better, more fulfilling, more all-consuming than joining the front lines of the ideological conflict against the most dangerous enemies of our nation and mankind? The CIA career I was entering seemed to be a job made in Heaven for me.

The group that assembled together at CIA headquarters constituted the incoming Career Trainee (CT) class, mostly younger but very-talented folks with high-level university educations, usually some work experience, and a demonstrated interest in foreign languages and international affairs. In fact, as the Agency staff members stated to us that first day, the percentage of applicants for CIA Directorate of Operations (DO) case officer positions who were accepted into the CT program was about 1/10th of 1%; during the one year of CT training, a significant percentage would also wash out of the program and either leave the Agency or get into a more compatible line of endeavor somewhere else in the organization. All of the CT's who were currently in that room had gone through an incredibly scrutinizing and comprehensive due diligence process; these were the "chosen few," kindred spirits of high capability, many of whom tended to possess quixotic tendencies of their own. In any event, this gathering contained an impressive group of talented young

Americans who wanted to make their mark on the world.

After our initial few weeks of indoctrination were completed, we went off to our respective "interim assignments," where we would be given a position with one of the DO area desks. These interim assignments were intended so that we would gain some on-the-job training and insights into how the DO and its overseas stations operated. Because of my previous experience and general interest in Africa, I asked for one of the Africa Division desks, and luckily my request was granted. This job provided an eye-opening first glimpse into how the clandestine world operated and it was a highly positive experience. The Africa Division had the reputation of being the "cowboy" division of the DO; they were a wild and woolly group of guys, and I really enjoyed working with them, as I would in my later assignment in an African station. My primary choice, however, was the Soviet/East European (SE) Division, but the official selection of home divisions was about half a year away.

After the first interim assignment was completed, the majority of our group was sent off to "The Farm" for the official CT course, six months of intensive training on how to become a DO case officer. This course was to train the CT on operational tradecraft, such as how to recruit and manage spies, how to communicate with them covertly in different operational environments, how to use covert technology to help do your job, and so forth. The instructor staff was made up of senior active duty case officers or retirees who worked on contract to help train this next generation of CIA officers. Although much tamer than Army Infantry OCS had been, the CT course was still quite a demanding, highly intensive training course, and we were all thoroughly challenged. When the lengthy course ended, a number of our classmates had been found to be lacking, mostly in their perceived ability to recruit and/or handle spies, and were dispatched to other parts of the organization where their skills might be put to better use. Although I was certainly not the oldest member of our class, I had more pertinent life experience than most of the CT's, and the training came relatively easy and natural for me. As a result, I was deemed at the end of the course to be one of five graduates with exceptional potential as a future case officer. Because a great deal of importance was placed on a CT's performance record at The Farm, this recognition was a nice pat-on-the-back to have in my record, especially during the competitive division and/or station assignment process.

During the latter stages of the CT Course, the various DO Division Chiefs and their staffs paid recruiting visits to The Farm to make their respective pitches to the class. Many of my classmates had not made any conscious decision in which part of the world they wanted to work, and they were, therefore, open to these recruiting presentations. My heart, however, was set from the very beginning on fighting our main Cold War enemy right on his doorstep. Obviously, my university education, work experience, and language abilities suggested that the SE Division would be my first choice, but it had to be a mutual decision; furthermore, SE Division had the reputation of accepting only the very best, so there was a great deal of competition for assignment to this elite group. Happily, the SE Division Chief and his staff agreed that I would be a good match for their team, and I was accepted. In addition, because of the very lengthy training and preparation process for assignment to any of the "internal" SE Stations, I was allowed to take my second interim assignment within SE Division in preparation for what I expected would be a posting to Moscow. Accordingly, at the completion of my CT course, circa June, 1981, I was assigned on my second interim to the USSR internal desk to begin that assignment preparation process.

I spent much of the next year assisting on the USSR desk and reading in on the operational activities of the Moscow station, but mostly I participated in additional training for the unique aspects of covert operations in a "hostile environment," such as Moscow. The term hostile environment meant that the threat of surveillance by the local counter-intelligence service was a constant reality; therefore, the aspiring internal station case office needed to get additional, more advanced, training in surveillance detection techniques, impersonal communications (indirect means of communicating with agents, rather than via personal meetings), technical communications, and so forth, than was offered at The Farm. The primary vehicle for obtaining this training was the SE Division Internal Operations (IO)

Course, which was an intensive, very challenging six-week course intended to give case officers being assigned to internal stations a realistic taste of operating under a constant threat of surveillance. It was also a final check-point to determine if a case officer should be allowed an assignment within the demanding hostile environment station where he/she could put someone's life at risk through the improper use of tradecraft; therefore, everyone took this training very seriously. In addition to the IO course, there was also extensive training in preparation for some of the unique technical operations that we had ongoing in the internal stations. Finally, although my Russian language skills were already fairly well-developed and because competence in Russian was crucial for effective operations in Moscow, I was also given the opportunity to take some brush-up Russian language classes during the course of this year of preparation.

As noted in a previous chapter, my cover job at the station in Moscow was to be a "clean slot," one that had not been occupied previously by a known CIA case officer; ████████████████████████████
██
██
██
██
██
██
██
██
██
██
████████████████. As a result, the SE Division worked covertly with the senior management ████████████████████████ to establish clean cover slots, ones not previously tainted by Agency officers, in an effort to deceive the KGB as to the case officer's affiliation; these positions were dubbed as "deep cover" slots, ████████████████
██
████████████████████████████████.

I was selected to occupy a clean cover position in the hope that I might receive less scrutiny from the KGB; ████████████████████

████████████████████████████████████

████████████████████████████████████

████████████████████████, the Agency investigated to see if a clean position might be established within the small ████ office in Moscow. Knowing also that the KGB kept track of all incoming ████████████ officers once their assignments were announced within the local community, usually several months in advance of their arrival, the Agency also arranged for me to assume a visible position at ████████████████ in Rosslyn, Virginia, prior to my relocation to Moscow. This assignment would offer additional evidence that I was a legitimate ██████ employee through telephone calls (always monitored) and unclassified cable traffic to and from ██████ Moscow. Thus, my final two months in Washington prior to my move to Moscow were largely spent at the ██████ office, where only one person, the ██████ Program Manager, was made aware of my true affiliation. In addition, on the Moscow ████████ side, only ████████████████████████████████

████████████████████████████████████

████████████████████████████; their ability to keep that fact secret was a crucial aspect in whatever success I might have in my real job. However, the most important factor determining success would be my ability to perform the role of Administrative Officer at the ██████ Moscow project so convincingly that the KGB would conclude it was my only *raison d'etre* for working in Moscow. Thus, with the adrenalin beginning to flow ever more rapidly, in early July of 1982, about 20 months after joining the CIA, my wife and I finally set out for Moscow to embark upon the challenge and adventure of a lifetime.

⚜ ⚜ ⚜

Moscow, July 1982 – June 1984

When we finally arrived in Moscow, our level of anticipation and excitement was incredibly high. There we were, in the bowels of the main enemy, with the opportunity to make tremendous contributions to the station's important mission. If we played our roles well and were able to persuade the KGB that we were just normal ███ ████████████ employees who did not pose an additional threat to the Soviet Union, we might very well be successful in the execution of our "part-time" responsibilities as members of the Moscow CIA station. The deep cover scenario, which was a relatively new approach to conducting successful operations in Moscow, had enjoyed some success already; however, everything would depend largely upon our acting ability, our absolute diligence, and our attention to detail in creating the impression to all, Americans and Soviets alike, that we were nothing more than regular ████████████████ folks.

Upon arrival, we were met at the airport by ███████████████ a colleague from the █████ office. We spent the vast majority of that first week going through normal new arrival check-in procedures, ████████████████████████, getting settled in our apartment, and becoming established at the ████ project office, ███████████ ██ ████████████. It was not until the end of that first week that I made contact with the station, using covert procedures that had been established prior to my arrival. During my initial meeting at the station into which I had been discreetly brought, I was welcomed and briefed on my activities for the next two to three months. In this regard, my assignment was to devote myself entirely during working hours to my cover job and accurately determine my surveillance status with the KGB, while getting out judiciously and attentively around the city during evening and weekend hours. This activity was a deliberate balancing act; it was crucial to learn how to get around the city, each time while employing enough of a planned route to be able to determine the presence, or lack, of KGB surveillance, while simultaneously not being out so often as to alert the KGB that we might be up to mischief. Accordingly, I would not be given any operational assignments until that point in time when we could determine that the KGB had come to the apparent conclusion that we were indeed not CIA officers with a hidden agenda.

The next two months or so were spent doing my cover job at ███████

which I performed with as much enthusiasm and dedication as I could muster, working at it 110% of my time. Like every department there, we had a large contingent of local employees, who were all either active members or "co-optees" of the KGB, and who were watching the American representatives closely. Because the Russian employees would be reporting daily on my activities, it was essential that they had no questions whatsoever about my purpose in being there. It would be their attestation to their KGB bosses that I was seemingly a hard-working member of the ████ staff that would enable me the opportunity to move more freely to do my real job when the time was deemed to be right.

As with all new arrivals, the KGB did mount surveillance on me several times during those first two months. Although all visible indications were that I was there solely to help ███████████ ███████, the only way for them to be certain was to take a look at what we were doing during non-office hours. As a result, we had a few week-long periods of constant KGB surveillance, in addition to other spot checks on a number of occasions; however, even though our SDR skills enabled us to ascertain whether we were being followed or not, we maintained our normal demeanor and did not alert the surveillance teams to the fact that we knew that they were following us.

Naturally, because the KGB also knew that the CIA does employ females as case officers, they were equally interested in what my wife was up to. However, we normally went out on our personal excursions together, and thus we kept it easy for them to keep track of her. Most spouses without children usually also looked for employment during their Moscow assignment; accordingly, very early in our tour, my wife got a job with the embassy General Services Office (GSO) as an assistant to the GSO Foreign Service Officer. Her desk was within the embassy complex, █████████████████████████████████ ██ ██ ██ ██ ██

██████████████████████████████████████

██████████████████████████████████████

██████████████████████████████████████

████████████.

Finally, towards late September, due to the ongoing, consistent lack of surveillance from the KGB, it had become apparent we had fallen off of their screen. As a result, I reported to the Station that we were generally surveillance-free, and, therefore, ready to become operational. The timing was good because there was a great deal of station business to be performed, and the other members of the station were largely getting full-time surveillance. Finally, it was time for me to begin executing the important mission for which the Agency, and we ourselves, had invested so much time, diligence, and resources; the window of opportunity was now open.

The period of October, 1982, through June, 1983, was an incredibly busy period for the station and for us. Because I was the only case officer who was enjoying the desired breaks from KGB surveillance, I was the action officer for handling almost all of the station-to-agent operations performed during that period. As concerns the passage of covert information in the other direction, from agent-to-station, there was an inherent risk in all such communications, such as the act of retrieving dead drops; the agent could have possibly been compromised thereby allowing the KGB to stake out the area of the dead drop to see who came to pick up the device. Because our ability to continue to maintain my cover depended on not placing me in a situation where my true identity could be blown, the other station officers were usually dispatched to make the more risky agent-to-station retrievals. However, whenever a station-to-agent dead drop needed to be placed in a predetermined spot according to the agent's communications plan, I was usually the one who would be tasked to emplace it.

As in all cases, my pre-operation briefing in the station, in advance of emplacing a dead drop and of marking the "have loaded" signal to alert the agent that a package was ready for his pick-up, was a clandestine operation in and of itself. During my discreet and always brief visits to the station, we reviewed the plans for the actual operation; I needed to commit the dead drop site to memory, as well as the have loaded signal site, and submit a suggested SDR plan for discussion in the station followed by approval from headquarters. Everything in conducting clandestine operations in a hostile environment such as Moscow was subjected to an incredible amount of pre-planning and scrutiny from Agency HQs prior to gaining approval to proceed. Once everything had received final approval, and the day of the operation had arrived, then there was the task to get the dead drop materials into my hands in a manner that would not seem unusual and possibly attract KGB attention.

Usually, on the afternoon preceding the planned evening activity, or on a Friday afternoon in preparation for a weekend operation, I was brought into the station for the final prep and the passage of the actual dead drop materials. Because the dead drop device itself (a concealment device, fake rock or otherwise, into which the clandestine materials would be placed) could compromise the agent's identity if it fell into the wrong hands, after leaving the station with the dead drop concealed in my briefcase or other suitable package, I needed to babysit the device closely until I could leave the office for home. I was never really comfortable having the operational materials in my office with Soviet staff coming in frequently, but that was one of the inherent risks we had to take in order to run such operations successfully.

As with the previously described agent meeting and Cable Tap cases, all operational outings largely required the same procedural process: (1) the conduct of a lengthy, logical SDR in order to determine the presence or absence of surveillance; (2) if free of surveillance, the parking of the car in a suitable spot; (3) getting away from the vehicle and discreetly changing appearance to look more local; (4) performing a secondary SDR while on foot or mass transit to the operational site; (5) emplacement of the dead drop in the designated site; (6) executing the have-loaded signal in the pre-designated spot for the agent to see; and (7) reversing the entire process to get back to the car, and then safely home, without alerting the KGB that we had been up to any mischief. Usually, these operations required about four or five hours, so our cover for action, such as an evening at dinner and theatre, movies, or whatever easily explainable activity we were attempting to convey, feasibly had to support the length of time we were out of sight.

We were so busy in the station at one point in May of 1983, with multiple operational requirements which needed to be handled, that I was once tasked to emplace two dead drops at two distant locations on the same evening outing. As far as we knew, this outing was unprecedented in the history of impersonal communications in a hostile environment; it also went against the prevailing security philosophy of successful clandestine operations, but we were under the gun, so the station and headquarters decided ultimately to proceed. It was about this time that I was going operational three to four times per month, and I was beginning to think that we were pushing our luck. Sooner or later, the KGB would certainly become curious as to why my wife and I were becoming more socially active and decide to take a closer look at us again. When I expressed my concerns the next time I was in the station, I inquired about the expected arrival of another case officer who was programmed to get another clean slot; I was informed then that this officer had failed a polygraph test, had revealed some serious security concerns in his personal activities, and had been fired from the Agency. The officer in question was Edward Lee Howard, who later volunteered extremely damaging information to the Soviets and compromised many of our Moscow assets.

Despite my concerns that we might be pushing our luck with repeated operational outings within a short time span, we mostly continued to remain surveillance free until the time in July when my wife and I departed Moscow for two weeks of R&R. We had successfully executed the Cable Tap operation in June, and I had met twice with our top agent during that first year. I had also gone out on two other anticipated meetings with the top agent that spring, only to get to the meeting site during the designated time window and find that he did not appear. These no-shows created quite an amount of concern at the station and in Langley, fearing that something may have happened to him; however, he later showed for another scheduled meeting, which allayed the concerns for the time being. In any event, when we departed Moscow for our R&R, we looked back with satisfaction at the job we had been able to perform. We had successfully maintained our cover for the first year and participated in over one-dozen covert operations; on the other hand, we were truly feeling the stress of repeatedly assuming the grave responsibility for those brave men's lives. So, needless to say, my wife and I were more than ready for a break.

After a trip home to meet with division management at HQs and to visit our families, we took a relaxing week's vacation in Ireland doing a drive-about B&B tour of the island. We then returned to Moscow in late July, ready to assume our dualistic roles. Upon arriving in Moscow, we discovered that, for some reason or another, the KGB had taken a renewed interest in us, and we endured a lengthy stretch of three to four weeks with almost constant surveillance. However, apparently having become persuaded that we did not constitute a threat, they left us free once again towards the end of the summer. Accordingly, we judged that we were again available to help the station with our operational requirements.

During that final year in Moscow, our successful operational outings were much fewer in number than the first year had witnessed. Although there were numerous stretches in which we were surveillance-free, the KGB decided that they would maintain a much closer watch on our activities during that second year. There were even several instances where we were forced to abort an operation due to the detection of surveillance during our pre-operational SDRs. Nevertheless, I was able to have one more meeting with our top agent in the fall of 1983 and to emplace several more dead drops during this second year at station.

One such operation in May of 1984 was particularly memorable. Because we had noticed that the KGB was generally leaving us surveillance-free on Sunday mornings, we planned one dead drop operation for such a day. Per usual, I smuggled the dead drop device out of the station on Friday afternoon, and then we babysat it in our apartment until it was time to go operational on Sunday morning. For this mission we took along our Golden Retriever, for the ostensible reason of a family outing in a park as our cover for action. As had recently been the case, our SDR proved to us that we were indeed surveillance-free that Sunday morning.

I had been driving throughout the SDR, as it was my primary responsibility to make the go or no-go decision; after making the final cover stop, however, we switched places and my wife took the wheel. Our route from that point took us through a heavily-wooded area where, at the pre-designated spot, my wife slowed down, and I jumped out of the car and tumbled into the woods, Indiana Jones style. As she drove from the area and proceeded to the large forest park where we would later rendezvous, I stayed concealed in the woods, monitoring the possibility of any undetected KGB vehicles that might have been following us at a discreet distance. After about 10 minutes, I decided that it was safe to proceed, so I made my way to the dead drop site, emplaced the dead drop, and placed the have-loaded signal at the distant site. I then made my way on foot to the park where my wife and dog were waiting for me. It was a huge forested area, but we had planned our rendezvous very well. I entered the forest via the back way (not from the road but from the rear of the forest park), and my wife and pooch were precisely where we had intended to meet. Being a typical Golden Retriever and certainly wondering why in the hell I had departed the car so unexpectedly, Christy was overjoyed to see me as I approached. After I assuaged her canine concerns, we packed up the picnic goodies my wife had brought, and made our way back to the car in the designated parking area for the forest reserve.

At the parking lot, we did notice that there was a surveillance team that had staked out our car, and we had company on our return route to the apartment. The possibility of this eventuality had been anticipated, but the mission had been executed in a pre-planned fashion, and the risk that the KGB might be able to backtrack what had transpired was deemed minimal. Although we were able to execute this operation successfully, from that point forward, the KGB surveillance teams were our constant companions, and my operational effectiveness came to an end. Nevertheless, we looked back upon the two-year assignment with a high level of personal and professional satisfaction. We had successfully operated under the noses of the all-powerful KGB and hit them where it hurt. As reward for a job well done, my division management had promised me the station of my choice, and I had requested a position in either ███████████████████ for our next assignment. There were unfortunately no available openings in ██████████, which was my preferred assignment, but █████ had an appropriate slot for an SE Division officer, so that was to become our next stop.

From the standpoint of professional accomplishment, the assignment to Moscow was to be the highlight of my Agency career. Mind you, I do not mean to suggest that it was the most enjoyable, but the tour certainly was the most professionally rewarding. All considered, it had been an incredibly stressful and anxiety-filled two years. Compared to future assignments, however, it was the Super Bowl of espionage, and, during those two years, our team managed to win the big game. Although my personal role was a major contributor to our team success, and I was given significant positive exposure and two awards by the Agency for my contribution, the dedicated and diligent efforts made by the station team to support my activities were gargantuan. They were the strategists, the coaching staff, and the offensive lineman clearing the way for me to be able to carry the ball on occasion, and the well-executed game plan worked well in the end. There were some scratches and bruises along the way, and I am sure that period of time is the point in life when my hair began to turn gray, but the opportunity to contribute to the nation in a major fashion made all the effort and stress worthwhile. Nevertheless, once we were finally out of Soviet air space on our departure flight home, my wife, who had been the consummate trooper throughout this two-year assignment, quietly turned to me and requested, "Let's please never do that again!" I chuckled and agreed.

Chapter 12

Espionage in Friendlier Venues

A City in Europe, October, 1984 – April, 1986

In preparation for my assignment to ████, we first went home for a few months; there was some cover position training at ████ ████████████, as well as a ████████ language brush-up course and a period to read-in on current cases. In mid-October, my wife, our trusty Golden Retriever and I packed up and flew to our new European home. Compared to the preparation which went into planning for a two-year tour in Moscow, planning for this trip to ████ was a piece of cake. This city was perhaps the farthest thing from a "hostile environment" we could imagine, and the living conditions were excellent. Other than the possibility of an occasional surly response from one or another city resident, there was nothing really negative to expect. From an operational environment, although this station was deemed to be an important one in our global intelligence efforts, the pace was much more relaxed. As a result, a person could expect to enjoy a well-balanced lifestyle in ████ if he or she chose to do so.

Inherently being a pretty gung-ho case officer and a romantic idealist to boot, plus having just left the high-tension, hostile environment of Moscow, the work in our new station required some real mind-set adjustment. The pace and modus operandi was simply different. Contrary to Moscow, in which the operational mission was to securely handle sensitive agents via mostly impersonal means, the primary mission in ████, like in all "external" stations, was recruiting and handling agents with direct or indirect access to information of interest to the U. S. Government. Agent acquisition (recruitment) was also the predominant factor in determining the overall effectiveness of a case officer in the non-hostile operating environment. The DO made allowances for SE Division officers who had worked in internal stations, where agent recruitment did not normally occur; however, once in a normal operational station, recruitment of key assets was the highest priority task for case officers as well as the key to promotion up through the ranks.

As an SE Division officer in ███████ station, I was assigned to the "hard targets" branch. Hard target was the term to describe ███████████ ████████████████████████████████████ countries to which direct access was limited, such as citizens of the USSR, the East European Bloc countries, China, North Korea, Cuba, and other nations, such as Iran or Cambodia, which were off limits to normal ███████████ interface. My primary mission in this station was to work to recruit hard target assets; however, if an American case officer attempted to proceed in this regard by directly developing the hard target, the chances for success were relatively slim. As a next best option, we attempted to identify and develop other people who had easier access to the hard target and to recruit them as "access agents" to the target of interest.

An effective access agent, who had direct contact with the hard target either through professional or personal means, could provide useful information that could contribute to recruitment efforts down the line. On occasion, an access agent might also provide intelligence of interest that he had elicited from the hard target. In general, every hard target nation had a large embassy located in ███████ with numerous employees. In addition, virtually every international Non-Governmental Organization (NGO) had an office there with many employees from hard target nations. NGOs were utilized by such nations as an additional vehicle through which to implant more of their own case officers, under NGO cover, as a means to beef up their intelligence operations in the host country.

Having just left the hostile environment of Moscow, in which the KGB had forced us to live and work in a fishbowl environment, I was eager to get to work against them and their Socialist comrades in a more USA-friendly location. I approached my assignment in this new station in a fanatical fashion and used every opportunity to come into contact with potential hard targets of interest in the diplomatic and NGO community. There were always diplomatic functions of one sort or another in ■■■■, as well as the Young Diplomats Club, which would have been more accurately dubbed the "Young Spies Club," where intelligence officers of every persuasion went to seek out potential targets in line with their own operational priorities. Naturally, I was not the only CIA officer who was in attendance at such functions, and all had the same basic desire, to recruit a hard target. As a result, case officer competition over a potential hard target was often akin to a young man trying to win the hand of the most beautiful female at the dance. As can be imagined, sometimes the approaches used to curry favor with the "new meat" in the room could become comical and a subject of some hilarity in the office the next day. In any event, it was all well intended and "for the cause."

In addition to trying to identify, develop, and recruit new agents, all incoming case officers had to assume management responsibilities for several ongoing agent cases, which were usually turned over to the new case officer from the previous one when he/she was about to depart the station. As did everyone else, I inherited a number of these agents, whom were turned over to me within the first few weeks after my arrival. Most of these cases were access agents who had been determined to have worthwhile accessibility to various hard targets within the local community. Within this stable of access agents, there were some who were quite useful and who provided worthwhile tidbits of information that would later prove to be of use in recruitment operations against a hard target. However, there were others who had been recruited on the premise of their ability to provide such useful information, but whom we later decided to let go from our stable of assets.

With the Moscow experience under my belt, where tradecraft was consistently practiced in a highly diligent manner, and where the case officer was always concerned about his surveillance status, I brought with me to my new station the same modus operandi for every agent meeting I had. The local operating environment was generally non-hostile, with little chance of an American case officer ever being the target of surveillance, and most of my station colleagues took a more relaxed approach to their SDR's prior to and following an agent meeting. I, on the other hand, continued to utilize Moscow Station tradecraft in the conduct of my operations. Following each agent meeting, case officers were required to write a meeting report that included not only the gist of the agent meeting, but also the security measures (SDR, etc.) used to and from the meeting, and my reports betrayed my use of extensive security measures. The other case officers in the Hard Targets branch liked to needle me about the extreme measures that I employed out of habit, but security for the welfare of the agent continued to be my utmost concern, and I tended to exceed the norm.

My new station city was also a popular transit point for many of our agents (hard target and otherwise) who were resident in other countries where internal agent meetings would entail a higher degree of risk. I was asked to meet with numerous of these during their transit visits to ██████, and/or other nearby European destinations, to debrief them, to report any suitable intelligence, and to manage the agent on behalf of his normal case officer. Because these agents tended to be assets of relative importance, I always looked forward to having the opportunity to play a role in these cases. These meetings provided a welcome source of adrenaline flow into what, otherwise, was a more mundane operating environment.

From the personal perspective, life in ██████ was highly-enjoyable. Both my wife and I appreciated the change of pace from Moscow, and we developed an active social life outside of my work requirements. Even our Golden Retriever enjoyed the new city. Our apartment was located very close to ██████████████████████████ ███████████████████████████. In the evenings, during our dog walks along the park-like streets in the area, like every Golden Retriever who ever walked the earth, Christy never knew a stranger and would by nature want to greet every person we saw on the evening promenade. This included the long files of prostitutes who lined up along one street every evening; Christy quickly became the hit of the local hooker population, and they would call her name and attracted her attention every time we walked by. I never took offense that they did not know me from Adam.

One more note about our trusty Golden Retriever. Our apartment was also quite close to ▮▮▮▮▮▮▮▮▮▮▮▮▮▮▮▮▮▮▮▮▮▮▮ the Soviet Embassy. On more than one occasion on the weekends, I walked the dog in the park close to the Soviet Embassy, in the hope that we would encounter potential targets of opportunity during our outings. On one such occasion, I heard a small group of people speaking Russian in the park not too far from their Embassy, so I took the leash off Christy and nudged her in their direction; as always, she ran immediately up to them and endeared herself instantaneously. I followed right along and caught up to her as the group was smothering her with affection; I began to speak with them in Russian, and, although they were initially quite receptive, as soon as they determined that I was American and thus a potential threat, they made a hasty retreat back to the embassy complex. Yes, even our loyal pooch was an operational asset in our attempts to execute our mission. Over the years, I actually employed her in numerous different scenarios. As long as there were new and different humans to meet, she never seemed to object.

Soon before our arrival in ▮▮▮▮▮▮, since we had been married eight years by this time, my wife and I decided that it was time to begin a family. However, after a lengthy period of unsuccessful attempts to do so and having come to the realization that "something ain't working," we subjected ourselves to the normal series of humiliating tests in an effort to identify the apparent problem. It turned out that my wife was diagnosed to have a severe case of endometriosis, and we were advised that our chances to conceive in normal fashion were highly doubtful. As a result, we began to look into the possibility of adoption. We had befriended a Counselor Officer at the Irish Embassy in the city, and, because I could prove to have Irish ancestry within three generations, we were qualified to apply to adopt an Irish child. So, just before Christmas of 1984, having decided that it was simply not our destiny to be parents to our own naturally-born children, we made our formal application to the Irish Adoption Board. As Fate would have it, however, during our Christmas vacation in Gstaad, Switzerland, the highly doubtful eventuality apparently took successful root, and our daughter, Kelly Lynn, was born that following September. Her birth just goes to prove that miracles do happen.

Despite that fact that we were generally happy in ████, especially with the birth of our daughter, I had begun to grow increasingly dissatisfied with my work environment. Life in this city, albeit very pleasant, had just become too docile to suit my romantic idealistic tendencies. Perhaps I was spoiled by the feeling of extraordinary accomplishment in Moscow, or possibly I had become addicted to the frequent adrenaline rushes from operating in that environment, but I started to believe that I was somehow wasting my life. I even thought very seriously about leaving the Agency and finding some other form of work to do. In any event, I discussed my feelings with my Branch Chief, a highly experienced and empathetic SE officer; we decided that I should convey my concerns to our Division Chief back at HQs, who was also a highly-empathetic gentleman and who cared deeply for his case officers. Soon thereafter, I was called back to Langley for meetings to discuss my future. Upon arrival there, I was informed that my former SE Division Chief had already investigated some other possible options for my consideration; one of these was to transfer to a city in Africa, where the Agency had decided to open up a new station. Upon hearing about this option, I thanked them for considering me for this interesting opportunity and told them that I would need to discuss it with my wife and think about it overnight, to which they agreed. Immediately after leaving the Chief's office, my first stop was in the CIA HQs library, where my immediate task was to try to ascertain exactly where in the hell this city in Africa was!

After discussing everything with my wife, we decided that this new adventure was too interesting to pass up. The idea of going to open up a new station where none had previously existed, located in a strategic region of Africa, captured my fancy entirely. This opportunity would offer me a completely blank canvas on which to paint my masterpiece, located in an area in which I was intellectually interested and which presented an incredible opportunity for new adventure. Obviously, my biggest asset in being able to take advantage of this opportunity was my always-amenable wife, whose sense of adventure was as finely-developed as mine; even the prospect of taking our newborn child to Africa did not deter either of us from the enthusiasm which this new opportunity engendered. The next morning, I officially accepted the new job and promptly returned to ▮▮▮▮ to finalize my obligations there. When we departed in April, 1986, to return to HQs to prepare for our assignment in Africa, we did so with some regret in leaving ▮▮▮▮▮, but with a tremendous anticipation of the adventure to come.

A City in Africa, June, 1986 – July, 1989

Whereas Moscow had been, and would continue to be, the professional highlight of my still-young CIA career, and our second tour was largely an enjoyable experience, this African post was to be our dream assignment. Never mind that this new station was in the country probably of least significant strategic importance to the U. S. Government on the face of the globe, to me it was the grandest assignment anyone could ever obtain. During the three years we were there, I often found myself recalling one of my favorite films, *The Man who would be King,* based on a Rudyard Kipling novel and starring Sean Connery and Michael Caine. Connery's character, Daniel Dravot, was also a romantic idealist who dreamed of ruling his own kingdom and was ultimately guilty of delusions of romantic grandeur. Although I do not believe that I ever became as delusional as Daniel Dravot, I confess that there were times in my new country when my romantic idealist mind-set did occasionally stretch to where I felt like I was governing my own remote African kingdom.

Between the time when we returned to WDC and the date of our departure for Africa, there was the usual assignment preparation in which to take part. My cover job was ▮▮▮▮▮▮▮▮▮▮▮▮▮▮▮ ▮▮▮▮▮▮▮▮▮▮▮▮▮▮ so I needed to take the ▮▮▮▮▮▮▮▮ ▮▮▮▮▮▮▮▮▮ officer course in order to learn the important procedures ▮▮▮▮▮▮▮▮▮▮▮▮▮▮▮▮▮▮▮▮▮▮ ▮▮▮▮▮▮▮▮▮▮▮▮▮▮▮▮▮▮▮▮▮▮▮▮▮

███████████████████████████████████████
███████████████████████████████████████. In my previous post, where my cover job was as an ███████████ officer, I had only minimal cover duties; however, as the ███████████ ███████████ officer, I had considerable and important cover duties in addition to my real job. Moreover, as a first-timer in running a station, I also had to take the Agency course in station management; the course included a great deal of training for administrative duties for which I had never previously been responsible as well as training to learn how to communicate securely between the station and HQs. Thankfully, I would have a highly-experienced Operations Support Assistant (OSA), who was primarily responsible for those day-to-day activities, but I needed to be sufficiently proficient in all such procedures in the event she was absent at any given point in time.

███████████████████████████████████████
███████████████████████████████████████
███████████████████████████████████████
███████████████████████████████████████
███████████████████████████████████████
███████████████████████████████████████
███████████████████████████████████████
███████████████████████████████████████
███████████████████████████████████████
███████████████████████████████████████
███████████████████████████████████████
███████████████████████████████████████
███████████████████████████████████████

███████. As a result, the CIA decided that it might be fruitful to establish a presence in this city, as an additional listening post for developments in this African region, as well as a potential hunting ground for hard target assets.

Despite the fact that ███████████ was of little strategic importance in the grand scheme of political priorities, the U. S. Government did have significant economic support programs in the country being managed by the Agency for International Development (AID) and the Peace Corps. In addition, there was a large international NGO population working on economic development and humanitarian programs.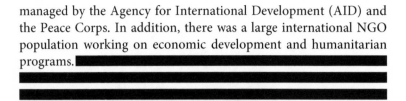

From the operational perspective, ███████ was certainly unique. As noted previously, I was the first case officer ever to have been assigned there; previously, intelligence operations in that country had been managed from distant ███████, but the country never had received much serious attention. In principle, the large hard target presence offered an excellent potential opportunity for new agent acquisitions; moreover, the small size of the diplomatic and NGO community provided easy and frequent access to potential targets of intelligence interest. However, greater access and a more visible hard target community is no guarantor of success. Otherwise, as concerns internal intelligence-gathering vis-à-vis the local political scene in ███████, and/or the situation in the region, in all honesty, there was as much useful information to be gathered in open discussions with local officials as there was to be derived from covert sources. Certainly, we had some covert sources of intelligence, which did on occasion provide intel that was not known from other sources, but I do not recall anything earthshaking having ever been produced by any of our station assets. At the time, we also enjoyed a close liaison relationship with the local intelligence service that, frankly, tended to share more useful information with us than we were able to obtain unilaterally.

Good liaison relationships with friendly host intelligence services can be an excellent source of information on topics of mutual interest, such as the hard target community, which was a common adversary for the local intelligence service and the USA. Naturally, they would officially draw the line on the sharing of any intelligence of a sensitive, internal political nature, but the hard targets were generally open game. Liaison relationships of this nature, especially in the third world, make a great deal of sense and can be mutually rewarding. For example, because I was basically a one-man operation, and there was only so much ground one man could cover, having the local service and their relatively large force working in partnership was a huge asset. Conversely, other than manpower, they traditionally did not have much equipment or high-tech resources at their disposal, and this was an area in which the Agency could assist in reciprocity for their operational assistance. In large part, this liaison relationship turned out to be a very satisfactory and productive one, which served the interests of both parties well.

Having had the experience of living in a fishbowl environment during our time in Moscow, and having resented it with all of my heart, I saw our nascent liaison relationship with the local intelligence service as a means through which I might be able to earn some payback. In essence, I wanted to bottle up the Soviets so completely within this environment that I would even know when someone in their Embassy passed gas. Although I will not comment on how effective we were in creating such an environment, let it suffice to say that I pursued this goal with single-minded fanaticism. I was working out of a motivation of pure revenge, of which I am not terribly proud, but, as most of us understand, both love and its opposite emotion can be highly-compelling and powerful motivators.

Because of my cover position ████████████████████████████
██

I had numerous instances where I would need to deal with the ██████
████████ Police Service that managed the ██████████████ border
station just a few miles west ██████████████████████████████████
██
██
██
██
██
██
██
██
██
██

[REDACTED] and where I would often need to meet with the commanding officer.

The officer in charge of the border station was a young Captain; he was a traditional Afrikaner, who initially came across as a tough guy and someone not generally happy with the U. S. Government stance on his country. As a result, although I was working hard to break the ice, our first meetings were not what I would describe as overly friendly, at least from his side. However, with time and persistence, I was finally able to convince him that, maybe, I wasn't such a bad guy after all, and we soon developed a fairly solid and friendly relationship. I honestly do not recall if I had ever mentioned the existence of this relationship to any of my Russian embassy contacts, or if they had simply assumed it, but the existence of this special relationship with the border post commander led to one very interesting development.

I recall being at home one Sunday evening in late October, 1987, when I received a call from a contact at the Soviet Embassy. Although we had grown rather friendly over the previous year, it was highly unusual for a Soviet diplomat to ever call an American [REDACTED] either at home or late in the evening. It was clear from the sound of his voice that something was amiss, for he seemed to be under some duress. He explained that he had something very important to discuss with me, which he did not want to address over the phone, and asked if it would be all right if he dropped by my house in a few minutes time. I told him that he was more than welcome to come right over and then hung up the phone, wondering what exactly he wanted to talk about. Was he coming over to "walk in" and volunteer his services in exchange for some gain? Although highly unlikely, was he possibly coming over to pitch me, to ask me to do the same thing? Was he in some sort of trouble that he needed to keep quiet from his embassy? All kinds of possibilities ran through my mind in the few minutes before he showed up at the house.

First, I made sure that my wife and daughter were exiled to the most distant room in the house, out of sight and earshot. Then, after his arrival, we convened to our living room with the beautiful cathedral ceiling and the floor to ceiling fireplace ablaze with a welcoming fire. After pouring drinks, we relaxed in front of the fire where, following the mandatory friendly chit-chat, I asked him what was on his mind. By this time, I had pretty much discarded the possibility that he was going to volunteer, ask to defect, or anything quite as exciting as that; furthermore, I had decided that there was no logical possibility that he was planning to pitch me. Nevertheless, something interesting was up, and I was certainly eager to find out what it was.

When he finally gave his answer, he explained that their Ambassador had apparently suffered a serious heart attack, and that he had come to request my assistance in this regard. As background, the medical services available in ███████ were not very well-developed, and the local hospital did not have a good reputation within the expatriate community. The Soviets did have a doctor in the city, who was serving with the local World Health Organization office, and he had been the first person they summoned when the Ambassador fell ill. Upon his examination, the Soviet doctor determined that the Ambassador required more state-of-the-art assistance than was available to him locally and he strongly suggested that the Ambassador be sent to nearby facilities in █████████████████████. However, because Soviet citizens were not allowed into that country in those days, what could they possibly do? Naturally, they decided to call the friendly CIA guy who lived on the hill; after all, he could do just about anything! In any event, I listened patiently to the dilemma in which my Soviet friends had found themselves and promised to see what I could do to help them out. His request wasn't exactly THE most interesting scenario that I had visualized, but it could prove to be highly useful in the long run.

After my Soviet contact departed, I immediately called the border post commander and asked him if he could meet with me as soon as possible at his office. I told him that it was an emergency, and he agreed to come right into the office to meet. About 30 minutes later, we were sitting in his office, and I explained the situation to him, that the Soviet Ambassador's life was in danger. After I was finished with my explanation, he continued to look at me, straight-faced and silent, as he obviously pondered how best to respond. Finally, he broke the silence and said, "Let's just let the bastard die!" Although I firmly believe that he was 100% serious, I treated his response as a joke, laughed a bit, and then said that, as attractive as the concept might be, we just couldn't do that; so, would he please see what he could do? He thought some more, finally said that he would need to check with his bosses and would get back to me in the morning. I thanked him, left the border office, returned home, and called my Soviet contact to tell him to standby.

Early the next morning, I heard from the Captain that he had received official permission to allow the Soviet Ambassador and one accompanying Soviet diplomat to drive through the border post and on to the hospital in ███████████████ for treatment. He further said that they could not drive themselves and that I would be required personally to drive the Soviets to ███████████████ and to deliver them into the hands of the responsible party on the other end. I wholeheartedly agreed and made arrangements to pick up the Ambassador and one embassy officer (my contact who had come over the previous evening) and drive them through the border post to the hospital. Accordingly, we left soon thereafter, and I was able to deliver them to the hospital before noon the same day.

Although this development did not turn out to be the intelligence breakthrough for which I had been hoping, it did make me into a bit of a hero in the local Soviet community. Naturally, they knew very well that I was still an official adversary and that they needed to conduct themselves cautiously with me, but they realized that I could be trusted as a human being. In the event that any one of them DID want to volunteer to help Uncle Sam, at least they knew whom to approach. Nevertheless, that info did not mean that they would henceforth open the doors of access wide for me; it just meant that they would show some signs of appreciation for what I had done to assist them in a time of crisis. After the Ambassador had been treated thoroughly in ███████████████, and allowed to return to ██████████, he did write me an official letter thanking me for my "friendly cooperation" in getting him to the hospital for treatment. The letter was more official than personal and less than glowing in its praise for my help, but I understood the game that we were playing; in the final analysis, he and his wife were genuinely appreciative.

In general, my work in my small African station in ███████ was very gratifying. I much preferred being a big fish in a small pond, rather than the other way around. Despite that fact that my station in ███████ was located in an area not considered a strategic powerhouse and that our intelligence reports were not on the top of the President's in-box the next morning, I received significant satisfaction from my time there. Life was comfortable, we developed a circle of good friends, and, although I worked very hard, the pace was not frenetic. Certainly nothing terribly earthshaking had come out of this station, but HQs seemed to be satisfied that I was doing a good job. I received due recognition as a highly effective case officer and station manager and was promoted soon thereafter.

In all, we spent over three years in this station; our tour of duty was originally planned for two years, but we had opted to extend for a third. As it turned out, my wife's initial problem with endometriosis had miraculously cleared itself up with the birth of Kelly, and our son, Brian, was born in November of 1987, seven months before we were due to depart post for an onward assignment. Although I had been selected to take over the top spot in our station in ███████ in 1989, we ultimately decided that we wanted to provide a more stable environment for the young kids by remaining in Africa for a third year. As a result, I declined the onward assignment. The new position would have required that we depart ███████ in the summer of 1988 to return home for a year of preparation, including a lengthy course in the ███████ language; in addition, because ███████ was still living under the grip of their communist government, and was still considered a hostile environment, we would have also needed to take the Internal Operations course once again. Furthermore, this move would have meant returning to a life of the stressful operational demands that we had experienced in Moscow, and my wife was not eager to do that, especially now that we had two small children. Ultimately, we made the decision to change plans and to stay in Africa.

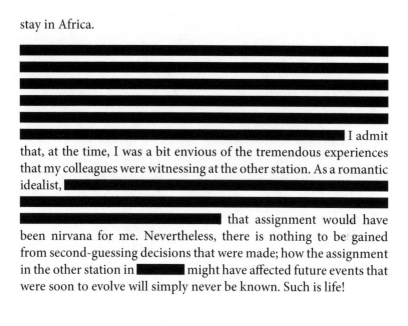 I admit
that, at the time, I was a bit envious of the tremendous experiences
that my colleagues were witnessing at the other station. As a romantic
idealist, ███
██
█████████████████████████████ that assignment would have
been nirvana for me. Nevertheless, there is nothing to be gained
from second-guessing decisions that were made; how the assignment
in the other station in ████████ might have affected future events that
were soon to evolve will simply never be known. Such is life!

⚜   ⚜   ⚜

The Farm, August, 1989 – September, 1990

Traditionally known as The Farm, the Agency had for years
conducted a great deal of their more important training at an off-site
facility that they owned and controlled. I had undergone my own
CT course there as well as some other covert training requirements.
Following our decision to extend in Africa for a third year, when the
time came to choose an onward assignment, we decided that it might
be an enjoyable change of pace to return home from overseas for a
tour as an instructor at The Farm. Frankly, even though it was highly
recommended for career case officers to return to Headquarters
at some point in order to better understand the inner workings
and politics of the organization, I just wasn't excited about that
prospect in 1989; thus, I applied for an instructor position. Because
I had a strong record from my overseas assignments, especially
the internal operations experience from Moscow, I was selected to

join the instructor staff, with the responsibility to train the current generation of CT's and to prepare them for their all-important overseas assignments.

The Career Trainee class at the CIA is reputed to accept only the best and the brightest of young Americans into its midst. CT's tend to graduate from excellent universities, and many have already attained a graduate degree by the time they enter the course. Most have studied extensively in foreign affairs or political science and may have at least one foreign language under their belt. Many have already lived abroad, so the prospect of working overseas is not an issue for them. Most also tend to have traditional American values, such as a love of country and a desire to serve something greater than themselves. As I was to discover, a large percentage of incoming CT's tend to come from families with strong religious backgrounds, even if they themselves may not be strong religious practitioners; I found that a significant segment of CT's come from either Catholic, Jewish, or Mormon families. Of greatest interest to me was the realization that they largely tend to be romantic idealists to one degree or another, and, as an instructor helping to train them for their future operational assignments, I was pleased to know that I was helping to prepare a class of kindred spirits for the challenges ahead.

As I had found during my time as a CT just nine years previously, the course which I joined in 1989 was a demanding experience, both for the students as well as the instructor staff. Each instructor had a full plate of formal tradecraft instruction that he/she would have to present, as well as the ongoing requirement to act as a role player in the constant situational exercises which the students would be tasked to execute. Perhaps the greatest responsibility was the need to mentor and advise our assigned CT's, usually one or two for each course, as they progressed through the training. The advisor tutored the CT on tradecraft disciplines that proved difficult, and was available for general advice as they began to plan their individual careers within the DO. Finally, each instructor played a key role in the need to provide opinions throughout the course on whether the individual CT's were demonstrating the skills and determination necessary to become a DO case officer; the attrition rate for those judged not to have what it took to become a successful case officer always tended to be significant. This latter job requirement was certainly the most emotionally trying, especially in the case of those CT's who were working exceptionally hard to qualify, but who simply didn't cut the mustard.

Despite the extremely demanding schedule, my work as an instructor at The Farm was enjoyable and gratifying. Although the job required that we instruct the CT's in all of the tradecraft disciplines, predominantly during the role play exercises, each of the instructors was also given platform time during which we made specific presentations to the class on one discipline or another. Because of my comparatively unique experience in internal operations, I contributed primarily to the formal lessons on surveillance detection and impersonal communications techniques; this task also included briefing the instructor staff, particularly those who had not served internal tours, to ensure that they were up to speed on current internal operations techniques. I took a great deal of pride in passing on the knowledge I had acquired in these important disciplines and found that I enjoyed tremendously the role of teacher to these eager and talented young students. However, although it certainly served the students well, the exuberance and zeal with which I approached these responsibilities tended to exceed my normal workaholic mind-set, and this tendency began to cause some serious problems in my personal life.

Although I will address this topic in greater depth in a later chapter, for the sake of chronological continuity, I should point out that some serious marital issues rose to the surface during this period of time at The Farm. It is my belief that the issues had been festering just under the surface for quite awhile and that they were largely subjugated during the previous seven years of living and working overseas. In any event, suffice it to say at this time that my wife and I came to the realization that life together was not going as desired; we went through marital counseling and tried to find greater understanding and the means through which to make the relationship work more successfully, but it did not seem to help. Towards the end of the first year at The Farm, the situation had become sufficiently unraveled to the point where we decided to live separately for a time. As Fate would have it, the Agency had a sudden operational requirement that they thought that I could fill, so the timing of the professional need and our personal dilemma tended to coincide well.

It was August of 1990. The Soviets had withdrawn from Afghanistan, and the country was on the verge of civil war; as a result, the CIA was keeping a very close watch on developments there and had formed an Afghan Task Force as the primary vehicle through which to keep tabs on Afghanistan. The Deputy Chief of Station (DCOS) at the time in ████████████████ was a highly respected Middle East veteran case officer, who was transferred back to Washington to assume command of this task force. To fill his spot as the DCOS, the External Operations Branch Chief in the station was promoted to DCOS, thereby creating a vacancy as branch chief. My former SE Division Chief at HQs was aware of my personal situation and believed that this job might be good for my career growth as well as a temporary solution to some of the personal issues I was facing. As a result, I was asked to assume the role of the external branch chief in ████████ station, initially on temporary (TDY) assignment for three or four months, to be followed by a three year permanent change of station assignment there the following year.

A City in Europe, September 1990 – December, 1990

The temporary assignment to ████████ seemed like a good idea at the time. First of all, the timing seemed to be a positive turn of events; our domestic life was in a bit of an uproar, personal feelings were badly bruised, and a short separation from the turmoil might provide a good cooling off period. Secondly, the position in ████████ sounded challenging, working as the branch chief for about a dozen case officers and support staff. In addition, I knew the Chief of the Station from an interim assignment at HQs and liked him, and I had a few good friends who were also working in the large station. Finally,

I had been personally chosen by the Europe Division Chief, who had formerly been my SE Division Chief and who had always been very supportive of my career in the organization; hence, I wanted to respond positively to his vote of confidence. What I had underestimated, however, was the tremendous impact that the separation from the family, especially the two children (Kelly was 5 at the time, and Brian would soon be 3), would have on my sense of well-being.

As with all arrivals at a new destination, there was a certain amount of excitement tied into my assignment to ▮▮▮▮▮. The station was large and active, and, therefore, I could expect a busy and challenging workload. In addition, the city could offer a world of interesting diversions. The station had two branches, one involved with internal operations ▮▮▮▮▮▮▮▮▮▮▮▮▮▮▮▮▮▮▮▮▮▮▮▮▮▮▮▮▮▮▮▮▮
▮▮▮▮▮▮▮▮▮▮▮▮▮▮▮▮▮▮▮▮▮▮▮▮▮▮▮▮▮▮▮▮▮
▮▮▮▮▮▮▮▮ and the external operations branch, to which I had been assigned. This year being 1990, the whole concept of external operations had changed since the height of the Cold War; with the dissolution of the Soviet Bloc and the impending break-up of the USSR, the traditional hard targets were no longer the primary focus of the Agency's operations. The major focus for the organization had shifted to counter-terrorism operations, and this European city, being a transit point for many of the world's terrorist organizations, was a suitable center for counter-terrorist activities. For me, having envisioned myself as a Cold Warrior on a personal quest to rid the earth of the Evil Empire, this evolution of the Agency's mission was a bit disconcerting. Although I certainly appreciated the importance of combating terrorism, I really never had much interest in the Middle East, its culture, or its politics. So, this assignment would require an entirely different mind-set from the one to which I had become accustomed.

The job of branch chief would be much different from an operational perspective as well. Previously, I had been either a case officer with a number of assigned cases, as in both Moscow and the other European city, and largely a one-man show in the African station; now I was responsible for the operational activities of a dozen energetic and industrious case officers, a job that emphasized effective management with a minimum of opportunities to get out on the street myself. Fortunately, I had inherited an excellent group of officers in the branch, and I did derive quite a bit of satisfaction from managing and supporting their operational efforts; however, I very soon came to realize that my heart was not as deeply intertwined in this enterprise as it had been in the past. Although I would get together with my old friends outside of work on occasion, and I made several new friends while I was there, I felt terribly alone and out-of-place without my family. Personally, I was miserable.

Having grown-up in a family in which my parents separated and divorced when I was at a young age, I had made the personal promise to myself that I was never going to be divorced nor to be the cause of the painful separation which divorce presents for young children. Despite the knowledge that life does not always concur with even the best of intentions, I felt a tremendous amount of guilt that I had not lived up to my own pledge, and this fact played on my emotions constantly. I was largely able to bury myself in the responsibilities of my work, and I worked long and hard in trying to accomplish my tasks, but my free hours were dominated by the underlying guilt and unhappiness I felt in my personal situation. Therefore, as I prepared to return home at the conclusion of the three-month TDY, I grappled with the difficult decision that I knew was forthcoming: either to return to ▮▮▮▮▮▮▮ after the holidays (most probably, without family) or to decline the permanent assignment.

Christmas, 1990

Having returned from overseas and after confronting a still-difficult situation at home, I came to the realization over the course of the Christmas holidays that reconciliation with my wife was not going to happen; thus, I had a major decision to make. As far as the Agency was concerned, I was programmed to return to ▮▮▮▮▮▮▮ to commence a formal three-year tour, and I was expected to return there soon after the New Year. However, I knew well enough by this time that a three-year tour overseas on separate status was not something with which I wanted to deal. Knowing also that declining an assignment under these conditions is not a "career-enhancing" move, I also felt that I needed some time to ponder life's direction for the future. The Agency had a program that allowed its officers to request an unpaid Leave of Absence to deal with personal or other considerations, so, after much introspection, I opted to request this allowance to see if I could work out the mid-life crisis in which I now seemed to be immersed. At this point in my history, I honestly did not know what to expect on the road ahead; I just knew that I needed some time to work things out.

Chapter 13

Bringing 'American Culture' to Poland

Madrid, Spain, Early February, 1991

After a period of introspective decision-making over the Christmas holidays, I did opt to take a one-year leave of absence from the Agency rather than return to ██████ for a three year tour. What may be illogical, however, is why I found myself flying into Madrid, Spain, in early February of 1991, preparing for a one-year stay. My decision may not make a great deal of sense on the surface, but I will try to put everything into proper perspective below. As for the title of this chapter, it too will make more sense towards the end, so I will need to beg the patience of the reader.

After returning from overseas for Christmas and with big decisions to make about the future, I was on an emotional roller-coaster going at a pretty high speed. It was very evident by this time that the marriage was over, so that valley had already been crossed. If, as I was leaning towards, I was to decline the three-year assignment to ██████, I felt that I really should go ahead and take the leave of absence to give myself time to sort out properly the issues in my life. However, if I were to take an unpaid leave of absence from the Agency and had to establish separate housing for my wife and kids, clearly I would need a solid income while I was trying to resolve the future.

As in all times of personal turmoil, having trusted friends with whom to discuss a situation can be a godsend. My roommate at Suffield Academy and close friend, Eduardo Fernandez, had packed up his family a few years earlier and moved to Madrid to build an entrepreneurial enterprise with his brother based on the successful fast food industry they had known growing up in the USA. They had loosely patterned their business, which they named "TelePizza", after pizza delivery companies in the States. In a nutshell, when they opened their new business in Spain in the mid-late 1980's, they had chosen wisely. The Spanish market was largely devoid of similar businesses, the Spanish economy was booming, and they had done their homework and business development plan very well; as a result, by February of 1991, TelePizza was prospering and building steadily.

During our conversations, Eduardo had mentioned that they were looking to develop their business outside of Spain by offering international franchises and asked me if I would be interested in going to Spain to assist them with this endeavor. The downside from the personal perspective was that it would mean going overseas again, and therefore being distant from the kids; however, I would have more flexibility in my travel than if I were to be in ▮▮▮▮▮▮ with the station, plus we were discussing a one-year proposition as opposed to three. Also, the compensation which Eduardo was able to offer would allow me to meet all of my increasing financial obligations while I tried to sort out my personal affairs. In the final analysis, we struck a deal, and I was soon off to Madrid to begin my next adventure.

Although I had traveled to Spain during my summer trek in 1975 and had not been terribly impressed with it, Madrid was a different kettle of fish. The city was beautiful, with historical and architectural wonders to explore, as well as a lively and enjoyable environment in which to re-engage life as a single man. In addition, although my budget was necessarily tight, I was not counting my pennies as I was forced to do in 1975, so I had enough to enjoy life while still meeting my significant financial obligations back at home.

The first two months in Madrid were largely spent learning the ins and outs of the TelePizza business, so that I could competently sell international franchises outside of Spain. TelePizza had instituted a very effective training program for potential Spanish store managers, so I was enrolled into the same program, actually donning jeans and my TelePizza polo shirt to learn the business from the bottom. This training included everything necessary to manage a store from making dough, spreading the dough (flipping the pie if one really became accomplished), building the pizza, cooking it in the assembly line pizza oven, preparing it for delivery, ringing up the sales, and cleaning the store, toilets, and anything else that needed care. The only task which I did not do was to deliver the pizzas around Madrid; my Spanish was not sufficiently fluent, my knowledge of the city not well-developed, and (the more important fact) I did not know how to drive the delivery scooters, so I was spared the need to participate in this aspect of the business. Otherwise, the training was 100% comprehensive and effective; my Spanish also improved significantly during this time period, especially my vocabulary that had anything to do with pizza!

After learning the pizza business from the ground up and becoming conversant in the commercial side as well, Eduardo and I began looking for target markets in which to spread the TelePizza gospel internationally. We looked at numerous potentially-interesting countries where we believed the market would be ripe for the pizza delivery business and started to advertise our international franchise opportunity in earnest. The franchise business start-up would necessitate a significant amount of capital investment. In the beginning stages, the investment would be limited to opening a store or two, while the materials and ingredients would be produced and supplied from TelePizza Spain's commissary to the new market. Because TelePizza had already proved itself to be incredibly successful and prosperous, there was a large level of business interest throughout the European markets where we advertised and visited.

At that time, I also had a good friend from Pullman days who was living in Warsaw, Poland. He had taken a position as Director of a western bank that had recently opened a branch in Warsaw. Being early 1991, Poland had already broken the grip of the USSR, and the country was in the early stages of the transition from a socialist, government-run economy to a free market model. When my friend heard about the new venture in which I had become involved, he believed that we should certainly take a look at Poland as a viable market for the business. Accordingly, he invited me to come to visit him in the "New Poland" and to take a long look for myself. Thus, in the spring of 1991, I flew to Warsaw to determine if the evolving

Polish free market might be a feasible one for TelePizza to consider.

As my friend had suggested, Warsaw was a city in motion, in transition from the shackles of economic oppression into a new and exciting "wild west" business environment. Everything was in the midst of monumental change, and entrepreneurs from all over the world flocked there to get in on the ground floor of the new economic development. My first week was primarily an information-gathering mission intended to determine the feasibility of starting a TelePizza franchising effort there. We also needed to investigate the legal and property-acquisition process to see if there were any insurmountable obstacles to getting such a business legalized and operational. My friend helped me in this effort by brokering introductions to legal and banking contacts with whom he was familiar. The rest of my time was devoted to initial market research, and, by the end of this first week, all preliminary indications were positive, so it was looking like my friend's suggestion to come to Poland was well-founded.

Also during that first week in Warsaw, I met a number of people who would later become instrumental in helping to get TelePizza Poland operational. On a visit to a Polish Bank to investigate opening up a foreign account, I met an impressive bilingual receptionist, who would later become my "right-hand-man" in establishing the business in Poland. We had discussed the business in some depth during our first meeting, and, because she was a full-time business student and just working part-time at the bank, she expressed an interest in working for the company herself. She also provided excellent advice on how to identify and recruit other solid employees in Warsaw, so our meeting was certainly fortuitous. Because I was scheduled to leave Warsaw the following afternoon, we agreed that we would continue our discussions by phone, and that I would plan a follow-on visit to Warsaw as soon as it was feasible.

Upon returning to Madrid and debriefing the TelePizza management team on what I had found in Warsaw, we all concurred that it sounded like a good potential market for a franchise and that the project deserved further investigation. Within a few weeks time, I was headed back to Warsaw to continue my market research, due diligence, and business development efforts.

The next visit to Warsaw was a bit longer and far more useful in many respects. One of the first destinations for me was the US Embassy Commercial Service (USCS) office, whose primary purpose was to assist American businesses to get established in the local country and to identify potential business partners. In retrospect, this visit was incredibly fortuitous for several key reasons: (1) the USCS local official with whom I met, a recent graduate from the University who spoke English perfectly, was incredibly interested in the concept; (2) this young man ended up being so consumed with the business concept that he eventually came to work for TelePizza himself (more on this later); and (3) he had recently been contacted by a Polish Company from Gdansk that had capital to invest and might be interested in looking at this franchise opportunity. This meeting alone, therefore, turned out to be a major turning point for the development of the business in Poland. Once the requirements for this trip were completed, I returned to Madrid and made my normal debriefing of the situation; in essence, I had become convinced that Poland was an exceptional opportunity for TelePizza. Moreover, I suggested that I should relocate to Warsaw myself to oversee the establishment of TelePizza Poland. Because we were making good progress and the project was moving forward positively, management agreed to my suggestion.

Our key to getting the business moving in Poland was the identification of a local partner / investor, and the solid lead we had obtained from USCS turned out to have excellent promise. Like many budding entrepreneurs in those days of economic transition, our potential Polish partners had carved out a niche in the market, theirs being the oil and gas business. They primarily imported these natural resources from Russia and distributed them within Poland. Their undertaking not only filled a drastic demand within Poland, but it also provided liquid capital, and lots of it, quickly. Our first meetings with the potential partner went very well, and we developed common ground quickly. The proposed plan was to open our initial stores in the northern seacoast region of Poland because this location was the center of their business activity and then to expand to the other major cities, such as Warsaw, Krakow, Poznan, and so forth. Once we had established our basic business plan with our prospective partner, we arranged for some of their key designated employees to go to Madrid for TelePizza's training program, while the rest of us remained in Poland working to get the business established and rolling forward.

Although the initial stages of our partnership went well, after about two months, we began to encounter differences in our operating philosophies that turned out to be irreconcilable. As a result, the partnership was dissolved. Nevertheless, we had already moved the business model significantly forward and continued to believe that the market indeed held the potential we envisioned, so TelePizza management decided to proceed ahead unilaterally. We endeavored to get the first stores opened as quickly as possible under company ownership and simultaneously continue the search for franchisees in the country.

The search for store locations was the most intensive part of the program. With the departure of the prospective partner, we now concentrated the store search primarily in Warsaw, but Krakow was an equally attractive option. Although the transition from government to private ownership of commercial properties was in process, and there were numerous excellent locations which were available, we had to apply for each property through a central Warsaw government office, where we soon discovered that cronyism and corruption were rife. We invested a significant amount of time and effort to qualify for numerous properties of interest that would have met our requirements quite well, but each time we were advised that someone else had won the rights to the property. There were no published bid results and never any explanations as to why our application had been declined, therefore, we eventually realized that we were not gaining any ground via this process. Finally, we were able to identify an excellent property in Warsaw, which was owned by an apartment cooperative outside of the normal city government process, and we were finally able to conclude a lease agreement for the property. By this time, it was early fall of 1991, and we had been looking for a suitable store location for months, but, as they say, better late than never.

Simultaneous to looking for store locations, we also invested a significant amount of time and effort trying to identify local sources for the raw materials we would need to support store operations. In Spain, TelePizza had their large and sophisticated commissary operation, which supplied all of the foodstuffs (dough, tomato sauce, cheese, meats and vegetables, etc.) as well as the paper and box materials for their Spanish stores. The international franchises, including Poland, could still import many of the canned and paper goods from Spain, but it was much more prudent to secure local sources where possible. We had identified an adequate cheese factory not far from Warsaw that had the capability to produce a good mozzarella cheese, and other local sources for suitable flour, and the meats and vegetables were eventually identified as well. As a result, the only product that initially needed to be imported from Spain was the proprietary tomato sauce. Otherwise, we were finally getting close to bringing the Poland operation to fruition.

While all of the logistical and store preparation issues were moving forward, we also sent our first team of prospective Polish store managers, including the former USCS officer, to Spain for training in how to operate a TelePizza store. All the while, our small team in Poland continued to develop the infrastructure we would need to move the project forward. However, by this point in late 1991, my official leave of absence was quickly approaching the end of the one year period, and, thus, decision time vis-à-vis the future was again at hand. I had various options to consider. I had been offered an equity stake in TelePizza Poland if I wished to stay on and manage the operation there, which certainly had some distinct financial advantages; on the other hand, although I had enjoyed my experience in Poland, I found that I missed my kids terribly. I also had the open option to return to work for the Agency, but I needed to let them know what my decision was going to be well in advance of the end of the one year leave of absence. Thus, some significant soul-searching needed to take place.

Ultimately, after serious consideration, I decided that I would return to the States to continue my work for the Agency. I made a quick trip home over the Christmas holidays, during which time I met with various Agency managers to discuss my options there, and we decided that I could return to be an instructor at The Farm. Because my kids were living nearby with their mother, this solution seemed to be the best of all available options, at least from my perspective. Accordingly, we decided that I would return to work with the Agency after I finished up in Poland and returned to the States. Although my friends at TelePizza were not overjoyed by my decision, they did understand my situation. In the final analysis, we had brought the Poland operation along positively, and I was leaving a strong local management team in place behind me. Thus, I departed Poland and resumed my work at The Farm in early February, 1992.

I would like to make one final footnote about my TelePizza Poland adventure. Returning to Warsaw in 2007, I noticed that there were numerous TelePizza stores in Warsaw, as well as in other Polish cities that I visited on that trip. Obviously, the faith we had shown in Poland as a venue for TelePizza had proven to be right on the mark. I even visited that first store that we had established 15 years previously and sampled the pizza, which was superb; the store was busy and obviously doing good business. As I was waiting for my pizza, I mentioned to the young manager that I had been the one who first introduced TelePizza to Poland 15 years earlier, but, frankly, he did not seem overly impressed. Nevertheless, as I enjoyed my pizza dinner in the store that evening, I chuckled to myself about the incredibly valuable "cultural contribution" that I had made to the nation during those transitional times in 1991 by bringing American style fast-food delivery pizza to post-Communist Poland. Humorous as the thought seemed, perhaps it was a fitting tribute for a man whose legacy was one of quixotic romantic idealistic pursuits.

Back down on The Farm, February, 1992, - July, 1993

Having resumed my instructor duties at The Farm, I was given a position working with the military training department, which had a similar course to that given to the Agency's CT's. For the most part, these students were active duty military intelligence case officers from all of the armed services, getting ready to be deployed to military intelligence units around the globe. The military training department also provided short courses in such disciplines as surveillance detection to outgoing ███████████████ who were being assigned to various sites abroad. The military students were generally older than the CT's and were usually in the middle of their military careers; they were always an enthusiastic bunch of students, with whom it was enjoyable to work. The training was also a less-pressure-filled exercise for them because they were not subject to being tossed out of the course if their performance was not up to par; they were simply there to learn to do their job to the best of their ability, and I appreciated their dedication.

After serving with the military instructor staff for the spring and early summer of 1992, I was transferred back to the Agency side of the house for the next CT class. Once again, I assumed my duties as the lead instructor for surveillance detection and impersonal communications, and we worked hard to properly prepare this next generation of Agency case officers. About that time, we were also entering the selection process for ongoing assignments, so, once again, I was thrust into the decision-making mode. For the same reasons which had influenced my thinking during my previous station assignment, I was honestly not sure whether or not I wanted to continue in this career path. My kids were living nearby, and I had been able to spend significant time with them since I had returned to The Farm. Although the job of case officer is most interesting when living and working overseas, I did not wish to go abroad on single status for a two to three year tour, during which, like the previous scenario, I would see the kids infrequently.

I did test the waters to see what overseas opportunities might be available, and there was one appropriate position opening in

██████████ that might have been very interesting under normal circumstances, but not with my prevailing family situation. Because I had been at The Farm for the maximum three years by that time, the only other stateside option would be to take an assignment at Headquarters, which did not excite me very much either.

Just about the same time, with Bill Clinton in the White House, there was an effort to reverse the growth that the Agency had enjoyed under President Reagan; therefore, case officers with sufficient service time were given the opportunity to take advantage of an early retirement program. A small cash incentive was offered as a means to make the decision more attractive to a larger number of officers, and I gave this option some serious consideration. Simultaneously, an old friend and colleague from my earlier days at Pullman had been asking me to come to work for him. He had a US-based company doing significant business in Russia, with a large operation in Moscow. After considering all of my choices, this option was beginning to sound a great deal more attractive. From the perspective of a romantic idealist, an opportunity to contribute to the transition of Russia from a Communist society and socialist economy to a free market democracy was alluring, thereby making the option all the more appealing.

As the summer of 1993 approached, it was time to fish or cut bait. I had enjoyed my time in the CIA (over 13 years by this time) and had certainly experienced some unique adventures, but it seemed to me that it was time to move on to other endeavors. I ultimately decided to take advantage of the early retirement option and to accept the US-Russia business position that was being offered by my friend. Following my out-processing from the Agency in early July, 1993, I prepared to make my permanent return to private industry, which will be detailed in the next chapter.

Upon parting from my career in the Agency, I looked back upon it with pride in my accomplishments and with gratitude for having been given the opportunity to serve the nation in this regard. Working in the CIA was a lofty privilege offered to very few, and the opportunity to participate in the highest echelon of national intelligence was indeed an honor. During my 13 years, I had worked with some of the finest people I would ever have the privilege to know, and, most of all, I would miss the camaraderie that I had enjoyed within this prestigious organization. To be sure, like all large government institutions, the CIA does have its inherent shortcomings; however, its ability to attract the best and the brightest, men and women whose most compelling motivation is to serve the nation to the fullest, is a tribute to the organization about which every American can be proud.

Chapter 14

Rebuilding from the Rubble

Early July, 1993

As any died-in-the-wool romantic idealist, having played a small role in bringing down the Iron Curtain, it was only fitting that I would want to help to rebuild that which we had tried so diligently to destroy. After all, such a mission would be the noble and humanitarian thing to do, right?

This was my mind-set when I accepted the offer from my old friend from Pullman days to join his company, Scott European Corporation. His business supplied products and services in the medical industry, the construction industry, and the oil and gas industries to the evolving Russian economy. I was offered the position of Vice President for Business Development, and my assignment was to help identify suitable development projects within the changing business environment in Russia. After a project was identified, I would then endeavor to find the financing and US-sourced equipment and technology necessary to bring the selected project to fruition. We decided that my most advantageous location would be in the Washington, DC, area where most of the potential sources of financing and US-Russia trade advocacy organizations were located. As a result, I settled in Reston, Virginia, a location that allowed ready access to downtown WDC, as well as to Dulles International Airport, from where direct flights to Moscow were available numerous times per week. It also kept me in easy driving distance to visit with my kids on weekends, which was very important to me.

Mid-1993 was not only a period of transition in Russia, but also one of serious opposition to the economic and political reforms that President Boris Yeltsin was attempting to implement. This was a time when managed chaos and power grabs were the norm, and the business environment seemed akin to that of the American Wild West. Corruption and strong-arm tactics were rampant as newly-emergent entrepreneurs competed to acquire assets previously belonging to the Russian Government and which were now being released to private ownership. In sum, this was an exciting time to work in this unpredictable environment, and I was looking forward to the adventure.

After joining Scott-European, which then had its main office in Montpelier, Vermont, I spent most of the first two months becoming acclimated to the company and the equipment manufacturers which the company represented in the Russian market. I also used this time to establish connections with the US-Russia Business Council (USRBC), the major player in promoting large scale trade with the emerging Russian market, and with other US-Russia trade advocacy organizations. In addition, I began to establish contacts within sources of potential financing and project support (OPIC, Export Import Bank, World Bank, US Department of Commerce, and others) located in the nation's capital. Because I had been largely absent from direct participation in the US-Russia business scene since the mid-1970's, my learning curve would be steep, but I approached the challenge with vigor and excitement.

My first trip to visit our Moscow office was scheduled for early-September, 1993. Because I had not been back to the USSR / Russia since I left my government assignment in June of 1984, I really had no idea of what kind of reception I might receive. Although the official dissolution of the USSR had taken place in late 1991, and Russia was now on the path to democracy and a free market economy, I knew that many of my former KGB adversaries were probably still in positions of responsibility. From my quixotic perspective, either I would be hailed as a hero upon my return by those who had sought liberation from the shackles of Communism or still be regarded as an enemy by those who may have lost their privileged positions in the recent current of events. Perhaps the country would be in such a chaotic state because of all of the massive and abrupt changes that no one would really notice my arrival, or, if they did, not really give a damn. Naturally, I was hoping the last possibility would be the case, but the level of anticipation of what to expect on my trip was high.

When I finally arrived in Moscow, everything went very well. There was no evidence that I was under any close scrutiny whatsoever, and I found myself absorbed in the excitement of seeing firsthand how Russia had changed and of witnessing this process of monumental transition. In all honesty, by this time, just one and a half years following the dissolution of the Soviet Union, there was not too much in terms of physical change to be noticed; however, the absolute changes in the manner in which Russian citizens dealt with me was earthshaking. Naturally, I was no longer ████████ representative of the US ████████ with whom any non-sanctioned contact was forbidden; that was my reality the last time I had been in Moscow. This time, the inherent distrust and hesitancy to engage in a normal conversation was completely absent, and I found this new situation to be the most significant, positive change in the years since I had last visited. Included in this new reality was the fact that I was no longer considered the "main enemy." Furthermore, I was now single and had no official sanctions imposed upon me against "fraternizing with the enemy." This new circumstance would soon introduce some real changes into my life.

In the interest of full disclosure, prior to my trip to Moscow, I had a premonition that I would meet a female of interest during this visit; in fact, I had even discussed this possibility with one of my Scott-European colleagues, so I may have unwittingly invited the Universe to provide the introduction based on my own predictions. In the end, Fate made it very easy for me to make my prediction come true, in that I had to look no further than the Moscow office to be hit by the "thunderbolt," just as it happened to Michael Corleone during his exile in Sicily in the movie *The Godfather*.

In fact, she was the second person whom I met upon entrance into our Moscow office. She worked as a receptionist, along with another engaging young lady, who was the first person I had met just seconds earlier. I have come to believe that this thunderbolt phenomenon tends to happen more to romantic idealists, such as myself, than to other, more normal people. It is always the way that love has happened to me, so at least part of my theory holds water. In this particular case, I was immediately struck not only by her physical beauty, but also her apparent *joie de vivre*, her engaging smile and distinctive, happy laugh, all of which captivated me from moment one. No doubt, I stared and smiled at her a bit more than polite interaction would warrant, but I do not believe that anyone took particular notice. Because I was in the company of my boss when the introduction took place, and I had been forewarned by him in no uncertain terms that romantic involvements within the office were not tolerated, I tried my best to be discreet. In fact, my previous training in covert operations later served me well in my ability to keep this relationship hidden.

This first trip was just one week in duration and largely intended as a familiarization visit to the Scott-European Moscow office to learn their operations (the company had several operating divisions, including an equipment distributorship selling Bobcat model skid-steer loaders) and to meet the key players and staff. It was a very busy week that kept me occupied throughout the day and evenings, but I also found a few sporadic opportunities to expand, discreetly of course, upon my acquaintanceship with the aforementioned receptionist who had so seriously caught my interest. Using all of my Agency-acquired and inherent relationship-building skills, I interacted with her according to a well-conceived strategic plan designed to offer plausible opportunities for increased personal interaction while simultaneously not revealing the fact that she had piqued my interest.

By the conclusion of the week in Moscow, I had developed a much better understanding of both the who-was-who of the Russia operation and the modus operandi of the company. I was also satisfied that I had not stirred up any political issues by virtue of my previous CIA employment. Finally, I felt that I had played my cards properly on the romantic front, so all was good as I returned home to the States.

The next few months turned out to be a very busy time. I was driving into WDC for meetings several days per week, traveling to visit with client companies, making trips to Moscow on a monthly basis, plus trying to spend as many weekends as possible with the kids. The newness of the endeavor very much appealed to me, and I enjoyed the free reign that I had with my schedule; moreover, I felt as if I had found a very appealing niche, the opportunity to help with the development of a free and democratic infrastructure in Russia. Not to be under-emphasized was the pleasant side benefit of having found a new romantic attraction in my life, and the irony that the budding relationship was with someone who was considered an adversary not too many months ago. I believe all of this irony must have contributed to the sense of intrigue that prevailed during the covert relationship building stage.

I made subsequent trips to Moscow in October and November of that year. During my absence from Moscow, I had kept the discreet communications channels open with my lady friend, a relatively easy matter because she was the focal point of all incoming and outgoing communications in the Moscow office. Keep in mind that this period of time preceded large-scale use of email and cell phones, and international communications were still very difficult; however, all of the phone calls and fax traffic went through her, thereby offering us an opportunity to interact every time I needed to contact the Moscow office. As time passed, still without having revealed my true intentions, the frequent contacts were becoming increasingly friendly, but still not to the point of being flirtatious.

By the time that my October trip to Moscow was being scheduled, the city was in the midst of a constitutional crisis. The Vice President of Russia, Alexander Rutskoi, had during the previous year become a vocal opponent of President Yeltsin's policies; in early September, Yeltsin chose to relieve Rutskoi of his duties. Later that month, however, with the support of the Speaker of the Russian Parliament, Ruslan Khasbulatov, and numerous other high-ranking Russian officials, Vice President Rutskoi took control of the Parliament Building. By an act permitted within the scope of the Russian Constitution, Rutskoi actually declared that he was assuming the position of President of Russia. This action led to a two-week confrontation between Rutskoi and his followers and the forces remaining loyal to President Yeltsin, including most of the Russian Army. During this confrontation, Russian Army tanks and soldiers surrounded the Russian Parliament and fired frequently at the Parliament building. From our office building just a few hundred meters away, snipers were also firing even while our employees were at work in the office. Finally, on October 4th, Russian forces stormed and took control of the Parliament building. Just before the building was finally subjected to a full scale attack, however, those occupying the building in support of the *coup d'etat* were given a last opportunity to evacuate. Among those last few people to leave the Parliament Building prior to the final attack was my lady friend's father, who had been a fervent supporter of Rutskoi and Khasbulatov.

Why is this piece of Russian history so important to my story? Other than simply the political atmospherics of the day, which made my presence there even more interesting for me, the events of the October uprising threw a real monkey wrench into my romantic plans for the October visit. First of all, my lady friend had become so worried and despondent about the events taking place and her father's participation in the support of the coup-makers, that, following the end of the confrontation, she felt the need to take several weeks off just to recuperate and calm her nerves. Unfortunately, the period of recuperation from her nervous condition coincided with the time of my visit, so I did not have the opportunity to see her at all. However, by this time our relationship had become friendly enough that I felt justified in calling her at home a few times during my visit just to inquire about her welfare and to express my compassion for the unfortunate events she had to endure. I had also brought a few CD's with me as small gifts of appreciation for the assistance she had given me on a particular project over the previous month, but I just left those in the office for her return. In any event, I would be returning to Moscow the next month for a trade show in which our company would be participating, so I hoped that we would be able to move the budding relationship dramatically forward at that time.

During the month that followed, our long-distance relationship evolved from just a friendly one into something clearly a bit more promising. She was extremely grateful for the expressions of support plus the gifts from the October visit, and the conversations between us simply became more personal and flirtatious. I was now mostly calling her at home instead of the office, and this made our dialogue less complicated. When I returned to Moscow for the November trade show, which was planned to be a two-week visit, my expectations were that we would be able to move the relationship to a more overt level, meaning finally overt between the two of us, but still covert in terms of the knowledge of anyone else in the company. She had also invited me to come to dinner at her home during my November visit to meet the parents, and we had decided that we should go together to see an opera or a ballet. Hence, the atmospherics of the budding relationship were clearly moving in the right direction.

Before we get to that point in history, perhaps a few atmospherics would prove useful to the full appreciation of the situation I was about to enter. First of all, although she did speak English reasonably well in those days, my Russian was better than her English, so we always conversed in Russian. Secondly, I was at that point 43 years old and an experienced and worldly middle-aged gentleman; on the other hand, she had just graduated from the University a few years previous, and was only 25. Thirdly, she came from a relatively influential and affluent, by Soviet standards, family. Her father had been a Deputy Minister of Culture under Gorbachev, and her mother was a former opera singer. Finally, her parents were quite protective of her, perhaps overly so. If one were to put himself in their shoes, one might guess that they would probably not be overly enthusiastic about the prospects of having a 43-year-old American suitor coming over to dinner. Of course, none of them knew the real irony of the situation, that a former CIA case officer was about to grace their dinner table with the intention to seduce their daughter. Can you imagine the possible reaction if they had known? Do you happen to remember the 1967 movie classic *Guess Who's Coming to Dinner*? It might have created a similar reaction and have been every bit as entertaining.

To make a long story short, the November visit took place; we lowered the veil of mystery between us as to the true intent of the courtship, went to the theatre a couple of times, had dinner with the parents, and came to the conclusion that we had something serious developing between us. As a result, I decided that I would come clean with my boss about us so that we would not have to sneak around so much in the future. I also had it in my mind to invite her for a visit to the states over Christmas, and I would need his support to organize the visit. Had we not been good friends for almost 20 years at this point, my boss might have fired me on the spot when I revealed how I had broken company rule #1; however, we were close friends, and we understood each other well, so there was probably not too much surprise on his part when I broke the news. In any event, we had successfully come out of the company closet, and, although we would not advertise our new relationship within the office, life from the personal perspective became a bit more normal.

During these forays into Russia, I had also begun to travel to some of the sites where ongoing or prospective projects were in the works. Because my previous travel in Soviet Russia had been severely limited, ███████████████████████████████████████ ██, I was excited to finally get the chance to see some of the unfamiliar areas of the country. Over the next few years, I made several trips into the Kola Peninsula region of which Murmansk is the capital, where we were developing several projects, including one diamond mine concession; to the Kuzbass, the main coal mining region in central Siberia, where Scott-European had equipped an entire hospital and where several other projects were being developed, including a large dairy project; to the oil and gas regions of northern Siberia; and to the Saratov region, where we were trying to assume a leadership role in the privatization process of several major manufacturing organizations, one in ball bearing production and the other in aircraft. Under the sponsorship of OPIC, I also made a trip to the Russian Far East, to include Vladivostok, Khabarovsk and Sakhalin Island; I was part of a large US Business delegation looking to investigate investment opportunities in this region, which was close to China and rich in natural resources, including oil, gas, gold and diamonds. Although the actual travel between Moscow and some of these outlying areas was often an adventure in and of itself, for the internal branch of Aeroflot Airlines and basic infrastructure to support travel in the outlying areas were primitive, I was fascinated finally to have the opportunity to get a glimpse into life in Russia outside of Moscow and Saint Petersburg.

Back on the personal front, developments were becoming exciting there too. My lady friend did pay a visit to me over Christmas of 1993, and, needless to say, the relationship at this point moved full speed ahead. I even had the opportunity to introduce her to my kids, who were eight and six by this time; happily, they all hit it off immediately. Over the next few months, after she had returned to Moscow and we resumed our long-distance relationship, interspersed by my periodic visits to Moscow, it became clear to both of us that we wanted something more stable. As a result, we began to make plans for her to obtain a business visa so that she would be able to come to the States for a longer period, ostensibly for training in our USA operation. In June of 1994, with the full support of Scott-European, we did manage to obtain the necessary visa, and she came to live and work out of my home office, which, by this time, had relocated from Reston, Virginia, to Annapolis, Maryland.

Over the course of the next year, life took on a whole new perspective. We were living together in my home-office in charming Annapolis, and our romantic relationship developed more deeply. Whereas I was still busy and traveling frequently, including necessary trips back to Russia on which she could not accompany me, we had a wonderful existence. She had her official duties to attend to throughout, and, when I was gone, she worked on her English language skills, primarily by watching re-runs of *I Love Lucy*. Thanks in large part to Lucy, we eventually got to the point where it was easier to converse in English rather than Russian.

Over the course of this year, from her arrival in the States in June of 1994 until the spring of 1995, life was truly good. My job continued to be exciting for me, and I felt as if we were making meaningful progress on some of the projects that we were developing. My lady friend and I were very happy in our existence, although my trips to

Russia every month or so had begun to wear on us; neither of us liked the separation the trips imposed upon us, and, thus, it was during this time that the conversation about doing something different in life began to become a more frequent topic. Also, during this time period, the USA-headquarters of Scott-European had relocated from lovely Montpelier, Vermont, to mid-town Manhattan, so I was also spending a significant amount of time in New York City, as well as weekends visiting my kids. All in all, it was a very busy but happy period in my life.

In the first part of 1995, we began to look at life from a more permanent perspective. First of all, we began to discuss seriously the prospect of marriage, which had obviously been our intent all along, but certain matters needed to be resolved beforehand. For example, although my former wife and I had entered into a legal separation agreement in 1991 and had split all of our assets, we had never formally filed for divorce. Because there were some tax advantages to maintaining legal married status, we had simply never felt the urgency to file the necessary papers. However, this issue was clearly something that now needed to be addressed. Secondly, if we were going to tie the knot, should we not seek to find a more permanent place to live? We loved the Annapolis townhouse that we were renting (we had a marina at the complex where I kept my sailboat), but it was beginning to make less sense to rent a home when we had the option to buy. Also, the lengthy weekend trips back and forth to visit the kids were largely illogical, and we decided that it would make much more sense to move closer to where they lived. Therefore, in the spring of 1995, after some major searching for suitable real estate in an area much closer to the kids, we bit the bullet; we purchased a nice home in Williamsburg, Virginia, and made the move from Annapolis with the full expectation that life would get even better.

At this point, a brief anecdote needs to be interjected. Russians, in particular Russian women, are very superstitious. One of the superstitions which Russians take seriously is the existence of the "House Spirit" who inhabits every domicile. When moving into a new home, the first task is to determine whether the House Spirit is a good spirit or an evil one; this task is delegated to the family cat. The feline is brought to the front door of the domicile, and, if he willingly crosses the threshold, then it is okay to move in; however, if the cat hesitates or refuses due to the presence of an evil House Spirit, it is clear that one needs to find another place to live. This particular superstition, which my lady friend took quite seriously, caused me some concern. Because we did not have a cat at the time we put a contract on the house, we clearly needed to get one before we could move in. At the time the contract closed, we still did not have a cat, so it was off to the nearby SPCA to find one to call our own. Mind you, although I am not a fervent anti-cat person, I could have very happily moved into our new house without satisfying the House Spirit issue. Because that was not going to happen, however, I needed to find a cat I could live with.

Luckily, the local SPCA had a large population of cats, and we looked at them all. There was one male tabby, about 9 months old, that was a handsome specimen and he caught my attention. When I asked the attendant to open his cage so that we could become better acquainted, I reached my hand inside to pet him, and he abruptly scratched and bit me. I immediately decided that I liked his spunk and that I could live with him, so we filled out the paperwork and took him to our new home. Because we had already purchased the house, there was no going back; whether the cat encountered a good House Spirit or an evil one, he was damn sure going to cross the threshold. So, when the time came, and we were positioned at the door of our new house, I ensured that the superstition was not going to affect us, as I more or less nudged him strongly (more accurately, practically threw him) across the threshold. Thus, we overcame the Russian superstition and, for better or for worse, officially moved into our new home.

As we settled into our new abode over the next year, life continued to be good. I was equally busy with my job, which still required a great deal of travel to Washington and to Moscow, but everything was working out well. Scott-European had decided to open up a new line of business catering to the increasingly important mining and minerals industry in Russia; I was assigned the leading role in identifying and recruiting US equipment manufacturers that would help us to fill our portfolio in servicing this industry. We had also hired several new Russian account managers to work with these clients, with me playing a major role in training and guiding these new employees. On the personal side, I finally got the formal divorce process moving forward, which was just a matter of filing the proper paperwork and brought that process to a close in the early fall of 1995. Finally, on December 7th, 1995, after much planning and preparation, my lady friend and I were married in a Russian Orthodox Church in Richmond, Virginia. Having married the first time in front of a justice of the peace with only two witnesses whom we had recruited in the Pittsburgh Court House back in 1976, we had decided that this wedding should be a more memorable affair. My new wife's parents were able to travel from Moscow to attend, and we also had many of our good friends present for the wedding and the reception, which was held at the famous Jefferson Hotel. This event was certainly more in keeping with the tendencies of a romantic idealist, and thus our new life was officially launched.

The next few months were blissful, despite the requirement to travel for extended periods to Russia. We were happy with our new home, and I even began to enjoy the company of our house cat, whom we had named Fred; I am not sure why we chose that name, but it seemed to fit. My job in helping to organize and manage our new mining and minerals division kept me very busy, and we were planning to participate in a mining trade show in Moscow to introduce the new companies that we had brought into the Scott-European stable of clients. The trade show was to take place in mid-March, 1996, and I was to supervise some dozen or so client company executives and sales reps at the show. When I departed Washington Dulles International Airport on March 15th for that event, little did I know how much of a life game-changer this particular trip would turn out to be.

Chapter 15

Persona Non Grata

Saturday, March 16, 1996

I had just arrived at Moscow's Sheremyetova International Airport from Washington, via Amsterdam. It was already late afternoon, and, after flying all night and day, I felt tired and grubby. Having deplaned, I finally reached my turn in the passport control line. The young passport control clerk was, to my delight, quite an attractive 25-ish blonde lady. I was confident that I would be able to quickly overcome the standard sluggish passport check procedure with a quick smile and the projection of my boyish charm.

After a quick greeting to her in my flawless Russian, which generated only a somewhat-less-than-friendly response, I noted how seriously she was studying my passport, then the computer screen, my passport again, and a quick glance up at me, all with a serious frown on her face. I remained silent while watching this drama, but finally my curiosity grew, and my patience withered to the point where I was compelled to ask her, "Is something wrong?" She ignored my question, and continued the same studied scrutiny.

After a short while, growing increasingly impatient, I asked her again (of course, in my flawless Russian) if there was some sort of problem. This time she answered, in her very-flawed, heavily accented English, albeit admittedly intriguing when coming from a comely young Russian lady, "Meester Morris, you have visa problem!"

My retort was instantaneous, my smile and charming demeanor unwavering, when I said, "No, there is no visa problem. I have a multiple entry visa which I've been using for the past year and a half!"

Her reply was equally instantaneous, her verbiage unchanging, with intonation slightly more dramatic, "Meester Morris, you have visa problem."

Once more I engaged in my insistence. "No, there is no problem. Take a look at the visa and all of the times I have already used it to enter Russia, and….."

This time she cut me off short, looked me straight in the eyes, and said with no hesitation, "Meester Morris, you have visa problem! Go seet down, over there, and vait!"

Not being too big a dummy, this time I understood entirely. Finally, after three years of unhindered travel to and from Russia, seemingly without anyone ever taking notice of the former American spook gallivanting around the country, someone finally took exception. But who, and why, and what was in store for me? I no longer had the ████████████████████████ to protect me, so what had I gotten myself into now?

For those of you who have not had the pleasure of flying there, Sheremyetova Airport is quite a distance outside of Moscow, very similar to the distance Dulles International Airport is from downtown Washington, DC. The way I figure it is that after my name came up on the passport control computer, and the alarm signal was activated, the lovely young clerk electronically notified the airport security police, who then notified the Russian FSB (Federal Security Bureau, in charge of counter-intelligence in post-Soviet Russia). In turn, the FSB called in two of their American Directorate case officers, who hurried to headquarters to find out what was happening, to read up on the Morris file, and then to make their unhurried way out to Sheremyetova. After several rebuked requests to the passport control lady to be permitted to move elsewhere, more than three hours passed until I was finally approached by an airport security officer who escorted me to a hidden-away meeting room where two gentlemen awaited.

I must admit that I had more or less expected an event of this sort since that time in July 1993 when I had retired from the Agency and decided to go to work with a company dealing in Russia. I assumed that sooner or later someone was going to try to harass me. Well, as I entered that dingy, small, and somewhat smelly meeting room, I correctly concluded that the long-anticipated time had indeed finally come.

The two men who greeted me were dressed for business. They wore expensive suits and looked like typical "new Russians," who were enjoying the relative prosperity of post-Soviet Russia. The younger one, who introduced himself as Sasha, spoke excellent, non-accented English and was a handsome young man in his mid-30's; he came across as a pleasant, friendly fellow, who, under different circumstances, might have been a good guy with whom to hang out over a beer or two. Sasha seemed to be a bit nervous over the circumstances and apologized to me for the lengthy delay in getting to me. The other man was about 10 years older and introduced himself as Alexander Vasiliyevich. He looked a bit more old-school, sporting his stereotypical gold tooth, and, although his demeanor also betrayed a hint of nervousness, he was clearly in charge.

Despite the fact we were on Russian turf, which was an obvious advantage to their side, the reason for their apparent nervousness was probably the fact that their American interlocutor was clearly not a happy camper. I suppose that my body language and facial expression may have betrayed the fact that I was really perturbed at having been detained for over three hours with no other explanation than the nonsense that I had a "visa problem."

The meeting was short and sweet. There was only minimal rapport-building, primarily led by Sasha, typical of a preamble to a normal business discussion. In fact, the foreplay was very short-lived, after which Alexander Vasiliyevich took over and got right to the point of our meeting.

"Mister Morris, we know that you have worked for the CIA!"

Living my cover as instructed during my 13 years as a member of the Agency, I immediately denied this accusation, and said to him, "You are mistaken." ████████████████████████████████
████████████████

"Mister Morris, we know that you worked for the CIA. If you lie to us, it will mean that you are still an enemy of Russia."

Again, I denied the accusation. "No, you are mistaken. I never worked for CIA, and I am certainly not an enemy of Russia, not now, not ever. In fact, I am here on business trying to help the development of the Russian economy. You should know that!"

"Mister Morris, please, we know that you worked for the CIA. In fact, people at your Moscow Station know me very well, so please do not deny the truth."

"Look, I don't know what I can tell you differently. ████████
██
██
████████████████████████████████████ There are any number of Russians who worked on that project with me who can attest to that. Besides, as you know, I have been travelling here almost monthly for the past three years, and no one ever questioned me before. Why are you doing this now?"

"Things have changed, Mister Morris," responded Alexander Vasiliyevich. "Your FBI is not allowing former Russian Intelligence Officers into the United States, and people here have decided not to let you in any longer."

"I don't know what else to tell you, other than your people are making a mistake. I have never worked for the CIA, not ever".

The meeting ended rather abruptly after that. Alexander Vasiliyevich closed the dialogue by saying, "You are lying to us. You are obviously still an enemy of Russia, and we have nothing further to discuss. You will no longer be welcome in Russia. *Do svidaniye!*"

At that, the airport security officer re-entered the room, my two interlocutors departed, and I was escorted to a holding area populated by a large group of transit vagrants, who were probably detained for any number of semi-criminal reasons. The security officer did arrange for my luggage to be brought to me from the baggage claim area, and then I was told to take a seat among the vagrant population with no further instructions.

I spent most of the next hour simply decompressing. Naturally, the "pucker factor" had been pretty high during the interrogation, and it took me some time to get my heart rate back down to near-normalcy. By this time, it was already approaching late evening. Several attempts to discuss my situation with the aforementioned security officer proved to be futile. I inquired if I could at least look into getting a ticket to depart Moscow, as instructed by the FSB officers, but he just ignored my requests. I began to wonder if this game was not yet over, and if they just intended to detain me in the vagrant purgatory overnight, and to begin the second half of the game the next morning.

Finally, feeling tremendous frustration and a bit of misgiving of what was to come, I got fed up, and decided to take action into my own hands. I picked up my luggage and started to walk away from the detainment lounge, heading to I was not sure where, other than just to get the hell out of that place. The security officer caught up to me rather rapidly and kindly asked me to return to the transit lounge. He was adamant enough to convince me that I should probably follow his instructions.

After about another hour among the great unwashed, a fortuitous event occurred. The original security guard, who had by this time taken a rather strong dislike towards me, was replaced by the night shift. The new, and younger, security officer in charge looked to be a decent chap, so I decided to take a somewhat less belligerent approach to him. When the time was right, I approached him and explained the situation, that I had been "asked" to leave the country, which I was more than happy to do, but that I had not been allowed to check into getting a ticket out of town. I explained that no one knew where I was, that people had been waiting for me at the airport, and that I had not been allowed to get word to anyone of my situation. Whether by pre-ordained design or that he was possibly more compassionate (i.e., less of a schmuck) than his predecessor, he acquiesced and escorted me out of the transit lounge to the airline ticket counter area.

The only available flight leaving Moscow at that late hour, about 2300 by that time, was a British Airlines flight to London. I gladly paid the rather exorbitant amount for a one-way ticket back to civilization, checked the bag, and was escorted to the aircraft that was already preparing for departure. Finally on board and safely out of the reach of my adversaries, I breathed a few deep sighs of relief, threw down a few hardly-tasted drinks, and passed out in my seat. The next instant I recall was landing in London and groggily awakening from my fitful slumber in the early morning hours of March 17th.

As noted above, I was flying to Moscow to participate in a mining machinery trade show, for which I had played a major organizational role. I was the primary point of contact for the dozen or so mining machinery company executives who would be arriving in Moscow in the next day or two to support the trade show, and now their primary contact was otherwise occupied. We had also had a company driver waiting for me at the airport, but I was nowhere to be found. Keep in mind that 1996 was largely the no-cell-phone era. In those days, I do recall having a huge Motorola brick phone, which was only effective in the USA, but nothing existed at that time like what we enjoy today with miniscule phones that operate globally. In essence, I had no capability to communicate with anyone.

Upon arriving in London, the first order of business was to inform my family and the company what had happened to me. Unable to locate me at Sheremyetova Airport, the company driver who was waiting for me advised the Scott-European execs that I had not appeared as scheduled. The company execs had then called my wife and asked if I had missed my flight. No, as far as she knew, I had made my flight to Moscow and had departed per usual; otherwise, she would have certainly heard from me.

Two days earlier, on March 15th, I had left my Williamsburg home by car and had made the three-hour drive to Dulles Airport. From there I had caught my flight to Amsterdam, arriving early morning on the 16th. After a layover in Amsterdam Airport, I then caught the connecting flight to Moscow, arriving there in the late afternoon, local Moscow time, which is eight hours ahead of the USA. After the event at Sheremyetova, when I finally made it to London, it was already the morning of March 17th, which was five hours ahead of the USA East Coast. By that time, therefore, I had been gone from my Williamsburg home, and out of touch, for about 36 hours. When I was finally able to call my wife to give her a sign of life, it was late night on the 16th her time and she was in a frazzled state-of-mind.

Everyone had apparently been frantic, having no idea what could have possibly happened to me. First of all, everyone knew that I would NEVER change my plans without informing folks immediately, so my sudden disappearance did not bode well. Those with less-dramatic inclinations assumed that I must have had a traffic accident en route to Dulles or experienced some medical emergency somewhere between Dulles and Moscow. Those few who knew my background tended to get more creative and believed that I could have been kidnapped or killed by Arab terrorists or some other Agency-related mishap. In any event, the collective conclusion was that something awful had transpired and that I may have gone onto the hereafter. The phone call to my wife, therefore, ended quite a worrisome period of uncertainty and distress.

Upon finally getting home much later that day and making all of the appropriate explanations, I then made arrangements to inform my former employer, through proper classified channels, of what had transpired. Once this task was completed, I then had to begin to tackle the next major problem created by this incident. The situation was that I was working in a responsible, well-paid position that required my presence in Moscow on a periodic basis, a place where I now was no longer welcome. I had a new Russian wife, a new and significant mortgage, and was working in the region for which I had trained myself during most of my professional life. All of a sudden, circumstances had evolved that would negate my ability to perform my job, as designed. Truth be told, I had already begun to tire of the frequent month-long-trips to Russia that were requirements of the job, so this sudden inability to do so was not entirely an unwelcome development. Nevertheless, how would I be able to perform my job if I were unable to travel to Russia? And, how would I be able to support my family? What could I do to somehow resolve this new dilemma?

First of all, because the President of Scott-European Corporation was a long-time friend, we were able to come to an easy conclusion; with my newly-found inability to perform the duties of my position, we agreed to ease me out of the company. In truth, as noted above, this new reality did not overly concern me because the inordinate travel requirements were not doing my new marriage any good. Accordingly, we came to a mutually-satisfactory agreement, and I concluded my employment within a few months. However, the more serious, long-term question was what to do from there? My education and most of my career had revolved around all things Russian, so this new situation obviously curtailed many of my employment opportunities, especially considering that there was significant investment attention being given to the post-Soviet Russian market.

One of the hallmarks of the romantic idealist mentality is that life must be fair and just. Obviously, the fact that I, the hero victor from the Cold War and philanthropic rebuilder of Russia from the ashes of Communism, could be singled out and treated so unfairly was inherently unjust. Moreover, despite this unfortunate and obviously misguided situation in which I found myself, certainly the forces of freedom and American justice would immediately come to my aid and vigorously help to resolve my dilemma. After all, I had diligently served my country for over 16 years as a Green Beret and CIA case officer; certainly people will be fighting among themselves in their haste to come to my assistance! Of this, I was absolutely certain. Alas, the next two to three years painfully convinced me that nothing could have been further from the truth.

I pursued vindication of this misguided circumstance with a passion. I communicated with all of the pertinent US Government Agencies (CIA, FBI, State Department, etc.), with all of my elected Senators and Representatives, with the US Embassy in Moscow, with anyone

I could think of on the American side. Although everyone expressed their sympathy with this unfortunate development and promised to "look into it" which I do believe some actually did, my US Government interlocutors in this quest were very insistent in their inability to assist. Elected representatives or at least their staffers did seem to take some action, but to no avail. Government Agencies that I contacted, in essence, largely turned a blind eye. This realization was indeed a tough pill to swallow.

The FBI made no response whatsoever. Although they were allegedly the instigators of the instance of reciprocity, there was no indication that they really gave a damn. Of course, FBI folks did not care much for CIA officers anyway and probably even less so for those who were cavorting on enemy soil, so they never even showed me the courtesy of a reply. Frankly, I had not expected much from them anyway. I expected even less from State Department, who tended to like CIA folks even less so than the FBI; State did, in fact, make some inquiries on my behalf, but with no positive outcome. This result was all predictable based on my knowledge of the organization; ██████ ████████████████████████████████████ ██████████████████████████████████ I knew their capabilities and predispositions fairly well.

The CIA was a different matter. Having worked my butt off for them for 13 years and having been one of their star players, I expected that they would mount their horses and make the cavalry charge to come to my aid immediately upon hearing of this unjust situation. Alas, there is no fool quite like the romantic idealist!

To be entirely fair, everyone whom I contacted at the Agency was genuinely interested and largely sympathetic; after all, as Agency employees, the very same thing could someday happen to them. However, they swore up and down that there was absolutely nothing they could do to assist me. I tried futilely to convince and cajole my interlocutors into some sort of action on my behalf; after all, I had done everything as instructed by my Agency bosses, I had done my job to protect my cover, and I played the game according to the rules. Now that I had held up my side of the bargain, what about you guys?

The canned response, and one which I inherently understood, was that they could not raise my case with their Russian counterparts for "operational reasons."

Certainly, some 12 years after I had departed my Agency assignment in Moscow, there was no secret on the Russian side that I had indeed worked for the Agency. The fact of the matter is that operational covers evaporate over time. I recall during my CT course being shown a thoroughly tattered t-shirt by one of the veteran officer-instructors, which he called a depiction of his cover after so many years in the organization. Just through the normal deterioration of cover over multiple overseas assignments, people knew who the hell I was. Certainly it was safe to say by this time that my true affiliation was 100% known to the Russians. Reflecting back on the Sheremyetova incident, here is the truth of the matter: I certainly knew that I was lying to them, they knew fully that I was lying to them, and yet we all played the role knowingly. Isn't espionage an interesting game?

The fact that the Russians knew my true background was even more evident because we had several traitors and defectors within the Agency ranks in the mid-1980's, a couple of whom were my training-mates in one or another course; they had undoubtedly revealed my handling of several sensitive cases during my tour in Moscow. In a nutshell, everyone not only knew who I was, but, in all probability, now knew most of what I had done for the Agency while working in Moscow. There really was nothing left to hide, was there? The Agency thought otherwise.

Finally, in answer to my final plea to give me the capability to discuss my dilemma with the Russian side honestly so that I would not have to continue to lie to them about my former affiliation, the Agency did acquiesce and allowed me to apply to have my cover status changed. Because I had retired from the Agency under covert status,

████████████████████████████████

████████████████████████████

████ they could elect to roll back that status to overt and allow me to admit to my true affiliation. They eventually did this favor for me. It was my misguided idea that if I could negotiate with the Russians honestly, they would realize ultimately they could benefit by having a diligent and resourceful American businessman assisting them to rebuild their economy from the ash-heap of history. Again, there is no fool quite like the romantic idealist! Not only did the Russians never reply to any of my inquiries, it is clear that none of them ever wanted to come to the aid of a former American Spook. By doing so, they might be smeared by association, so, needless to say, none of my numerous inquiries ever generated one word of response.

This entire process of trying to get justice for the injustice I had suffered consumed much of a period of two to three years. Obviously, I embarked on other ways to support my family, and I will address a few of them in later chapters, but I readily admit that I invested an inordinate amount of time and energy into this futile pursuit of justice. Not only did this activity absorb much time and energy which could have been better invested into revenue-generating activities, but the unfairness of the situation also affected my mind-set and negatively altered my outlook on life. Thus, my dogged pursuit of justice along the romantic idealistic path not only adversely affected my ability to support my family, but also negatively impacted my family relationships because of my preoccupation with this futile quest.

As I write this chapter, I have not been allowed to travel to Russia since 1996. I have traveled to former Soviet Republics, such as Ukraine and Azerbaijan, and numerous times to Georgia, but never again to Russia. Indeed, I have ultimately resigned myself to live with this fact. I do remain highly interested in the political and economic activities in Russia, am highly curious about how the country is evolving, and continue to follow developments there. However, I will never travel there again, and, to be perfectly honest, at this point, I do not particularly wish to. Nevertheless, it remains a country into which I devoted a significant part of my adult life, both professionally and personally, and one that has impacted me greatly.

Chapter 16

Searching for Meaning

Following my expulsion from Russia, it became quickly clear that I would be unable to continue to perform the required tasks of my job with Scott-European, so my boss and I agreed on a phase-out from the company, which took place at the end of June, 1996. Although I had begun my efforts to attempt to get my travel rights to Russia reinstated, I knew in my heart that this effort would ultimately be unsuccessful, so I needed to find something else to do to provide for my family. I decided to form a consulting company, which I dubbed Robert O. Morris & Associates although, other than Fred the cat on occasion, I had no one else in my home office. The mission of the company was to do business consulting for the Russia market, where ironically I could not travel, and the East European countries. Based on my wide circle of contacts, however, and a number of dependable surrogates in Russia, I was able quickly to find a couple of retainer clients who were looking for business development assistance.

The first consulting agreement that I finalized for Russia evolved from an old friend, who was at this time President of a street sweeper manufacturer located in North Carolina. The company was looking to expand their international market, and my friend knew me from Pullman days when we were representing his former company in the USSR. My father-in-law became my key surrogate in Russia for this project, for he had excellent contacts in the municipal maintenance market in Moscow, including friends who were executives of ZIL, a large Russian truck manufacturer. We knew that local content would make the product more marketable within Russia, so we began discussions with ZIL about the feasibility of mounting the US sweeper equipment on a Russian truck chassis for the Russian and former USSR markets. Over the course of 18 months, we did succeed to produce the prototype of this jointly-produced machine, and then

ZIL took over the long-term marketing of the product.

Simultaneously, my close friend from prep school and TelePizza days, Eduardo, had since sold his shares in TelePizza and moved to Nicaragua to embark upon his childhood dream to become a farmer. Among the many farming enterprises which he started was a cigar tobacco farming operation, which soon became one of the largest in the country. His initial plan had been to produce high-quality tobacco for the many cigar producers in Nicaragua, but, once his farming operation became well established, he decided that he would branch out into the production of his own cigars. In this regard, he wanted to learn more about the distribution of cigars in the US market. Knowing of my passion for cigars, he invited me to partner with him to produce a cigar brand for the US market and to distribute it through the normal US market pipelines. We initiated this undertaking with mixed success, and it will be addressed in a later chapter.

The main enterprise that developed during this time period, however, was a project that was jointly the brain-child of my Russian father-in-law and myself. When my wife's parents came to the United States to attend our wedding, we took them several times to visit Colonial Williamsburg, with which my father-in-law had become immediately enthralled. Having served previously as the Deputy Minister of Culture in the Russian Federal Soviet Socialist Republic (RFSSR), he was intimately familiar with the tourist potential of the many Russian cities that possessed tremendous architectural and historical importance. Although these towns had significant tourist potential, they largely lacked the necessary infrastructure to appeal to western tourists. When he learned of the evolution of Williamsburg from a small run-down village with historical and cultural significance into one of the major tourist destinations in the United States, it occurred to him that Williamsburg could serve as a model for similar development of selected locations in Russia. We discussed this concept over the course of several months and more than a few bottles of vodka, until we compiled a proposal which we thought might be of interest to the leadership of the Colonial Williamsburg Foundation.

For those unfamiliar with the evolution of Colonial Williamsburg, a full description of the history of its development is available through the Colonial Williamsburg Foundation (CWF) web site. In a nutshell, however, the original idea of developing Williamsburg and to preserve the historical and cultural significance of the location was the dream of Reverend Dr. W.A.R. Goodwin, the pastor of the local Bruton Parish Church during the late 1920's and 1930's. Dr. Goodwin saw the potential of developing and preserving the 18th century colonial capital and hub of the American Revolution and approached famous businessman and philanthropist, John D. Rockefeller, Jr., with his ideas. Dr. Goodwin was persistent in his appeals to Rockefeller and finally convinced him of the merits of his dream. Ultimately, Rockefeller invested significant funds to support the refurbishment of old buildings that had long-since fallen into disrepair, to rebuild old buildings that had vanished, and to support the infrastructural development to transform Williamsburg into a tourism destination. Over the decades of the 20th century, Colonial Williamsburg thus developed into a booming economic model, creating jobs and economic growth for an entire region.

My father-in-law and I felt that the Colonial Williamsburg economic development model could be applied to similar Russian locations with the same end result. The next time my father-in-law visited us to celebrate the birth of our daughter, Sasha, in July, 1997, I arranged an appointment with the then President of CWF, Bob Wilburn, to run our ideas past him. What we proposed to him was for CWF to sponsor a Conference for Cultural Tourism Development in Russia to which we would invite the Russian Minister of Culture and selected Governors of Russian regions where the potential for cultural tourism development existed. In addition, we would also invite a plethora of American and European investors, western companies involved in tourism infrastructure (hotels, transportation, communication companies, and so forth) and other interested parties to expose them to specific tourism development projects in Russia. The business plan that we presented was a win-win situation for CWF; they would provide the facilities for the conference, training for the Russian participants, and assist with publicity for the event, and we would raise the funds from event sponsors to cover those costs. In addition, CWF would earn revenues from conference participation fees, hotel and meal charges from the event and positive publicity for having sponsored such an internationally-oriented activity. In fact, my father-in-law and I were the only ones assuming any financial risk, for the only compensation we were proposing was commissions on all revenues earned from the event. The only additional consideration was that, if this first event was judged to be a success, then CWF would agree to a longer term program in International Cultural Tourism Development, which we would manage under a consulting agreement. President Wilburn agreed, and, in the late summer of 1997, we got to work.

Based on his previous service as Deputy Minister of Culture for the Russian Federation, my father-in-law was a friend and colleague of the incumbent Russian Minister of Culture, Natalya Dementieva. Because such a project would fall under her jurisdiction from the Russian perspective, we needed to solicit her agreement to the concept, which was quickly obtained. We also needed the Minister's input concerning which of the Russian Regions to invite to make presentations at the conference. Once we had a list of potential participants, then my-father-in-law would lead the next effort, which was to speak to the Governor of each potential region to measure his interest. For the previous several years, my father-in-law had been working as a consultant to the Russian Federation Council (similar to our Senate), which included all of the Governors (elected Administrative Heads) of each region (state) of Russia. As a result, he personally knew all of the Governors on the list and worked in the same building with them during the sessions of the Federation Council, so this task was also accomplished rather quickly and easily.

Within a short span of time, the final regional choices had been confirmed: the regions were Novgorod, Pskov, Yaroslavl, Karelia, Leningrad region, and the city of St. Petersburg. Each of the regions was to prepare several project presentations for the conference and to appoint a select team of specialists to represent the region; for budgetary reasons, these teams were limited to four persons each. In addition, there would be a small team from the Ministry of Culture to include the Minister and a few other dignitaries. Overall, the delegation to come to the Conference from Russian Government circles would be 30 people. Because there were no funds available within the Russian Government budget for such projects, the task to identify and recruit sponsorship for the event to cover the costs for this group fell to me. In addition to transporting the group to the USA and back, lodging and feeding them while they were here, and covering other miscellaneous expenses, we also arranged for a two-day cultural tourism training program for the Russian delegates to be put on by CWF. The costs for this event, including a number of Russian interpreters, were also to be covered by sponsors still to be determined.

All in all, we needed to identify and secure sponsorship funding in the neighborhood of $100,000 in order to pull off the Conference, and, as noted above, that task was mine. In this regard, I was quickly able to solicit the assistance of the US-Russia Business Council (USRBC) leadership, whom I knew well from my Scott-European days; they were able to supply names and points of contact for all of their member companies, which numbered in the hundreds. In exchange for this assistance, USRBC would become a non-cash contributing sponsor and, by doing so, would provide significant credibility and additional publicity for the event. This development was a major initial step in pulling the event together.

The second sponsor that was identified was FINNAIR, which agreed to transport the Russian Government delegation to and from the United States gratis, in exchange for the positive publicity and Russian good will that they would receive from the event. The most obvious choice for filling this role would have been, of course, AEROFLOT Russian Airlines, but we never succeeded in getting any proper responses from the company. In any event, FINNAIR provided our delegation with exemplary service, and we were pleased and honored by their agreement to support the event.

The last piece of the puzzle was not so easy to fill. With the free trans-Atlantic transportation having been offered by FINNAIR, we still needed to raise close to $70,000 to support the remainder of our budget requirements for the Russian delegation. From the historical perspective, as we were looking far and wide to solicit US corporate sponsorship for this project, the last half of 1997 and the first half of 1998, precisely the period in which we were seeking project sponsorship, was a time of financial difficulty in Russia. In fact, the situation in Russia led to a full scale financial melt-down in August of 1998. Nevertheless, we pushed on, and, because corporate sponsorship interest was low, we began to investigate the non-profit NGO world to identify sponsors. Finally, after soliciting just about every philanthropic organization known to support programs for Russia, we finally succeeded with the Open Society Institute (OSI).

We had begun by contacting the OSI headquarters office in New York City, and they in turn put us in touch with the OSI office in Moscow and their local Director. Fortunately, OSI-Russia did have a mandate and a budget for cultural projects, and their Director agreed that cultural tourism development seemed to fit that mandate well enough. If they were to contribute funds to support the project, however, OSI-Russia wanted to have a say in the content of the conference, to which we agreed. After extensive discussions, debates, and joint decision-making over a period of several months, we reached a final agreement, and OSI-Russia provided the remaining financial obligations for the support of the Russian delegation.

Support for the Russian delegation also included the weekend training session to be held for all of the Russian members, including the OSI team, on the CWF Cultural Tourism Management Model. This two-day event would expose the Russians to the entire CWF complex and would include a seminar on how to manage a living museum such as CW, how to raise funds to support such an endeavor, how to create tourism interest and infrastructural development, etc., etc., etc. This training segment was a major selling point in obtaining OSI's agreement to sponsor the event. At that point, having determined the entire program for the Russian delegation, and having successfully solicited the required financial support, the only remaining task was to provide a suitable audience for this unprecedented event. With the aforementioned financial crisis having befallen the Russian market and western interest towards investing there having largely disappeared, this task proved to be the most challenging of all.

As they say, timing is everything, and the reality of the Russian financial crisis put a real damper on the level of enthusiasm to be generated from the US and western perspective. Nevertheless, with the help and support of the USRBC and with my own personal list of contacts who were active in the Russian market, we eventually succeeded in attracting a high-quality, sufficiently large list of participants to attend the Conference, which was to take place November 16-17, 1998. The final list of US and western attendees included dignitaries from the US Department of Commerce, especially those involved with US-Russia trade, NGO officials, executives from several private and governmental financial institutions, hotel companies, and numerous other assorted US companies involved in business development in Russia.

The Conference itself was spread over two full days. Day #1 saw welcoming remarks by the President of CWF, Bob Wilburn, followed by remarks by the Virginia Secretary of State, and then by Russian Cultural Minister Dementieva. During the course of the day, formal presentations for cultural tourism development projects were made by the Governor of each of the six Russian Regions in attendance. These presentations had been well-prepared, and they outlined a number of highly interesting areas for joint ventures and project development in the regional tourism infrastructure. Lunch and dinner speeches by US Government dignitaries accompanied the superb meals prepared by CWF, and the evening post-dinner activities included a singing competition between Russian and American participants; knowing from past experience that Russians cannot and will not retreat from such a challenge, I presented the singing competition to the Russians, knowing in advance that their contributions would be far superior to ours. I also knew from past experience that it would be a hell of a lot of fun, as it truly was.

Other than recuperating from the previous evening's singing and simultaneous drinking festivities, Day #2 was devoted to two panel discussions; one covered the realities of potential tourism development issues, including real estate reform, tax incentives for development projects, and so forth, while the other panel dealt with potential sources of financing for the types of cultural tourism projects which we were discussing. The afternoon of Day 2 was set aside for the individual Russian regions to hold private meetings with potential investors and/or business partners, and then closing remarks were made by Mr. Wilburn and Minister Dementieva. All in all, the Conference was determined to have been a huge success, especially considering the unfortunate timing of the event, which coincided with the financial crisis which had befallen Russia. Unfortunately, we did not attract investors with funds in hand ready to disperse or hotel developers prepared to begin construction in any of the featured Russian Regions, but this first of its kind conference did break ground into an entirely new realm of endeavor. Many worthwhile discussions that would eventually lead to progress in Russian cultural tourism development projects began at this event and continued to evolve in subsequent years. In our final collective analysis, the conference was judged to have been a very successful event, and one in which everyone involved took a great deal of pride.

As agreed with President Wilburn, the success of this initial effort did lead to a full-time consulting agreement with CWF for International Cultural Tourism Development, which covered the following two years. In addition to this initial conference, during 1999 we also were able to mount a similar event that was devoted to a week-long training session conducted by the CWF staff. This course dealt with the philosophies and practices of Colonial Williamsburg in developing and managing a successful cultural tourism destination. The event was attended by cultural specialists, museum managers, and other various officials from a diverse number of countries, exclusively from nations of the Former Soviet Union and Eastern Europe. Included in the group were representatives from Georgia, Azerbaijan, Uzbekistan, Kazakhstan, Mongolia, Ukraine, and Poland. Sponsorship for the attending students was once again covered by OSI, but this time each individual OSI national office covered the training fees and travel expenses of the representatives from their respective countries. This event did not turn out to be nearly as large a revenue generator for CWF as the Russia Conference had been, but it did prove to substantiate, once again, the demand for knowledge of the cultural tourism development model as CWF had so masterfully developed.

We had also initiated discussions for cultural tourism development projects with the World Tourism Office (WTO) in Spain, as well as in Poland with the Polish Ministry of Culture and Tourism. Word of CWF's initiatives in international cultural tourism development also began to spread around the global tourism community. For example, in late 1999, CWF was invited to participate in a Global Conference on Tourism Development sponsored by the US Commercial Service Office in Athens, Greece; I was dispatched to deliver a speech on our cultural tourism development program as part of the conference agenda, which was well-attended by tourism officials from dozens of countries throughout Europe and Asia. Ours was still a unique concept in the global scope of tourism development, and our presentation drew significant interest from numerous attendees.

One such attendee who was captivated with the concept was the young, dynamic mayor of Lviv, Ukraine, who invited me to visit the city in the forthcoming months to discuss how we might be able to apply the CWF model to his beautiful city. The visit, which took place in the winter of 2000, was a very interesting one, and I was well-received by the mayor and his staff. The mayor had a great vision for developing tourism in his historic city, considered one of the top cultural centers of the Ukraine. Although we maintained a steady post-visit dialogue about possible tourism development projects, unfortunately, our desire to mount some major efforts in this regard was cut short by changes within CWF's priorities.

Whereas Bob Wilburn had envisioned a potential role for CWF within the international theatre, when he departed CWF for a position at another major museum, the new leadership at CWF did not necessarily share that vision. Furthermore, although we had generated significant revenue with the Russia Conference, augmented by the 1999 training seminar, we had not succeeded in producing enough of a consistent cash flow to justify continuing the program past 2000. As a result, we amicably decided to terminate our consulting agreement, which I fully understood intellectually, but about which I was highly disappointed. Available funding for such programs was always severely limited, and we had found from our experience over the previous three years that finding sponsorships for individual events was a major effort in and of itself, and unfortunately not always successful. So, it was with deep regret that I departed from this role which I had grown to appreciate so much. It was also about this same time that some serious issues were developing on the home front, which will be covered in the next chapter.

Looking back on a lifetime of various endeavors, the creation and successful implementation of this unique program, most especially the Russia Conference, is something in which I still feel a tremendous amount of pride and satisfaction. I know that my father-in-law felt the same way, and it was a pleasure to work so closely with him in developing this program. It happens to be a concept which I believe still possesses excellent development potential. As Colonial Williamsburg has grown into one of the world's leading cultural tourism destinations, one which has prospered and provided economic benefits to an entire region in southeastern Virginia, so too can many other magnificent cultural tourism locations across the globe. The basic prerequisites of historical and cultural significance already exist; what is needed is the foresight to envision the end result and the passion and dedication to attack the challenge of finding the support to fund such an the effort, just as Dr. Goodwin had done in the late 1920s and early 1930s.

Chapter 17

Life is a Slippery Slope

In the words of a famous anonymous American philosopher, "Shit happens!" And, as Friedrich Nietzsche once said, "What doesn't kill us makes us stronger!" From my personal experience in the period roughly between 2001 and 2004, I can attest that both quotes seem to be equally wise and true. As you may have guessed already, this chapter deals with some unhappy moments, which, as we all know, are simply an inescapable part of our life's path. So, where to begin?

Perhaps the most logical point at which to begin this brief, yet unhappy, chapter is with the reality of career uncertainty and its negative implications. At its point of origin, this reference beckons back to that fateful day in March, 1996, at Moscow Sheremyetova Airport, when I was declared persona non grata. This unfortunate development threw my career pursuits and life into a tailspin. As indicated previously, instead of simply acknowledging and accepting that my path had been unalterably changed, for a period of three years I invested too much time, energy, and emotional capital into my futile attempts to get the Russians' decision reversed. The romantic idealist living in my head just refused to let go of the perceived injustice, and "he" continued fighting windmills at every opportunity. Although this effort obviously did not totally preoccupy me for those three years, it did consume more time and energy than a more logical man would have allowed. As a result, it significantly detracted from other projects on which I was working, thereby creating financial difficulties and also a negative impact on my mind-set. Taken all together, among other detriments, some marital strains developed that probably could have been avoided.

Being somewhat of a self-appointed expert on the topic, having done it three times, I will address my philosophical musings on marriage in a later chapter. However, for the purposes of chronological continuity, I feel that I need to address this topic briefly at this juncture. Whereas my first marriage of over 14 years had dissolved, by mutual agreement, based on the existence of irreconcilable differences, my second marriage ended based more on a unilateral decision. We had met in Moscow in 1993, we married in the States in 1995, our daughter was born in 1997, and my wife filed for divorce in early 2002. In retrospect, one might be able to make a solid case that the relationship may have been ill-conceived from the beginning, but that is honestly irrelevant. I fell in love with a beautiful woman, we had a wonderful first few years together, and, somewhere along the way, difficulties arose, and she decided to pursue another course. Although it was clear by 2001 that our relationship had suffered over the previous few years, and she openly stated that she wanted out, I had hoped to persevere and somehow make our marriage work. In brief, her will prevailed. We sold the house, separated our assets, set her and my daughter up in a new home and I then packed up my suitcase and left. For the purpose of this chapter, that information will suffice.

For those of us who have been unfortunate enough to experience it, divorce is almost always a very painful (especially when there are children involved) and costly exercise. Although a person can usually survive one such experience without too much major fallout, a second one can be devastating, from both the emotional and financial perspective. On the positive side, those who have been blessed with good friends and solid family support normally can weather the storm more easily. In this particular instance, just as he had ten years earlier, my good friend, Eduardo, came to my assistance and asked me to help him in one of his new endeavors. His cigar tobacco farming and production business had been steadily growing over the previous three years, and he was now considering the purchase of a large cigar distribution business in the US market. He asked my assistance in performing due diligence on some of the possible candidate companies for acquisition, and hence, in late 2001, I took off for Miami to begin the process.

From that time when my wife had declared that she wanted to file for divorce until January 2004, when I departed for an assignment in the Republic of Georgia, I was honestly in a consistent state of emotional chaos. In my mind, my life was in tatters, and I was honestly working in survival mode. Having vowed to myself as a young man that I would never be divorced and never subject children of mine to that which I had experienced as a child, I had not only broken that pledge once, but twice! This realization caused me significant pain and guilt, and I tortured myself unmercifully for this failing. Financially, the two divorces had collectively taken me from a situation of reasonably strong net worth down to the brink of bankruptcy. I had assumed a considerable amount of debt from the second divorce, but, now, thanks to Eduardo coming to my aid, I was at least able to cover my many monetary obligations and to keep my head barely above water. However, there was absolutely no financial cushion whatsoever in this situation. I was back where I had started after graduation from Georgetown, 30 years previously, and making ends meet on a month-to-month basis. So, here I was, single again, living a thousand miles away from my three kids, financially challenged, emotionally distraught, and feeling like an absolute failure as a husband and father. "How can life possibly get any worse?" I asked myself. The answer would soon be forthcoming.

Towards the late summer of 2002, a couple of new realities arose. First of all, my son was encountering some difficulties in his relationship with his mother, and it was clear that he really needed to come live with me. About that same time, I heard from another friend about an interesting start-up opportunity that was developing in the defense industry, and for which he could broker an introduction for me with the entrepreneur behind it. The job responsibilities in Eduardo's new cigar business had me on the road about 60% of the time, which was not conducive to being available for my son. In addition, although I was making ends meet financially, this new opportunity offered a "get rich quick," pot-of-gold-at-the-end-of-the-rainbow, scenario and it immediately caught my attention. I did make arrangements to meet with the entrepreneur in question on two occasions; from these meetings, I was suitably impressed with him and his business plan, as he described it to me. His goal was to build up the company over a few years time, make it appealing to larger defense companies, and then to flip it, making a substantial profit for himself and his key team members, of which I would be one. In a nutshell, the appeal of a quick potential resolution to my difficult financial situation, plus the ability to help my son through a difficult period with his mother, won out. As a result, I pulled up stakes from Miami, rented a home in Northern Virginia, where the new company was to be located, and moved with my son into our new environment, with high hopes for the future. I had been sliding hopelessly down a slippery slope, but I luckily had come upon a branch to which I could cling, stop my downward fall, and try to climb up the slope once again. Unfortunately, the branch shortly broke.

For the benefit of the reader, I should state at this point that I am neither proud of, nor happy to reflect upon, the period of time which followed. It clearly covers the absolute low point in my life, which I would never wish upon anyone; however, as will be shown later, it may have been an unfortunate but necessary development in the evolution of life. Sometimes, a person simply needs to fall to the very bottom of the deep ravine in order to regroup and to begin the long and difficult climb back to the surface.

After we had settled in northern Virginia, I enrolled my son in his new school and started to work with the new entrepreneurial venture. Soon after beginning the new job, it became quickly apparent that something was amiss. Although I had been assured that the new venture had identified investor capital to support the start-up, this was apparently not the case. Upon further examination and with eventual collaboration from others, it became clear that the entire venture was a hoax, and that the technology which would allegedly be developed did not even yet exist. Within a few weeks, the stark reality that I had not performed sufficient due diligence before making the jump, and that I had been lured into a scam, hit home. Thus, I found myself sliding briskly back down the slippery slope, and the bottom of the ravine was not yet in sight.

There I was, living in Northern Virginia with my son, with my expected source of income and eventual financial fluidity now having disappeared, and with no visible resources to support us. Added to those woes, to put it mildly, this new situation contributed to disintegrate my already fractured sense of self-esteem, and I plummeted to a level of unprecedented emotional lows. At that point, it might have been an easy decision to simply give up and succumb to the perceived forces of cruel nature, except that my young son was alongside, depending on me to find a resolution to our situation. Over the course of the following eight months, in addition to helping to obtain just desserts for the scam-artist in question, I desperately sought out new sources of revenue, while selling every possible asset which I still had to my name; I also had to resort to appeals to family and friends to help me financially to weather this storm. I have never prayed so hard for help as I did during this period, and, with the love and generosity of family and good friends, and prayers that were answered, we were able to keep afloat.

During this difficult period, I also came to the painful realization that, without my son being there and depending upon me, I may have simply given up. My only remaining asset was a life insurance policy that was large enough to cover all of my debts, plus some, and also allowed for the eventuality of suicide. As much as I am ashamed to admit it, in the depth of despair, I gave serious thought to this option.

On the positive side, because I was unsuccessful in finding another suitable job during this period, I was available to devote myself fully to the welfare of my son. I became a better, more involved parent for all of my children, and I played a more active parental role in my son's school activities. Mind you, things were tough, for both of us, but, as a result of this difficult time, we developed a much closer bond between us, one that perseveres to this day. I now shudder to think of what might have happened had he not been with me, depending on me to make things right. For fear of becoming too dramatic, I honestly believe that his presence during those days saved my life, for had he not been there with me, it might have been too easy to give up.

Towards May of 2003, I finally succeeded in identifying a couple of jobs that would enable us to begin the climb back out of the deep ravine. One was with a local defense contractor which would have enabled us to stay put in the area, and the second was a more lucrative, two-month gig with a separate defense contractor in the Republic of Georgia. Whereas the former certainly had appeal, I felt that Fate was beckoning me to accept the second one. Hence, at the end of the school year, we moved out of the house in Northern Virginia, and my son went to spend the summer in the Virginia mountains with my sister. The gradual and difficult climb up the slippery slope, albeit with a minor slip or two back downwards, had begun.

Chapter 18

Georgia on my Mind

Mtskheta, Republic of Georgia, Sunday, August 10, 2003

Since mid-June, 2003, I had been part of a Mobile Training Team (MTT), recruited by an American defense contractor, for a program to train Georgian Army Officers in Officer Personnel Management; the program was coordinated by the US Office of Defense Cooperation (ODC), under the auspices of the Georgian Ministry of Defense (MOD). My position on the MTT was as an Area Specialist, while the other members of the MTT were retired US Army Officers who had spent their Army careers as Personnel Officers. After two weeks at the US contractor's office to compile and coordinate the content of the training course, we were deployed to Tbilisi in early July to begin the course for designated Georgian Army Officers.

This trip was my first to Georgia, and I became enamored with the country from the outset. We stayed at the local Sheraton Hotel in Tbilisi for the duration of our visit, and, from the view off my hotel balcony, I could look out over the city and see architectural gems dating back as far as 1,400 years. From the historical perspective, Georgia's Christian heritage is recorded as far back as the third century, and the ancient churches and other historical and cultural monuments of old Tbilisi are highly impressive. The city of Tbilisi is relatively small, only a bit more than one million people, but it is a bustling one, where good restaurants and clubs abound, so there was always something to do after-hours. More importantly, however, the Georgian people are extremely hospitable by nature and go to great lengths to make foreign visitors feel welcome. We also found that the expatriate community in Tbilisi was considerably larger than expected, especially Americans. In fact, there was a significant USA sponsored Georgian Train and Equip (GTEP) program in which US Marines were training Georgian Armed Forces in infantry and mechanized tactics.

We conducted our training course in Officer Personnel Management within the Georgian Defense Academy, and we had about 30 students, predominantly males ranging in rank from Lieutenant to Lieutenant Colonel. Although a few of the Georgian officers spoke some English, we had a team of interpreters to assist with simultaneous translation of the course presentations. Because the officers also all spoke fluent Russian, I often spoke to them in Russian, which helped from the rapport-building perspective. Overall, the course went exceedingly well, and the Georgian officers and their higher command all seemed to be pleased with the results. After decades of domination by the USSR, their military command policies were all of Soviet extraction, but they desperately wanted to adhere more closely to the ways that western Armies managed their personnel policies. Because promotions and advancement within the Soviet model depended more upon Communist Party membership and cronyism than on competence, the Georgian officers, especially the younger ones, definitely wanted to implement a system that based officer promotions on ability rather than political influence.

Towards the end of the course, the Commanding General of the MOD J1 (Joint Staff Department for Personnel and Manpower) sponsored a picnic for all of the course participants and the staff members within the J1, probably about 100 people in all. The picnic was held on a Sunday outside of Tbilisi, near the picturesque ancient town of Mtskheta. Already well-accustomed over the previous six weeks to Georgian festivities of the like, we were prepared for a great time, with lots to eat and drink, lively music, and excellent company. Being a single man at the time, naturally, I was looking forward to spending the day with a multitude of beautiful Georgian ladies; however, I was honestly not prepared for the type of thunderbolt occurrence that transpired that day.

After everyone had arrived at the picnic site, which was in a wooded park outside of Mtskheta, about 20 kilometers from Tbilisi, the designated chefs began their extensive preparation for the lunch feast. In the meantime, a group of us took a bus tour of Mtskheta and its beautiful churches and museums. It was there that the "bolt" hit me when I noticed a beautiful young lady who had volunteered to be a tour guide for the foreigners during the outing. As seems always to have been the case during my lifetime, I was immediately smitten. I was unable to attract very much of her attention during the morning tour, but, as I watched her from afar, I was thoroughly taken with her ready smile and her extremely attentive and caring demeanor as she ensured that the small group of foreign guests received the full dose of Georgian hospitality. Amazingly enough, when she was paying closer attention to the other Americans than she was to me, I felt a twinge or two of jealousy! There is nothing like the romantic idealist to blow reality entirely out of proportion.

When we returned to the picnic area and prepared for lunch, I made a point of singling the young lady out for a face-to-face conversation. It turned out that she, a medical doctor by education, had just that last week joined the MOD J1 staff as a medical consultant. Because her self-taught English language capabilities were minimal, and my Georgian was limited to a few words and phrases, our ability to converse easily in Russian helped a great deal. The more we spoke, the more captivated I became so, when it was time to move to the lunch table, I asked if she would be kind enough to sit with me and to help translate the endless litany of toasts that would be offered during the meal by the "Tamada," the designated Georgian Toastmaster. She kindly agreed.

A wonderful two to three hour feast ensued, interspersed with no less than 30 traditional Georgian toasts covering almost every topic imaginable, each followed by the traditional consumption of copious amounts of Georgian wine. I had been able to continue the conversation with my new lady friend during much of the remainder of the afternoon, after which everyone boarded his or her respective means of transportation for the trip home, all well-fed and sufficiently-affected by the unending supply of wine. En route back to the hotel, my primary dilemma was that I had become hopelessly enamored with this beautiful young Georgian doctor, but we only had three more days in Tbilisi before we had to board a plane to return to the States. As we departed the picnic, I knew her name was Maka and that she worked somewhere within the MOD J1, but very little else. "How cruel Fate can be!" I thought, but I did know that I definitely wanted to see her again before we were to depart on Thursday.

As always, having been a well-trained case officer in my prior life, I was able to concoct a clever game plan through which to attempt to arrange one more meeting with her. My co-conspirator in this plan was one of our MTT interpreters, Nana, with whom I had become friendly over the past six weeks. She knew Maka, albeit not very well, but well enough to assist me. When we were at the offices of the J1 on Monday, the day after the picnic, I asked Nana to see if she could locate Maka within the office and to try to get me a phone number where I could reach her. She succeeded, and I called Maka at home that same evening.

It is important to note that Georgians, especially Georgian women, are extremely traditional and conservative in their upbringing. They are certainly not accustomed to the much more open and aggressive mannerisms of Americans in our style of courtship, and the idea of formal dating after one brief meeting certainly goes against accepted norms. However, probably thanks to Nana having done some prepping prior to my call, when I called Maka and invited her to dinner the following evening, she kindly accepted. We agreed that she would pick me up at my hotel, and we would drive to a near-by restaurant for a quiet dinner prior to my departure a day and one-half later.

The dinner was absolutely delightful, and there was dancing to be done as well. We were able to build upon our brief interaction of the previous Sunday and we enjoyed the evening immensely. Again, we were playing by Georgian rules, so the entire evening was quite proper and according to local etiquette. Because we both had to work early the next morning, we called a relatively early halt to the evening, and she drove me back to the hotel. When I asked her if she would permit me to kiss her, she broke into a big smile, extended her right hand to me, palm down, and allowed me to kiss her hand. The recollection of that scene makes me chuckle to this day, but, after all, those were the "Georgian Rules."

The MTT team departed Tbilisi during the early morning hours of Thursday, August 14, and, some 20 hours later, we arrived home very late that same night. It had been a very enjoyable and highly-rewarding experience, and I, for one, now had the motivation to see if I might be able to follow up this gig with something similar. Before I had departed from Georgia, I had become aware that there were several potential US-sponsored programs that were due to kick-off in the country within the coming months, and I decided that I would very much like to pursue them. I certainly was not sure that everything would fall into place, but I was definitely going to give it my best shot.

After I returned from Georgia, I further learned about several specific companies that were bidding on one DoD contract to supply a US-Contractor Team to assist the Georgian MOD in their transition from Soviet to western style modus operandi. This program was in keeping with the Georgian desire to become a member of NATO. The project was also very timely from the US-Georgian cooperation perspective because the fall of 2003 marked the time leading up to the "Rose Revolution," which was the November 2003 political revolt that led to the resignation of President Eduard Shevarnadze, and the rise to power of new President Mikheil Saakashvili. From the historical perspective, over the 11 years or so since Georgia had become independent from the USSR and survived their two-year civil war, the country had floundered, both politically and economically. Shevarnadze, the former Soviet Foreign Minister, who was ethnically Georgian, was the President of Georgia from 1995 until 2003, but, under his rule, the nation suffered from serious infrastructure problems, high unemployment, and rampant corruption. The Rose Revolution and the accession of the young and talented Saakashvili to the Presidency boded well for the possibility of increased US support for this former member state of the USSR.

Having returned from Georgia in mid-August, soon thereafter I began the application process for this new Georgia project. Meanwhile, I was able to identify a short-term defense contract assignment in

Hampton, Virginia, which offered financial support while I waited for the job in Georgia to open up. Psychologically, this was quite a difficult period for me, for I was still struggling emotionally from the financial and personal chaos into which I had fallen during the previous year. I was basically living out of a suitcase that fall of 2003, until future job prospects could work themselves out. In short, it was essentially a continuation of the very difficult mind-set of the previous year, despite the brief respite I had enjoyed during the Georgia MTT, and the fact that Fate had shown me a glimpse of hope by guiding me to meet Maka. However, I honestly had no way of knowing if I would ever see her again.

During this fall of 2003 while I was back in the States, Maka and I maintained steady email communications, augmented with an occasional phone call. The spirit of the communication was still more friendly than romantic, although there was a slight sense that there might be more than simply friendly interest. Nevertheless, until there was some indication that another opportunity might arise that would allow me to return to Georgia, neither of us could know whether the relationship would ever amount to anything more than just friendly emails back and forth.

Meanwhile, mired in a situation of uncertainty, I was still just trying to make ends meet. Towards the end of November, my temporary gig with the defense contractor came to a close, so finances again became critical; furthermore, I still had no word, one way or the other, as to whether I would be able to secure a position on the new Georgia program. Once again, it seemed as if life had hit rock-bottom, with no glimpse of sunlight on the horizon. However, as I have come to believe quite firmly over these past few years, we are never alone in moments of strife and desperation, and there are unseen forces that will never really allow us to take the total plunge. This particular phenomenon will be expounded upon in the next chapter.

In the meantime, as November passed and we started to move closer to Christmas, I finally heard that there was an opening for me to join the project team going to Tbilisi, and I was asked to be ready to deploy soon after the beginning of the New Year. This news was highly welcome and hinted that life might be starting to take a turn for the better. The well-paying and interesting position in Tbilisi was about to come to fruition, and I would also be able to see if my current romantic inclination was more than just a passing fancy.

I arrived in Tbilisi under the new contract in early January, 2004. I was to work as one of two Personnel / Administrative Officers assigned to assist the J1 in the MOD's quest to transform the Georgian Armed Forces from a Soviet model to a western-oriented military. The Georgian leadership hoped this would enhance their future possibility to qualify for membership in NATO. Our entire team was comprised of about one dozen members, most of whom were retired Army or Marine officers, with specific expertise relevant to one or another of the MOD Joint Staff functions. The group which had been assembled by the US contractor company was a fairly well-qualified team, and largely a good bunch of guys. Some of the team, like me, were approaching this job in the spirit of the true romantic idealist, helping Georgia evolve from the dark shadows of the Soviet Union; some, on the other hand, were just there to make a buck.

The first few days were mainly spent getting settled in and learning the parameters of our team assignment. It was good to return to see the J1 Commanding General and his key staff members, with whom I had become friends during the summer MTT course. It was almost as if I had not been absent for the previous five months. We were all glad to see each other and to have the chance to work together once again. Naturally, I also had a pressing ulterior motive for my return to Georgia and, thankfully, I was able to meet up with Maka on my first full day at the MOD. It was wonderful to see her again! As noted previously, we had maintained email communications throughout the previous five months, but these were mostly friendly chit chat in nature. Although I knew that my interest went beyond just casual friendship, I still had no indication as to whether she felt the same.

After all, we had only two get-togethers, five months previously, and there was a major age difference between us. Perhaps this fantasy existed only in my head? Time would certainly tell.

When it became clear that I had been accepted to join the team going to Tbilisi, I had emailed Maka to give her the news and to ask her for her help in researching furnished apartments available in the city. After I arrived in Tbilisi, I registered at the Sheraton Hotel, where I had stayed during my previous visit, but I would be able to save quite a bit of money and have a much more pleasant and comfortable living experience, if I could rent an apartment in the city. When I saw Maka that first day, she already had done quite a bit of research and had a list of suitable apartments; moreover, she was kind enough to assist me as we visited the list of apartments over the span of the next week. We did not have to look at too many before I saw one which met all of my needs. It was conveniently located right in city center, not far from MOD and close to many good restaurants. Spacious with room for guests, the apartment had a comfortable sitting room with a fireplace and an outdoor patio to accommodate my occasional desire for a cigar. Thus, within the first two weeks, I was set up, and ready to see what Fate had in store for me.

As far as the job was concerned, it became clear from the beginning that the evolution of the Georgian MOD was going to be a slow and grueling process. Because Georgia had been under the domination of the USSR for over 70 years, their entire military had been formed and managed under systems developed by the Soviets. Change from the old system into a completely new manner of managing their national defense was going to be a difficult and lengthy process. It also had become quite clear that, even though the United States Government had generously allocated funds to send the contractor team to Georgia to assist with the process, our actual influence in bringing about change would be minimal. Contrary to my romantic idealistic mentality, that I would be able to help to transform Georgia magically into a NATO juggernaut within the matter of a few months, reality sometimes just doesn't conform.

Challenging as it might be to transform a Communist-trained

Armed Forces into a Western-oriented one, it might be said that this is no less a daunting task than to win the heart of a traditional Georgian maiden. Certainly, there were some similarities in terms of the amount of diligence and concentrated effort required to make such a change come about; however, challenging and frustrating as the heart-winning exercise may have been, it was, at least, a highly enjoyable one.

In any event, over the course of the next month or so, Maka and I saw each other quite often during the work day at MOD as well as during our free time and weekends, although there was still not much to indicate that the relationship was going anywhere fast. We truly enjoyed each other's company, and I was even invited to a family dinner to meet her parents and siblings; nevertheless, I began to think that the romantic interest was unfortunately only one-sided.

The situation came to a head one late February evening when the Commanding General of the J1 had a party at a local restaurant for the J1 staff and foreign advisors. Maka and I were both there, but I had seriously begun to believe that our relationship was just a figment of my imagination and that, although we were good friends, it was not going to go past friendship. During this typical Georgian supra (feast), which abounded with great food, lots of wine, good music, and dancing, everyone was having a good time. Maka and I had spent a lot of time together during the party and had danced a few times, but she spent an equal amount of time dancing and hanging out with other people and apparently really enjoying doing so. After watching these shenanigans for a reasonable amount of time, I simply decided that I had seen enough, and, unhappy and feeling a bit depressed, I left the party for home.

Sometime later, not seeing me anywhere, Maka began to look for me, couldn't find me, and had been advised that I had left earlier. She was perplexed that I had simply left without saying good-bye and was apparently was a bit worried, so she gave me a call on my cell phone. By that time, I was already at home, feeling more depressed than before, and trying to drown my sorrows in drink. She asked me what had happened, where I had gone, and why, but I was vague and evasive in my responses; nevertheless, it was clear to her that I was upset, so she decided to come to the apartment to talk with me.

In a nutshell, when she had arrived, we had a "come-to-Jesus" meeting of sorts, during which straight talk and honest conversation became a welcome substitute for what had become a stalemate in our ongoing dialogue. The full scope of our feelings for each other were openly expressed and acknowledged for the first time, and our romantic, versus friendly, relationship officially began from that point forward. Mind you, we were still living by the Georgian calendar of romantic progression, so I can honestly say that the earth didn't move that evening, but we had now at least broken down the invisible barriers that had corralled us, which would now allow the relationship to progress more normally and to grow deeper.

Over the next few months, the situation in the workplace became increasingly frustrating. The MOD staff was in a state of constant change with many officers being purged primarily for political differences with the newly elected and instituted administration. In addition, our team was having less-than-desired results in our collective efforts to help enact change for the better. For the normal guy (of which I was unfortunately not one), it was enough to be the beneficiary of a nice compensation package, to live in a foreign country, and to enjoy the benefits of the expatriate lifestyle; for the romantic idealist, however, we were falling far short of what we should have been building in the wake of Communism.

Fortunately for me, I was not the only quixotic character on the staff, so I at least had a few others in whom to confide. However, by the end of my third month there, although the defense contracting company which sponsored us was making a healthy profit, and most of the team were satisfied that they had a decent job and were making good money, I was beginning to feel that the mission of our team, at least as I perceived it, was somewhat hopeless. In my mind, although I was truly enthralled by my romantic relationship, I was coming to understand that I might be wasting my time from a work perspective. I simply did not feel that our presence there was going to bring about much, if any, positive change within the Georgian

MOD. Simultaneously, some issues were developing at home with my kids that weighed heavily on my mind, and I was beginning to feel increasingly guilty that I was not more available to them. If the reader is beginning to sense that being a died-in-the-wool romantic idealist is an affliction which can lead to real inner conflict, then I must be making the point accurately.

About four or five weeks later, when the situation wasn't improving and the other issues playing on my mind had grown more troublesome, my frustration level finally boiled to the surface; I had a serious falling out with the chief of the team, and we reached a mutual decision that it was time for me to leave. As one might imagine, the most serious downside of this development, outside of walking away from a good income, was that my relationship with Maka would face a serious turning point. I stayed on in Tbilisi for a few more weeks to wrap up my business-related affairs, and, most importantly, to discuss with Maka where we would go from there. Obviously, this change would dramatically complicate things, but we decided if our love was real, and if Fate was kind, everything would all work out in the long run.

I departed Tbilisi for my return to the States in mid-May of 2004. I did so with a heavy heart in that my romantic relationship would now be put to a test; however, I had also come to the realization that everything would work out as Fate intended it to. As the next few months passed, Maka and I kept in close communication and continued to look ahead. We managed to obtain a visitor's visa for her to come to the States for a 10-day visit in August of that year, during which we came to the conclusion that we deeply wanted to spend our lives together, and we began to plan accordingly. Upon her return to Tbilisi, we initiated the proper proceedings to obtain a K-1 Fiancée Visa for her to come to the USA permanently. This process required mountains of paperwork and a lengthy period of time to bring to a conclusion. However, by early March of 2005, the visa had been approved, and Maka prepared to join me later that month to begin our new life together.

The terms of the K-1 visa dictated that the intended marriage be consummated within 90 days of the arrival of the fiancée in the USA. Therefore, on June 1, 2005, Maka and I were married in our new home of Virginia Beach. We had decided to keep the ceremony simple and we were married in front of a Justice of the Peace in a beautiful outdoor setting near the beach. As I write these words, we have been married now for six wonderful years, and I can honestly say that I have never been happier. As the reader may also conclude in chapters yet to come, the circumstances which brought us together and which allowed us to enter into this blissful state of marriage were certainly a matter of Fate at play. Going back to our chance meeting on August 10, 2003, to the circumstances and timing surrounding the follow-on assignment to Georgia, and everything that transpired afterwards, I am unwavering in my strong belief that everything in life does happen for a well-defined and intended reason. I have also come to believe that, despite any challenges or personal difficulties which we may face in life, Fate is ultimately kind as we endeavor to make sense of our existence on earth.

As I reflect upon the happy events of these past eight years, I am often reminded of the lyrics of the famous Ray Charles song, for I forever have "Georgia on my mind," and, as it turns out, deeply imbedded in my heart as well.

Part IV

Observations on Life

Prologue to Part IV

A Life-Changing Revelation

One Particular Day in the Fall of 2003

I once attended a lecture on the philosophy of the ancient Sufis that addressed their stages of spiritual development. I was particularly struck by the premise that in order to transcend to a level of spiritual enlightenment, a person must first pass through the level of despair. Now, I certainly do not profess to have reached anywhere near a level of spiritual enlightenment, but the events of one fateful fall day in 2003 did provide me with a firm belief that there was truth in that ancient philosophy.

As noted previously, during a certain period in 2002-2003, I had found myself in a very difficult and undesirable state of mind in which I had come to believe that life was looking pretty hopeless. In retrospect, I believe that I had become my own worst enemy in that I began to envision myself as having been victimized by a steady course of negative events. My unwanted divorce had been finalized, my financial situation was catastrophic, and I seemed to have completely lost my way in life; therefore, on this particular fall day, with things having taken a perceived turn for the worse, I was feeling quite overwhelmed and hopeless. As I had done previously, I allowed my thoughts to dwell on the possibility that, because my life insurance policy permitted payment for suicide, my family might be better off if I were dead. I am ashamed of that mind-set now, but, right or wrong, that was the unfortunate state of mind in which I found myself trapped on that day.

I was living in Virginia Beach at the time. On that day, during which the despair seemed the most demonic, I recall feeling the desperate need to leave the house for a very long walk on the beach; I walked for hours, mostly in a mental daze, and on the return route home, I eventually found myself passing the Edgar Cayce Association for Research and Enlightenment (A.R.E.). Because I had walked about nine to ten miles, I had the urge to rest, so I sat down in the A.R.E. Meditation Garden, a very peaceful spot just outside the main building. In line with the purpose of the setting, I began to meditate and to pray for help and the spiritual guidance to deal with my plight. Amazingly, during this meditation, a vision suddenly came to me that had a life-changing impact and helped me to climb out of the state of despair into which I had fallen.

The vision was vivid and as clear a message as I could ever imagine. In the vision, I saw Jesus Christ making the transformation from spirit to man and from man back to spirit again. The experience was fleeting, but impactive, and the clarity which came upon me was instantaneous. Contrary to what I had been taught to believe in my childhood religious education, the understanding was revealed to me that this one life in which I found myself was not the end of the road. I was offered the glimpse that life was not a one-and-done shot, but rather a series of incarnations on earth. Having been in an intense mind-set of pain and failure, the impact of this revelation felt like a millstone being lifted from my shoulders; rather than "burning in the fires of hell," as Sister Alexis had preached in grammar school, could the vision mean that I would be offered the opportunity to try to do better in the next life?

This revelation and the understanding that evolved from it all happened in an instant. Suddenly, as in the words of the hymn *Amazing Grace*, I felt that "I once was blind, but now I see." Still quite amazed by the intensity of my vision and epiphany, I left the Meditation Garden with a feeling of wonder and indescribable relief. Having been mired in a state of despair, my prayer had apparently been heard, and the understanding of the important message had been clearly conveyed to me. Thanks to my unseen spiritual guides, this revelation created a light at the end of a long tunnel, which now had become visible for me and which offered me hope.

As a result of this occurrence, even though my actual circumstances were largely unchanged, I found renewed enthusiasm for life, and I began intensive research into the theory of reincarnation. The close proximity of the A.R.E. library, the second largest metaphysical library on earth (the Vatican Library being the largest), offered me a tremendous resource through which to delve more deeply into this phenomenon; I also began to participate actively in the various activities at A.R.E., which I found to be reinforcing. All along the way, I felt a spiritual presence guiding me down a path that might eventually lead me to a station of inner peace.

On that one particular day in the fall of 2003, as I was held tightly in the grip of despair, my prayer for guidance was gracefully answered. That fateful day blessed me with an understanding that ultimately has provided me with a much higher level of personal well-being and contentment as well as the will to live this life, and those in the future, to the fullest.

Chapter 19

The Vision Quest

Although I had experienced spiritual yearnings throughout my life, it was during the mid-1990's when I began to feel a compelling need to become closer to my spiritual side. Because I was then in my mid-40's, I suppose some people might call it the beginning of the mid-life crisis. Whatever the reason, I could not ignore the strong inclinations that I was feeling and I began to delve more deeply into my spiritual needs.

My first such experiment in my search was the result of the recommendation of a friend of mine, who had met a spiritual therapist while seeking to address some of her own demons. My initial meeting with the gentleman was interesting and eye-opening, and I decided that he could possibly help me as well. After the introductory session, he invited me to attend one of the workshops he was conducting for other like-minded individuals in search of meaning in their lives; I decided to participate to see where it might lead.

The first such workshop was an introductory weekend program held at a facility in Washington, DC. Although I had agreed to give the session a shot, it was indeed a very different, yet certainly a thought-provoking, experience. There were numerous exercises in meditation, yoga, the value of truth-telling in our everyday existence, and other assorted sessions. One exercise in particular I found to be particularly strange and a bit uncomfortable; however, in retrospect, it offered a valuable insight into understanding that we are all part of a universal spiritual community separated largely by physical and ego-driven differences.

We were seated, cross-legged on the floor, in two lines facing each other, knee-to-knee and face-to-face; we were to conduct this brief exercise several times, facing a series of individuals, moving down the line after having completed it with one person to another. When facing the individual across from us, we were instructed to look directly into the other person's eyes, avoiding the normal human inclination to look away, especially at such close proximity. The idea was to begin to view the person opposite you as another spirit, versus a physical being, by looking deeply into the eyes, the window to the soul. This method would enable us to "see" them strictly as one spirit to another, rather than as a human of a different race, a different ethnic background, or a different gender. When faced by this other spiritual entity, we would then alternate by speaking the words "you love me" to the other as a demonstration of the spiritual love that all members of the human community can or should feel for each other. If the reader is already getting a sense for the potential discomfort that this exercise might cause, hold on, it gets better.

The most instructional aspect of the exercise occurred for me when I was seated across from an East Indian gentleman, who was wearing a turban and who was, in terms of physical attributes, quite "appearance-challenged," which is politically correct (PC) for downright homely. However, after staring into his eyes (hence, into his soul) for several long minutes, in complete disregard of his physical appearance, all-the-while stating the mantra "you love me," I had to admit that the lesson of the exercise became clear. That is, if we can look past our physical differences and learn to appreciate all members of the human community as simply another spirit inhabiting a suit of skin and bones, then there might be less strife in the world and more human understanding. In order to appreciate the value of this exercise, we only have to watch the news on any given day to learn that, somewhere in the world, people are fighting and killing each other simply because of tribal, ethnic, racial, and/or religious differences. Might all of this war and chaos be alleviated if we learned to concentrate on our spiritual unity rather than our apparent physical differences?

For the sake of contrast, one of the other persons across from whom I lined up that day was a highly-attractive, gregarious, younger female. The exercise was entirely the same, but it was equally, if not more, uncomfortable. As hard as I tried to look solely into her eyes and to concentrate on her as only a spirit with the same diligence as I had exercised with the Indian gentleman, I suddenly realized that I was failing. As she and I proceeded with the same exercise, stating alternatively "you love me," I found to my dismay that I was becoming quite physically aroused. Oh well, sometimes you win, sometimes you lose! Nevertheless, the lesson from that day was a valuable one that was not entirely lost on me; it is one which I try to remember every day of my life, although, I admit, not always successfully.

I was sufficiently interested from this initial workshop to take two more from this gentleman over the ensuing few years; these were longer, week-long workshops that greatly expanded upon the principles initially offered in the shorter session. Again, these workshops concentrated on truth-telling in our everyday existence, meditation, yoga, and many other worthwhile lessons geared towards gaining spiritual enlightenment and inner peace. In addition, the workshops concentrated on developing a life mission based on bringing creativity into our lives. These sessions were also very instructive and eye-opening, but they were especially worthwhile from the perspective of creating our life's mission. Although I had experienced other senses of this yearning in the past, it was here that I first began to formulate actual plans for writing a book. It would still require another 13 years or so to bring this plan into fruition, but, as we all know and appreciate, Rome was not built in a day.

Jump ahead to 2001. The yearnings for spiritual growth had continued to increase, and, with my marriage in a state of flux, I felt the need to get more serious with my pursuit. I had heard of another workshop, conducted by a different organization, which was called "Vision Quest" and which was held in a northern wilderness area of Ontario, Canada. As described by the program, the "Vision Quest is an age-old rite of passage valued by all great religions where individuals go alone into the wilderness to seek a vision from God for themselves and for the benefit of the whole community. Our ancestors knew what we have long forgotten, that at times of crisis and transition, we need a ritual that reconnects us with who we are, what we are about and with the Wisdom of all life." At this point in my history, this workshop presented precisely what I felt that I needed to address, so, in mid-August of 2001, I drove up to Northern Ontario to embark upon my own Vision Quest.

The eight-day program was conducted in a Spartan camp with no modern conveniences, located on an island in the middle of a pristine lake in the northern Ontario wilderness. In addition to the Vision Quest itself, which was preceded by the Native American purification ceremony of the sweat lodge and other preliminary rituals, there were also frequent sessions conducted by the workshop staff in dream interpretation and other spiritually-oriented instruction. The real beauty of the program was the spirit of community involvement and partnership of the 50 or so other students and staff to assist each attendee in working through those individual issues that prompted participation in the Vision Quest. It turned out to be a tremendously impressive experience in many ways.

The numerous sessions on dream interpretation were both highly enlightening and useful. Whereas all of us experience dreams, which we usually forget upon awakening, the recollection and understanding of the content of our dreams, which are in essence messages from our subconscious, can be incredibly instructive. Without going into a long narrative on what I discovered, I can attest that I learned to appreciate how incredibly useful dream interpretation can be in our quest to understand and embrace our spiritual needs.

The Vision Quest itself was quite a unique experience. After the purification ritual of the sweat lodge, we paddled our canoes across the lake to the deserted area of our choice and identified the site for our individual vision quest. There we spent the next 48 hours in complete isolation (except for the occasional moose or squirrel), seeking a "vision," an encounter with the Mystery and Wisdom of all life. Thus, I spent two days in observance of nature, quiet meditation, and contemplation of my mission in life, diligently seeking the answer.

After two days of solitude, a good 60% of which was spent in the rain and cold, I honestly did not experience any particular vision, nor did I feel that I was the recipient of any new or earthshaking wisdom;

however, having spent two days in quiet reflection and meditation, I did come away with a whole new appreciation of life with self and of living in the moment. I began to understand better how a life of consistent meditation and simply taking the time to "smell the roses" can lead to a much higher feeling of inner peace. Rather than allow ourselves to be caught up constantly in the ego-driven need to do something, meaning to act as "human-doers," the ability "to be" in the moment, as a "human being," devoid of mind-motivated stress, anxiety, anger, and/or resentments, was a tremendous lesson in how to live a better life. As one of the instructors so aptly pointed out before we departed the island, the "longest journey a man can make in his life is to go from here (pointing to his head) to here (pointing to his heart)." When I find myself getting caught up in the daily stress and strain of life absorbed in a stream of mental chatter, I always try to recall the meaning, and wisdom, of those words.

Having completed the Vision Quest program and departed from the pristine beauty of the northern wilderness, I returned back to the reality of life and all of its many challenges. Despite the wisdom and glimpse of inner peace that I had just encountered, the situation of a wife who wanted to go her separate way and the financial difficulties that were visible on the horizon brought me quickly and painfully back to reality. As depicted in previous chapters, the period of 2002 – 2003 yet to come would seriously challenge whatever inner peace I had managed to find during the Vision Quest experience. Nevertheless, the need and search for spiritual strength and contentment continued, largely without much notable success, until that fateful fall day in 2003, at the A.R.E. Meditation Garden in Virginia Beach, which was covered in the Prologue to Part IV.

With the life-changing vision that came to me on that specific occasion, and the motivation and excitement that accompanied it, I thrust myself into the A.R.E. community in an attempt to take better advantage of the wonderful resource that was just blocks away from my home. In addition to the metaphysical library and the exceptional wisdom contained therein, I began to attend classes and conferences on topics of interest to me, such as meditation and reincarnation. In so doing, one of the tools that A.R.E. opened up to me was the idea to experience a "Past Life Regression," through which a person could gain a glimpse into prior lives experienced during the process of reincarnation and perhaps even gain insights into the current one. A.R.E. had a list of licensed hypnotherapists who were qualified to conduct these sessions, so I went through a selective process and finally chose one to approach.

Past life regression is a technique that uses hypnosis to enable the subject to recover memories of past incarnations. The therapist utilizes hypnosis to place the subject into a relaxed state and then leads him through suggestion back in time to a place where the subject spent a past life of some personal significance. There is nothing of a predetermined nature in this process, and the subject simply is drawn into an envisioned environment of some apparent importance to his ongoing spiritual development. I had no anticipatory expectations whatsoever of what, if anything, would result from this exercise; however, from the incredibly impactive experience that I encountered therein, I came away from that three-hour session a firm believer.

After a lengthy process of bringing me into a relaxed, hypnotic state, the therapist guided me down an imagined time-line into my past lives, along which I stopped and viewed a past incarnation. Soon, and quite surprisingly, I envisioned myself in a mountainous environment, which appeared to be a small European alpine farm. There were no distinct revelations about the specific date and place of this memory, but from the looks of the area and the domicile, I concluded that I had found myself in about an 18th century setting, perhaps in rural Austria. The farm house in which I lived with my wife was quite modest, with few furnishings. My clothing looked much like I would envision a European farmer to be dressed in those days, and my wife did as well. She was busy knitting at the time, sitting silently in a rocking chair with a child's empty crib nearby. We were not communicating and the sense I felt was that our marriage had become loveless, with little interaction between the two of us. As the therapist talked me through the scene, it provoked a memory that our young child had recently died and that his death was the source of the apparent rift between us.

It was at that moment that I became besieged by an onslaught of extreme grief, and, although still in a state of hypnosis, the feeling that overcame me was as real as anything I had ever consciously experienced during my lifetime. I felt an intense physical pain and began to weep uncontrollably, gasping for breath as I dealt with this state of hysteria. At this point, the therapist began to reverse the process and to bring me gently back to full consciousness. However, after I woke up, I was still very much shaken by the intensity of the experience that I had just had. Eventually, as I relaxed and recovered from the episode, I came to the realization that I had felt some strong personal guilt for the death of our child, plus the sense that my wife held that incident against me. I was amazed by the very real atmospherics I had experienced through that glimpse into my past life, and it took me quite awhile afterwards to begin to put the experience into proper perspective.

In a nutshell, if a person studies the precepts of reincarnation, our series of incarnations on earth are all progressively intertwined; a person's karma from a previous life becomes a focal point for the next, providing issues on which to work and improve. For example, if a person departs a past incarnation with unanswered needs or a feeling of guilt for one shortcoming or another, then that issue may be subconsciously important to the individual in a future life. Having come to such a realization by virtue of this past life regression, it also helped to explain why parts of this life had seemed so important; in this particular case, my apparent issue from this past life explained clearly to me why the care for my children had been such a high priority in this life. It also seemed to clarify the reason for my previous pledges never to suffer a divorce, and hence never subject my children to the pain of such an event. The past life regression experience further explained the severe level of guilt I felt as a result of having broken those pledges. As painful as the insights gained from the regression may all have been, however, it did help to bring some clarity to life, and this was obviously welcome.

The time period covered by the aforementioned events and programs spanned nearly 10 years; clearly, the pursuit of spiritual growth is a slow, deliberate, and evolutionary process. As noted in the Prologue to this part, as believed by the Sufis, the state of spiritual enlightenment mandates that one first pass through a phase of true despair. As learned from my personal experience, I interpret this philosophy to mean that a state of despair strongly motivates the search for meaning and sincere prayers and meditations to help seek resolution. In short, it means actually taking measures to understand and nurture our spiritual side, for, as the philosophy of reincarnation defines, we are spiritual beings incarnated perpetually into human form, our suit of skin and bones that surrounds our true spiritual selves. Our bodily existences begin and end as we return to dust, but our spirits live forever.

Since that time when the events noted above transpired, the past seven years have truly witnessed difficulties and challenges of their own; such is the inescapable reality of our lives on earth. However, despite those realities, during these past seven years, I have also felt a much higher level of well-being and happiness than I heretofore experienced. The hand of Fate certainly played an undeniable role in blessing me with my current wife, Maka; Fate led me on that path to Georgia and back which brought her into my life. Moreover, the overall spiritual development that has transpired over the past years has made my life much more blessed in so many ways and has brought me a semblance of inner peace that so frustratingly evaded me in my younger years. It has also brought me the wisdom to become a better husband, a more-involved father, and a better friend. Along the way, I have found that the influence of many good friends who are also invested in their own quests for spiritual development, and the assumption of "an attitude of gratitude" for life's many gifts and challenges, also have been instrumental in my own steady progress.

The journey is far from complete; this is an odyssey that will last until my last breath in this incarnation and will almost certainly continue into the next. However, my sincere hope is that each of us will endeavor to make that long spiritual journey, from mind to heart, an odyssey that will ultimately lead to a greater level of inner peace and contentment.

Chapter 20

Life is a Good Cigar Shop

Okay, because this chapter has been placed in my "Observations on Life" section, perhaps a few words of explanation in advance might be appropriate. Although the title of this chapter will probably be understandable to most cigar aficionados, for the reader who is not a connoisseur of premium cigars, and, therefore, not a frequent visitor to good cigar shops, it may not make a great deal of sense. Therefore, please humor me as I attempt to explain.

One of my favorite movies of all time is *Life is a House*. For those who haven't seen it, and I encourage all to do so, this is a movie about passion, building supportive relationships, and simply living life to the fullest. Hence, the title of this chapter is a take-off on the name of that excellent movie.

For the past 15 years or so, I have been regularly frequenting what I consider to be good cigar shops. My definition of a good cigar shop is one that serves much more of a purpose than simply selling cigars. In such shops all across this country, I have consistently witnessed conducive environments in which men and women, who share a passion for cigars, gather together in the spirit of community, commonality and camaraderie, regardless of any differences in race, religion, politics, and/or social standing. The phrase "The Brotherhood of the Leaf" is often used to describe the bonds created in these locales and within the industry in general, and, from my experience, this expression describes the community well.

Within Native American cultures, tobacco has a traditionally sacred purpose; it is used as a purifying element prior to important gatherings, to show respect for visitors and to give spiritual protection. As I am informed, the Pipe Ceremony is a sacred ritual for connecting the physical and spiritual worlds. The smoke which is exhaled from the mouth symbolizes the truth to be spoken, and the plumes of smoke provide a path for prayers to reach the Great Spirit and for the wisdom of the Great Spirit to travel down to Mother Earth.

Stating that cigar smoking fills a similar cultural and/or spiritual need in our society would be an exaggeration; however, there are some real similarities. For example, whenever I have the need to ponder a particular issue, or when I feel the urge to reflect upon life, I have always found that a cigar helps to quiet the mind and assists the reflective, meditative process. I believe most avid cigar smokers would agree with that concept. Looking at this premise strictly from the social perspective, the assemblage of kindred spirits that are typically found in any good cigar shop nurtures a sense of community and brotherhood in which meaningful discussion of life's issues commonly takes place. Just as often, a gathering of cigar smokers might typically just be for reason of raucous fun while watching a football game or playing a game of cards, but the key ingredient that forms the foundation of all such events is the bond of the community.

The "Cigar Boom" is a phenomenon that began in late 1992 and coincided with the publication of the glossy and glamorous *Cigar Aficionado* magazine; the 5-6 years which followed marked incredible growth, in all respects, in the cigar industry. During the years prior to the cigar boom, the cigar industry in the United States was largely stagnant and relatively unattractive, and good cigar shops were rather rare. However, during the boom years, the industry began to witness an evolution in the appearance and modus operandi of cigar stores; these evolved from simple retail outlets offering over-the-counter-purchases of tobacco products to full-service facilities with a wide range of premium, hand-rolled cigars, well-stocked walk-in humidors, and comfortable seating and entertainment to accommodate customers. In essence, during that time period, the cigar store began to be more of a local social destination, rather than merely a store in which to purchase cigars.

I worked in different capacities within the cigar industry over a period spanning about eight years, and I can honestly attest that I have never enjoyed any other endeavor quite as much. Although I started smoking cigars regularly during my late 20's, my exposure to and knowledge of the industry was quite limited. After becoming involved in the industry in 1997, thanks to the initiative of my good friend and prep school roommate, Eduardo Fernandez, this exposure provided me with a whole new appreciation of the science and artistic flair that goes into the creation of a good, hand-rolled premium cigar. In this regard, the essentials for producing a quality cigar product are almost identical to those that go into the production of wine: sound agricultural technology, extensive nurturing of the crop during the growth process, strict attention and proper aging during the fermentation process, and then expert blending, production, packaging, and marketing of the final product.

Whereas the production side of the cigar process is an amazing one, of which I am still very much in awe, from my perspective, the real joy of the industry is on the distribution side, primarily in dealing with the cigar retailers and their customers. Each cigar store tends to have its own personality; however, whereas the clientele may differ somewhat from store to store, the underlying sense of brotherhood and community is the consistent hallmark of each.

During the final two years of my work in the industry, 2004-2006, I assisted Eduardo with a US distribution company that he had purchased in Miami. As Regional Sales Manager for the eastern half of the country, I managed and supported the seven to eight independent sales representatives through which the company marketed and sold its cigars to tobacconists throughout the region. Working and travelling with these sales reps, I was able to spend a significant amount of time in hundreds of cigar stores from Maine to Florida, from Wisconsin to Mississippi, and everywhere in between, and got to know many of their customers. Although some stores were more upscale and more conducive to the development of a loyal local community, the vast majority of all of the cigar stores into which I entered were typical of that which I described above, a welcoming gathering place for the kindred spirits comprising the Brotherhood of the Leaf.

In addition to the enjoyment I derived from working that job, I also was blessed to develop numerous close friendships that still exist to this day. I have come to believe that everyone, through the course of his life's existence, comes into contact with other human beings who have been put into his path for a reason, to help to achieve some personal development need. As previously indicated, this trend has been true throughout the entirety of my life; however, I found this to be particularly true during the years of my involvement in the cigar industry. Granted, this was a time in which I was evolving through an especially challenging period in my own existence, and I was clearly more sensitive to the possibility of kindred spirits entering my life; nevertheless, the Brotherhood of the Leaf did introduce me to numerous folks who played a major role in the manner in which I looked at life.

First of all, I have mentioned that my old friend, Eduardo Fernandez, was the one who got me involved in the industry in the first place. He has been a close and loyal friend since we first met in prep school some 46 years ago, and it was a pleasure to work with him in his new endeavors in the cigar industry.

Thinking back to our prep school days, I remember one Sunday afternoon when we were discussing what we wanted to do when we grew up. Eduardo's response was funny at the time, but prophetic in the long run. Eduardo was born in Cuba, and his family fled to the USA after Fidel Castro assumed power. His father was a respected attorney in Havana, and his mother a highly-regarded architect, and the family was very well-off within Cuban society. Like his brothers, Eduardo was being primed to assume his rightful place in American society and was expected to pursue a career as a lawyer, banker, architect, doctor, or some other distinguished position.

So, back to the aforementioned Sunday afternoon discussion of our preferred career path, in reply to my question, Eduardo responded with, "I want to be a farmer."

I laughed and told him that he was full of shit. "Besides," I said, "your family would never allow it!"

After graduation from prep school, and going to one of the nation's top universities to study business finance, Eduardo enjoyed successful careers as an international banking executive and entrepreneur. Nevertheless, fast forwarding some 30 years from the day of that prep school conversation, he had indeed established one of the largest multi-faceted farming operations in Nicaragua, employing thousands of people. His story just goes to demonstrate the incredible power of having a dream and of taking the steps, however illogical or improbable, to achieve that dream. Eduardo's story has continually inspired me over the years and is one of the major reasons why I am finally writing this book.

In Las Vegas during the 1998 Retail Tobacco Dealers Association (RTDA) trade show, in which I was participating, another person who would have a strong and lasting influence upon my spiritual development came into my life. Bob Greenwood is a Native North American from Canada and a clan leader from the Mohawk tribe. He and I hit it off immediately, became fast friends during the short time of the trade show, and have kept in close contact over the years. As we got to know each other well, I found in Bob a positive spiritual influence. In keeping with his Native American heritage, Bob has a very strong spiritual side and connects with nature and with people intuitively.

Because tobacco played such a significant role in the cultural and spiritual life of his people, it was fitting that Bob had found himself in the tobacco industry. Within a few years of our initial meeting, when life had taken a severe turn south for me, Bob's friendship and mentorship became very important as I was trying to work my way through my period of personal despair. We made a few trips to Nicaragua on cigar business, and we visited each other several times, both in Canada and in the States, during which time he assumed an increasingly influential role as a spiritual mentor and guide. In fact, my attendance at the Vision Quest in Canada and my initial exposure to A.R.E. in Virginia Beach were largely influenced by Bob. To this day, I often recite a prayer to the Great Spirit which Bob said had often helped him through times of personal challenge, and it helps me as well. Although we do not see each other quite as often these days, Bob remains a valued friend and spiritual mentor in whom I place a great deal of importance.

In the spring of 2005, when I was working as a regional sales manager for Eduardo's distribution company, we invited a small group of important retail store customers to a tour of our tobacco and cigar facilities in Nicaragua. During that week-long trip, I met Don Barco, a cigar store owner from Tampa, Florida, with whom I immediately made a connection. Don and I were about the same age, with a similar sense of humor, and we spent most of that week laughing uproariously and just having a good time. We kept in close contact afterwards and I made a point of visiting his store in Tampa as frequently as my schedule allowed. About three months following the Nicaragua trip, Don experienced a couple of serious life challenges. First he was diagnosed with prostate cancer followed soon thereafter by the sudden loss of his son; hence, I was compelled to try in any way possible to support him as he worked his way through those extremely difficult times. To this day, Don expresses his appreciation for the support that I allegedly gave him; however, to be honest, I believe that I drew more spiritual strength from the manner in which he managed to survive those challenging times than I ever contributed to him. In any event, it was another of those instances in which the Brotherhood of the Leaf made a strong impact on my spiritual journey.

Finally, it was in Don's cigar shop, King Corona Cigars, where I had my most memorable cigar-related spiritual experience. My wife, Maka, and I had dropped into the store to visit with Don and to spend the afternoon there with him. Don was not there at the time, so we sat down at the sandwich bar in the store and awaited his return. About that time, a gentleman sat down at the bar next to us, smoking a cigar. He was alone, and I noticed that he seemed distraught, so I started a conversation with him. As it turned out, he was in Tampa on a business trip, but he was still overcome with grief from losing his teenage son in a traffic accident just a few months previously. We spoke for several hours, and I shared with him what

I had recently come to understand about myself while dealing with my own difficult times; the discussion seemed to have a positive impact upon him. When he left the store a few hours later, I know that he did so with a less-heavy heart and an appreciation for the fact that his son's passing, albeit painful and unfair, was part of our life's plan. Before he left, he hugged me and thanked me profusely for sharing my insights with him; however, his presence there was equally important for me, and an opportunity to connect spiritually with another soul along life's path. I firmly believe that his presence there was not accidental, and I conclude that the venue for the interaction, a good cigar store in Tampa, Florida, couldn't have been more appropriate.

Although I am no longer involved in the industry, Maka and I continue to frequent our local cigar store and to attend cigar events whenever possible. The predominant appeal is simply to gather among like-minded members of the cigar community, where brotherhood and camaraderie of the sort are unwaveringly present. Over the past few years, this involvement has become increasingly important to us, as the runaway forces of political correctness in America are attempting to make such venues and such opportunities less likely as they endeavor to pass anti-tobacco legislation in every state. Although the smoking of cigars and pipes is a decidedly different matter than cigarette consumption and is far less hazardous from a health perspective, the fanatical legislators are blind to the fact that cigar smoking is altogether a different kettle of fish. As a result, cigar-smokers have banded together under the leadership of several political action associations to try to preserve our rights to enjoy these products in good cigar stores. If we fail, and the PC-ers have their way, the most unfortunate side effect will be the dissolution of such venues where community, commonality, and camaraderie prevail and where the Brotherhood of the Leaf can enjoy, and share, the human experience.

Chapter 21

On Marriage

"Lust is fleeting, romantic love can fade, but true friendship is eternal"

\- Robert O. Morris

I jokingly claim to be somewhat of an expert on the topic of marriage. After all, having done it as often as I have, even the most unwise of folks should have learned something, right? In any event, I do indeed believe that I have accumulated some small pieces of wisdom on the topic of marriage, and, because you've already acquired the book, you might as well take a read; it won't be very lengthy or terribly profound, but I believe that it holds water.

First of all, here are some rather unusual facts about the topic of marriage as practiced by some of my ancestors and me:

- My maternal grandfather, Owen B. Winters, married 5 times before he died at age 49.

- I have been married three times, and, although one of my wives was an American, I met each of these women within the boundaries of the Former Soviet Union.

- Each of my marriages evolved from an event of "love at first sight."

- My initial courtship of each of these women, even the American, was conducted in a foreign language, Russian.

- Although some people call me crazy, we often celebrate family events with all three wives together, and each event is always an enjoyable occasion.

I am certainly no Dr. Phil or any other formal authority on marriage.

What I have learned has been through the sometimes painful process of trial and error, but I will submit my humble thoughts and debatable wisdom for what they are worth.

All of the circumstances of my three marriages have already been depicted in the previous chapters, but I will recap them briefly for the sake of continuity.

I met wife #1 in Leningrad in the summer of 1975, where we were both participating on an American student exchange, an intensive Russian language program. I first spotted her in the university dining room one evening and I felt the thunderbolt effect immediately. My first interaction with her was during a field trip to the island of Kizhi, when she unwittingly stepped on me while she was maneuvering for a good photograph of an old wooden church; I was lying face down on the dock, trying to wash my face with lake water and sober up from the previous evening. Because we were obliged to speak only Russian during the program, our conversations that first day, most of which occurred during the hydrofoil ride from Kizhi back to Petrozavodsk, were conducted solely in that language. That encounter in late June was our final one until we communicated when each of us was back in the USA about three months later. As I wrote that summer in my journal, in the true tradition of the romantic idealist, I had already come to the conclusion that Fate intended for us to be together; and so it happened. We were married in Pittsburgh in 1976, lived and worked in numerous countries, had two wonderful children together, and separated in 1990.

I also met wife #2 in Russia, this time in Moscow, in August of 1993. By that time, I had retired from CIA and gone to work with Scott-European Corporation, where she was a receptionist in the company's Moscow office. Once again, I was struck by the thunderbolt when I saw her that first day in the office; however, since inter-office fraternization was seriously frowned upon by the boss, this sudden interest did not bode well for a normal relationship. Nevertheless, things seemed to work out. Similar to the first, this long-distance courtship evolved slowly over the span of about three months. Once we were both committed to the relationship, I finally revealed the situation to our boss and arranged for her to come to live with me in the States in June of 1994. We were married 18 months later in December of 1995, and our beautiful daughter, Sasha, was born in July of 1997. Unfortunately, problems eventually developed in the relationship, and against my wishes, we separated in 2001; the divorce was finalized the following year.

I met my current wife, Maka, in August, 2003, in Tbilisi, Georgia, just four days before I was due to leave the country at the completion of my contract. As is typical for me, it was once again a case of being struck by the thunderbolt (are you seeing a trend yet?), and it was, at least from my perspective, love at first sight. We maintained long-distance, predominantly friendly, communications for the subsequent five months until I secured another contract in Georgia and arrived there in January, 2004. Although I was present in Georgia and saw her almost daily, our relationship developed slowly and methodically, and turned romantic only two months after my arrival. When I returned to the States in May of 2004, we again maintained our relationship via long-distance communications. She came to the US for one visit in August of 2004, during which we decided that we wanted to commit ourselves to each other. Accordingly, we obtained a fiancée visa for Maka, she moved to the States in March of 2005, and we were married on June 1st. We have enjoyed a wonderful married life for more than six years, and we look forward to spending the remainder of our lifetimes together.

So, what are the differences, if any, in these three relationships, and why is one successful where the others were not? They all started from a very similar "love at first sight" beginning, and all developed slowly over time and distance. Clearly, there was no rush to judgment in any of these scenarios. Neither of the unsuccessful marriages was perpetrated by any of the typical reasons for marital break-ups, so what were the issues?

I have come to believe that success in marriage depends more upon the existence of a solid friendship than on love alone. In retrospect, I believe that the key element that was largely missing in my first two marriages really boils down to not having enough in common outside of the initial romance and our shared love for our children. After the time when the flourish of the romance began to fade, there was little that we really enjoyed doing together. In the mind of the romantic idealist, love conquers all, but the sad reality may be that love is not altogether enough. As my former wives might attest, perhaps the real moral of the story is that one should simply never marry a romantic idealist, but that's another topic altogether.

At the time of this writing, I have three unmarried children. If any of them were to ask me what I believe to be the most important ingredient of a successful marriage, the answer that I would give is "your prospective spouse, first and foremost, should be your best friend." I have come to understand this reality primarily because Fate was so kind and generous as to allow Maka to enter my life's path. I am forever grateful for this gift. In essence, we have absolutely everything in common. Despite a significant difference in age, we like virtually all the same things in every regard. We have the same tastes in food, the same preferences in entertainment, in vacation destinations, in sports, in decorating the house, in nearly everything. We enjoy each other's company immensely, and we like nothing better than simply hanging out together. After a long day at work, when we both get home, the thing we enjoy most is sitting on the front porch, lighting up our favorite cigar (which is usually the same brand), and catching up on the day or simply sitting together in contented silence. It is uncanny, but absolutely wonderful.

As mentioned previously in this book, I had made the pledge to myself as a young man that I would never be divorced; the fact that my parents were divorced had a major impact on my thinking. I especially remember the loss of not having both parents around when I was growing up, so my desire was not to subject my children to the same reality that I had experienced. Obviously, I failed miserably in this regard, and the guilt with which I live in this respect never totally disappears. Nevertheless, I have come to understand that all things in life happen for a reason, and that everything works out for the best in the end. Staying married when the relationship has deteriorated seriously, and is simply not working, is not a good solution. Divorce is painful, and serves no one well, but sometimes it can be the better recourse.

I have entirely reconciled the relationships that I have with my ex-wives, although this was not always the case. Truthfully, my first wife and I do not actively seek out each other's company, but we now get along well enough, and I believe that we have again come to appreciate each other. My second wife and I actually get along quite well now, and we do enjoy each other's company. Thankfully, we are all equally pro-active and cooperative on matters concerning our children. And, I can honestly say that I really do enjoy celebrating Thanksgiving, or other family festivities, with all of us together. As in any human relationship, I believe that the most important element, which I will discuss in a later chapter, is the ability to forgive. Forgiveness is key, not only the ability to forgive others for any real or perceived wrong doing, but also the sometimes more difficult ability to forgive ourselves for one's own mistakes.

When it works, there is nothing more satisfying than a strong and thoroughly compatible marriage. I love my married life, and I pray that my children will experience the same level of marital bliss that I have been so fortunate to feel with Maka. There truly is nothing better in life than when one's best friend and lover are one and the same person.

Chapter 22

On Fatherhood

"You are the bows from which your children as living arrows are sent forth.

The archer sees the mark upon the path of the infinite, and He bends you with his might that His arrows may go swift and far.

Let your bending in the archer's hand be for gladness;

For even as He loves the arrow that flies, so He loves also the bow that is stable."

- From *The Prophet*, by Kahlil Gibran

There are a great many different reasons for me to write this book, but the topic of fatherhood is a major motivator. To begin this chapter, allow me to explain why.

I had a father whom I loved, and with whom I enjoyed spending time; as far as I am concerned, I consider him to have been a good father. My parents were divorced when I was four; accordingly, my father was not around all of the time and that was an unhappy reality, but I do not recall feeling that I was terribly deprived in that regard. I would certainly have preferred that he had been there every day, and I undoubtedly experienced emotional pain from his absence, but I did not dwell on this fact. Following the divorce, my father continued to live in the same town for the majority of my childhood, and he was always available to visit. He attended most of my athletic events, and we spent a lot of enjoyable time together. As an adult, although I saw him less often, I continued to enjoy spending time with him and my half-siblings and can honestly attest that we had a good relationship.

On the other hand, I feel that I never really understood my father or what made him tick. Although we spoke about a lot of things, mostly sports and other normal father-son topics, we never really had what I consider to have been a heart-to-heart discussion. I truly do not have much knowledge as to why he made the life decisions that he did, and I can only guess at what may have been the most important things in his life. I do not recall ever seeing him become emotional about any particular subject and have concluded that he simply had a difficult time expressing his innermost feelings or showing his emotions. The one instance I do remember where he may have been caught up in his emotions was at my high school graduation, where I noticed him walking off alone at a distance from me and the other family members in attendance; however, because I could not really see his face or read his mind, I am only guessing. I certainly do not hold this trait against him, but I would have very much liked to know him better under the surface and to have had a clearer understanding of his life's philosophy, his dreams, and his regrets.

Now that I am a man in my 60's and well into the autumn of my life, I want to ensure that my three wonderful children have a better knowledge and understanding of their father than I had of mine. In large part, this book is an effort to ensure that there is a record of my life, the events that took place in it, and the reasons behind how and why they transpired. This effort is especially important because my life has been such a quixotic odyssey, a journey different from that of most people, and includes a number of chapters about which they otherwise might have never known. Just as I never sat my father down and implored him to tell me the secrets of his life, none of my kids have directly asked me either. In their case, perhaps the issue is not that vital to them, but it is my assumption that someday it may be. I do believe that I may have done a better job than my father in sharing some of my innermost feelings and philosophies along the way, but I know that I have only scratched the surface. Accordingly, if the urge does arise to know and understand more, this written record will exist for them, for their children, and for those who follow.

I became a father for the first time 26 years ago at the age of 35, and my youngest child was born when I was 47; both divorces occurred when the kids were quite young, in each case before they began school.

As a result, especially with my frequent absences caused by overseas travel, I missed much of the everyday activities of their youth. Under the circumstances, I tried as much as possible to stay involved and to spend as much time with them as I could, but, obviously, I was not as much a part of their lives as I would have liked to have been. Fortunately, in both cases, they had loving and attentive mothers, as I had, and I felt entirely comfortable that they were not being deprived in terms of parental support and caring guidance. However, especially considering the pledge I had made as a young man not to subject my children to the reality of divorce, this situation caused me immeasurable guilt and pain, and countless tears, as I lived with the realization that I had failed to live up to my own expectations.

As I write this, my children are aged 26, 23, and 14. Despite the somewhat limited role that I have played in their lives thus far, they are all well-rounded, healthy, and talented. They are loving and caring human beings who have been graced with compassionate and creative spirits. In this regard, I am fully cognizant of how deeply I have been blessed and I am unwaveringly grateful. My pride in how beautifully they have developed, and my unconditional love for them, knows no end. I am also eternally grateful for the mothers in their lives, not only for their natural moms, but also for the unselfish, nurturing roles their stepmothers have played in their upbringing; my kids love and appreciate their stepmoms without question, and the two oldest seem to take pride in the fact that they have three moms instead of just one. All in all, despite the guilt and pain I have felt for my own perceived short-comings as a father, I know in my heart that everything has worked out for the better, and that I can derive solace and satisfaction from the way life has evolved.

As I note above, this book is written mainly for my children, as a gift from their father. Although this book has a finite number of chapters, I hope and pray that my role as a father will have many more chapters in which to contribute to their lives and, hopefully, to the lives of their children as well. Despite any lingering grief and regrets from the past, I have come to realize that "now" is the only time that is important, for I understand that I have the unobstructed opportunity today, and every day to follow, to ensure that I play my role as father to the fullest. As will be addressed in a subsequent chapter, I am also blessed by having developed the ability to forgive, not only my ex-wives and others for whatever unhappy events may have occurred in the past, but also to have finally learned to forgive myself for my own perceived failings. For me, the latter point has unquestionably been the more difficult attitude to develop, but I have ultimately learned that forgiveness is a vitally important element for the foundation of one's ability to love and to give of oneself. Thus, I am far better prepared now than in the past to fulfill my role as a father to the utmost, and I am unwaveringly grateful for the continued opportunity to do so.

My bucket list contains several items that pertain directly to my role as a father. I want to live long enough to witness my children at their weddings and to dance with my daughters, and daughter-in-law, on those happy days. I want to take trips with my kids to places which have special significance for each of them and to develop indelible memories from each journey. I want very much to witness the birth of their children and to share in the joy of those births, just as their births gave so much joy to me. Most of all, my daily bucket list contains the wish that I live every day as a loving and caring father, and that my children know unquestionably in their hearts that their father loves them deeply and will be there for them, as Gibran states above, "a bow that is stable," now and for always.

Chapter 23

On Forgiveness

To err is human, to forgive is divine.

\- Alexander Pope

Let me begin by saying that I am far from an expert on the topic of forgiveness. Nor can I make any claims that I am able to convey any earthshaking or novel insights into the life-changing nature of forgiveness. I will also readily admit that I still am far from having perfected my own ability to forgive, and occasionally I still allow old resentments and grievances to pop into my mind and fester. However, I apparently have succeeded in understanding and practicing forgiveness to the point where I can usually clear my mind quickly of the negative chatter of old issues and return to a level of contentment and relative inner peace, which is the ultimate purpose. This topic refers back to the passage to which I referred in Chapter 19 about the longest journey a man can make, that being from his mind to his heart, and I will attempt to explain it in my own terms.

History is full of ancient animosities that have prolonged hatred and killing to unbelievable proportions over the course of decades and centuries: Shia versus Sunni, Hutu versus Tutsi, Hatfields versus McCoys, Red Sox versus Yankees (joking here!), but you see the point. These are cases of organized, traditional, perpetuated, and endless hatred, all created and evolving from the act of resenting another human being for some real or imagined ill. These are clearly some of the more extreme examples of how hatred gone amuck can be a destructive force, but I have been surprised in recent years even by how family members and loved ones can be so resistant and unmoving when offered the opportunity to forgive. Fathers and sons who love each other, but who cannot bring themselves to forgive and forget old issues, brothers and sisters who become adversaries over inheritance matters, and, the worst of all examples, former spouses who not only carry their grievances to the grave, but also spread their resentments to anyone who will listen in the hopes of poisoning the well for the other. In all of these cases, as I have witnessed myself, it is ultimately the unyielding bearer of the resentment who suffers the most from the inability to forgive; as such, this inability is truly a form of self-persecution.

I would like to make the issue of forgiveness even more pertinent, as it relates to the title of this book. From the perspective of the romantic idealist, who is inherently prone to create ideological and other assorted enemies from within his deluded mentality, the ability to learn forgiveness is absolutely necessary if he ever wants to experience inner peace or any level of contentment. Otherwise, the romantic idealist can perpetuate his or her resentments right to the edge, to the level of complete self-destruction. Accordingly, as a died-in-the-wool romantic idealist, I have learned that to practice forgiveness was much more than simply a nice thing to do; it was, and remains, necessary for my basic well-being.

Forgiveness is not a new concept. Throughout the Bible, the message of the necessity and sacred nature of forgiveness is constant. If one isn't much into reading the Bible, then just check any of the bookstore shelves in the New Age category where you can find dozens of examples that deal wholly or in part with the topic of forgiveness. There is a consistent message in all of these texts; our hatred and/or resentments are stories that we ourselves create and perpetuate in our own minds. They cause only damage to ourselves and not to the person(s) against whom we hold the animosity.

Here's a simple example that should certainly make perfect sense in these days of political strife. Each one of us probably has at least one particular politician who causes us to become resentful, stressed, irritated, and possibly angry to an emotional extreme. Clearly, these feelings are all negative ones that can have detrimental effects on our own emotional state; however, looking from the standpoint of the recipient of all of this negative energy, how are these people affected?

Do they even know that they are the beneficiary of our resentment? The obvious answer is "No," for the only real presence of the negative energy is in the mind of its creator, you or me. We create the story ourselves, and we may choose to perpetuate it to others, just as disease may be spread from one person to another; but we, the bearers of the resentment, are the ones dealing with the presence of the negative energy. The object of our resentment doesn't know the difference.

There are hundreds of books and articles readily available in bookstores or online that deal with forgiveness, so I will not go into much additional detail in this brief chapter. I will only emphasize how much better my life has become since I began to appreciate the wisdom of living a life of gratitude for what I have been given, both the good parts and the not-so-good, and because I have found the ability to forgive those against whom I have held grievances. For me, as it would probably be for any romantic idealist, this change was by no means an easy evolution. It came only after seeking to delve more deeply into my spiritual side, and repeatedly reading the works of philosophers so much wiser than I will ever be, that I began to comprehend the concept. After beginning to put the actuation of forgiveness into practice, I truly began to notice the physical and emotional benefits within myself. And, as it turns out, the philosophy behind the practice of forgiveness is not rocket science.

I recall how a wise man once asked me, "Morris, do you want to be happy?"

Naturally, I responded, "Of course, I want to be happy!"

His advice to me simply was, "Then, BE happy!"

I assume that most people would have the same reaction that I first did upon hearing such simple advice, protesting that I just can't decide to BE happy; some outside force or someone else needs to initiate some sort of measures to help make me happy. Such seems to be the prevailing impression, but actually nothing is farther from the truth. Years after first hearing the wise man's advice, I still find that I am not always in a happy state; however, I have come to understand that I am the one creating the unhappy image in my own mind, and, just as readily as I created it, I have the innate ability to make it go away.

The same phenomenon seems to hold true for forgiveness; despite how strongly and indelibly we may have etched one or another resentment of a human being into our minds, we have the innate ability to move to a state of forgiveness. For me, the process becomes easier when I visualize the beneficiary of my resentment just as another human being, who, exactly like me, is struggling to make sense of life as best he can. He or she makes the same mistakes, occasionally takes the wrong path, and has suffered from the same realities in life as I have; in essence, he or she is just another soul struggling to seek enlightenment. By visualizing him or her so, the other becomes a fellow traveler along life's journey, rather than one who may have perpetrated some perceived ill towards me. This explanation may seem simplistic, but it appears to work for me and helps to relieve any stress, resentment, or anger into which I may have slipped.

Going back to the "longest journey" metaphor noted in chapter 19, it really does create the perfect visual image to consider the concept. With the average man, the actual distance from the brain to the heart is only about 18 inches; therefore, it is so ironic that the vast majority of human beings never successfully make that journey from living predominantly within the confines of one's ego-driven mind to a life completely dedicated to living from the heart. It is even more surprising when the ultimate ability to make that transition boils down simply to the conscious decision to do so. As I have found out after years of trying, the practice of forgiveness is not at all easy in execution, but, in principle, nothing on earth could be simpler. In essence, it boils down to making the decision to do so, and to live that decision through consistent practice and application.

As touched upon in the previous chapter, the ability to forgive one's self is potentially even more difficult and ever so important, especially for the romantic idealists of the earth. The romantic idealist lives in the imagined world of chivalry and noble pursuits, and envisions himself to be a knight on a white horse, a hero of deistic proportions, who, by definition, is above the ability to fail. Therefore, when the romantic idealist does fail, and he often does, the self-retribution can be purely ruthless; thus, there is an absolute necessity to understand and to practice forgiving one's self on a consistent basis.

As promised, there is nothing earthshaking or terribly enlightening in what I have to offer on the topic of forgiveness; however, if the reader of this brief chapter feels that the shoe fits, that he or she may in fact possess strong resentments for another human being, then I might humbly suggest that the benefits of working on forgiveness of that person are immense and can bring you a much higher sense of well-being. If my theory rings true for you, then I would urge that you pick up a book or two from any one of dozens of established writers in the so called New Age Philosophy and to read and ponder; or, alternatively, pick up the family Bible, dust it off and read from the New Testament, which will convey precisely the same message. As Christ preached so many times, "Love your enemy." His words are not a commandment but rather a strong recommendation as a means to relate to humanity, thereby finding peace and well-being. Whatever resource you might use as most appropriate for the task, from my own experience in trying to make this journey, I can recommend the effort highly. Living life in a spirit of gratitude and forgiveness is simply a better way to exist; contentment and inner peace beat the hell out of a life full of resentment. Like I said, the practice of forgiveness is not rocket science, but it's certainly well worth the undertaking.

Chapter 24

Live Like You are Dying

"And I loved deeper and I spoke sweeter,

And I gave forgiveness I'd been denying.

And, he said: some day, I hope you get the chance,

To live like you were dyin'."

- From the song, *Live like you were dying*

- Sung by Tim McGraw

The lyrics noted above are from a popular country song performed and released about seven years ago by Tim McGraw. I like the song and its message very much. It concerns the response from a father when his son inquires what he did when he found out that he was dying from a terminal disease. As many people know, there are also two other lines in the chorus about going "sky-diving, rocky mountain climbing, and going 2.7 seconds on a bull named Fu Manchu." However, I have had my share of sky-diving and have done some mountain climbing, although I am always up for more, but there's no way in hell I am ever getting on Fu Manchu's back, so I left those two lines out. As far as I'm concerned, the remaining four lines ring very true for me though.

Every day of our lives, we are all in the process of dying. From the first breath we take, we have begun to roll down the hill towards the ultimate destination of death. Naturally, we normally don't dwell on this fact, and it would probably be counter-productive to do so; however, I do believe that it is worthwhile to remain cognizant of the fact that any day could be our last and to try to live life as if it were.

This book is being written very much in the spirit of that song. I have had the desire to write for over 35 years and have only now taken the steps to bring that dream to fruition. In my case, it has always been too easy to subjugate that desire to the necessities of earning a living, of taking care of financial obligations, and/or of not having the ability to multi-task and to find the opportunity and energy to write in my free time. For me, the kicker came when my brother passed away from cancer at the age of 66; he had worked hard all of his life, retired from the Army as a Lieutenant Colonel after 25 years, and then worked another 20 years in private industry before he finally decided to retire. He had put both of his sons through college, and had done very well to provide financially for his family. His retirement goals were to work on his golf game (which truly needed it), and to spend as much time as possible with his five (now six) grandsons. However, Fate had other plans for him, and he passed away within the first year after he retired. For me, this painful experience made it clear in my mind that I really needed to   take action if I wanted to have the time to achieve some of my life's unfulfilled dreams, such as writing. As a result, I made the decision to retire from my corporate job and, finally, to get with the program.

There are many instances of which I have become aware of people who have gone through near death experiences and then completely turned around the manner in which they lived the lives that were so nearly taken away from them. In their cases, the reality of the ultimate destination of death became immediately clear, and it thus became much easier for them to recognize the merit of living each day as if it were their last. However, why should it take a near death experience to make such an impact? I wrestled with that question for some time before I finally made the all-too-difficult decision to break away from my normal mode of thinking and take the steps to pursue my long time dream. On their death beds, I think that most people have regrets about only what they have not done in life; I intend that this will not be the case for me.

As defined in one of the previous chapters, I have a bucket list for several important facets in my role as a father. As Tim McGraw sings in his song, the unquestionable wisdom to "love deeper, speak sweeter, and give forgiveness which I've been denying," rings very true to me. As a father, husband, friend, and human being, I can think of nothing as noble. The process of writing this book is providing me with considerable pleasure and personal satisfaction as I create something that is an act of my innermost passion. I consider each day in which I complete another chapter to be incredibly rewarding, and I find myself completely immersed in a sense of gratitude that I was able to make one more forward step towards my ultimate goal. For sure, there are days in which the words do not come to my satisfaction, and I sometimes feel a sense of frustration. The task, therefore, is to continue to seek the inspiration to work towards what, I believe, Destiny has intended for me to do.

I have come to believe that life happens precisely as it was planned to happen. I also believe that living in the past, and having regret for the challenges and unhappiness we faced, is a waste of life's gift to us. I have come to understand that holding on to resentments we previously felt is self-destructive, and an impediment to inner peace. I have come to realize that living in "the now" is the key to happiness; after all, the only guarantee we have in life is the moment in which we find ourselves, so why not make the most of it? I have not always had these beliefs, but I am full of gratitude for having come to embrace these attitudes towards life. In the spirit of the romantic idealist, my hope is that these modest words may possibly help the reader to enjoy the higher level of inner peace and contentment which I thankfully enjoy now. This is my humble, yet sincere, wish for all.

"Nobody can go back and start a new beginning, but anyone can start today and make a new ending."

- Maria Robinson

Epilogue

Virginia Beach, Sunday, October 30, 2011

After a lifetime of living the "quixotic odyssey," I can honestly state that these last 6 years have been the most settled and normal ones that I have experienced in my life to date. Although a person can never completely exorcize the romantic idealist mind-set, thankfully, I do believe that I have largely managed to subjugate its dysfunctional influence in favor of a more typical, less chaotic existence over these past few years.

Since our marriage on June 1, 2005, Maka and I have been living happily and continuously in Virginia Beach. With the exception of his time spent training in the Air Force plus one deployment overseas and his time away at the University, our son, Brian, has been living with us. This life segment has all been a wonderful change of pace from what had become a somewhat unpredictable and disjointed lifestyle for so many years previously.

Employment wise, for the vast majority of the past six years before retirement, I worked in the defense sector, the last four in international sales with a manufacturer of communications equipment for military and government customers. Although I enjoyed my work with this company, and it provided us with a very good lifestyle, I left my corporate job on July 1, 2011, so that I could finally pursue my lifelong ambition to write on a full-time basis.

This book is the first of many works that I have in the pipeline; the only real limiting factor in this regard would seem to be the amount of time I will be granted in which to get all of them written. However, in keeping with the spirit of the previous chapters, the only moment we have on which we can totally depend is "now", and my goal is to live the now as if every breath could be my last. However, as I understand and accept, Fate will be the final determinant of what the ultimate results will be.

I have a definite bucket list of things which I still hope to accomplish. As already mentioned, I have some specific, very important goals to achieve in my role as a father, but I have an equal number of significant bucket list items that revolve around my role as a husband and a friend. I have a special interest in reconnecting with old friends and to share with them some of the wisdom and lessons learned from what we experienced over our respective lifetimes. Perhaps this theme will even be the topic of a later work, still to be determined.

At the conclusion of Chapter 10, the one written in honor of my good friend, Johnny Burke, I suggested that the true meaning of life is making a positive impact upon one's immediate community. Because of my ever-changing locations and somewhat chaotic past, I have felt quite remiss in this regard, and it is my sincere intention to become a much more effective and positive influence in those communities where I have a potential function. Be it simply taking a more active role in my neighborhood or participating more fully in alumni associations, charitable programs, or whatever, I believe that I am being called to become more participative in community causes. For the record, I do believe that this book is a positive first step in that regard, and my hope is that it will provide a springboard for many such opportunities.

I recall many years ago having a conversation with my first wife about death, my legacy of life, and where I wanted to be buried. As I write this book, I am 61 years of age; however, at the time of that conversation with my first wife, I must have been somewhere in my mid-30's. During that time in my life, I was truly convinced that I would never live past the age of 50, so the conversation was not so inappropriate. Moreover, I was equally convinced that I was going to play such a significant role in the history of my country, that my burial ground would be a topic of some popular debate. Thus, in reply to my wife's question as to where I should be buried, my response was, "Let the people decide!" Because I was only half-joking, by definition, my declaration meant that I was indeed half-serious. Perhaps no other quote better represents the somewhat delusional mentality of the romantic idealist.

So, here I am, already well past 50 years of age, with a bucket list that will require at least another dozen years, so one goal is to live life in a manner which will make my desired longevity an achievable reality. There will be lots to do within those dozen or more years, memorable experiences with my wife, my children, and my friends, many contributions to be made to my communities of choice, and numerous books to write and/or to publish. My goal is to live each one of the days to come as if it were my last, to maintain an attitude of gratitude, to practice unwaveringly the art of forgiveness, and to pursue continually spiritual enlightenment in my life. I truly believe that these goals are highly worthy ones within any individual life pursuit.

Finally, at this point in my life, I believe that it is quite safe to say that the topic of my burial ground will not be a matter of public debate; no doubt, my descendents will quietly make that decision themselves. However, I have often wondered what I would like to have written as the epitaph on my tombstone, and I believe that the following may be fitting:

Warrior, Wanderer,
Seeker, Dad

As I continue to ponder the appropriateness of those words, I honestly believe that, for better or for worse, this maxim pretty much says it all.

The suggestion of my epitaph notwithstanding, my life story is far from complete. As noted above, there are many chapters yet to come, bucket lists to be fulfilled and community contributions still to be made. Although the compelling need to fight windmills has subsided with the acquisition of wisdom and the realization of human limitations, the mentality of the romantic idealist never entirely dies. The focus and energy of my quixotic pursuits will merely be re-channeled towards more fruitful goals, with the undying wish that the odyssey of one may ultimately benefit those who find some personal relevance in the telling of this story. May Fate continue to be so kind.

Made in the USA
Middletown, DE
17 December 2017